# ACES

## TRUE STORIES *of* VICTORY *and* VALOR
## *in the* SKIES *of* WORLD WAR II

### BILL YENNE

CHARTWELL
BOOKS

Quarto
Knows

Inspiring | Educating | Creating | Entertaining

Brimming with creative inspiration, how-to projects, and useful information to enrich your everyday life, Quarto Knows is a favorite destination for those pursuing their interests and passions. Visit our site and dig deeper with our books into your area of interest: Quarto Creates, Quarto Cooks, Quarto Homes, Quarto Lives, Quarto Drives, Quarto Explores, Quarto Gifts, or Quarto Kids.

This edition published in 2020 by Chartwell Books,
an imprint of The Quarto Group,
142 West 36th Street, 4th Floor
New York, NY 10018, USA
T (212) 779-4972 F (212) 779-6058
*www.QuartoKnows.com*

Chartwell titles are also available at discount for retail, wholesale, promotional, and bulk purchase.
For details, contact the Special Sales Manager by email at *specialsales@quarto.com* or by mail at
The Quarto Group, Attn: Special Sales Manager, 100 Cummings Center Suite 265D, Beverly, MA 01915 USA.

10 9 8 7 6 5 4 3 2 1

ISBN: 978-0-7858-3834-0

LIBRARY OF CONGRESS CONTROL NUMBER: 2020938512

PUBLISHER: Rage Kindelsperger
CREATIVE DIRECTOR: Laura Drew
MANAGING EDITOR: Cara Donaldson
EDITOR: Leeann Moreau
COVER DESIGN: Andrea Ho
LAYOUT DESIGN: Lauren Vajda

Printed in Singapore

Finnish ace and Knight of the Mannerheim Cross, Lieutenant Hans Henrik "Hasse" Wind, climbs into his cockpit for a mission on September 12, 1943. *Wikimedia Commons*

# CONTENTS

**INTRODUCTION**

**FIGHTER PILOTS HAVE ALWAYS BEEN THOUGHT OF AS THE KNIGHTS OF THE AIR.** Since World War I, they have been seen as a breed apart, fighting their battles high above the mud and muck of the battlefield, fighting one another man-to-man like the knights of the medieval joust. A special folklore grew up around the knights of the Middle Ages, and the code of chivalry that defined knighthood created a special vocabulary. This was also the case with the knights of the air. Most important in this modern lexicon is the term "ace," which was coined to describe the knight who had achieved a level of expertise beyond that of his fellow knights of the air.

**WHAT IS AN ACE?** Technically it means a pilot of a fighter aircraft who has shot down, or destroyed in the air, a total of five enemy aircraft. An ace is defined as a fighter pilot who has achieved five aerial victories. An ace can also be described as a fighter pilot who has dueled to the death with five other fighter pilots, and has survived.

Similar to the knights of old, however, the knight of the air does not necessarily seek to literally kill his opponent, but rather to destroy his aircraft. If he dies in the process, he dies heroically, but if he survives, the code of the ace abhors the fighter pilot who would shoot at a man hanging helplessly in a parachute. While this did occur, it is, and always has been, roundly condemned by fighter pilots everywhere. It was much more common that the victorious pilot flew past his victim with a salute or a wave.

Other examples of the level of chivalry among aces occurred on two occasions in 1941 and 1942, when the British aces Douglas Bader and Robert Tuck were shot down over France. In both cases, the German ace Adolf Galland, who was also a Luftwaffe group commander, invited the men to dine with him at his officers' mess. In the air, Galland would have considered them enemies. Elsewhere, they were colleagues. After the war, Galland and Bader were reportedly close friends. For many years after the war, numerous surviving aces from opposing sides met and mingled at reunions and other events, as though they were all part of a band of brothers.

The term was coined in 1915 when French newspapers described Adolphe Pégoud as l'As (the Ace) after he became the first pilot to down five German aircraft. He was killed in action in August 1915. The term is also widely associated with French daredevil aeronaut turned military pilot, Roland Garros. He was also prominent as an ace in the French press in 1915, but it seems that he only scored four aerial victories before he was captured in April 1915.

Aces were popular in World War I because of the glamour involved. They fought high above the filth of the terrible trenches and they fought one-on-one like the knights of old. They inspired just about the only chivalrous tales to come out of that terrible war.

In World War II, aces were equally colorful, though aerial combat had become more sophisticated technologically, more routine and much more deadly. Far more individuals were involved in aerial combat and far more became aces. Also in World War II, the recording of aerial victory data became an official part of air force record keeping. It had been so with the German and the French in World War I, but it was much more informal with the air services of other countries.

While the maintaining of data relative to aerial victories was more formalized in World War II, there were still differences and variations from one air force to another. An ace was universally accepted as someone who has scored five aerial victories, but each of the air forces involved in World War II had a different method for calculating exactly what constituted an aerial victory.

In World War II, as in World War I, Germany had a strict "one pilot, one victory" rule. One pilot was given a victory credit for each enemy aircraft shot down. If he was assisted by another pilot, the other pilot got no credit to his overall score for the "assist." If two pilots shared

equally, then the credit went to the staffel (squadron) and to the overall tally of neither pilot. To claim a victory in the German Luftwaffe, the claimant had to have a witness—preferably two—and he had to formally fill out a comprehensive victory report which was followed by a combat report. For this reason, German victory totals in World War II are considered very accurate, and in cases where there might have been a discrepancy, the totals are definitely on the low side. The Germans even went so far as to recognize only pilots with 10 or more victories. Such pilots were referred to as an "experte."

The Americans are considered to have been the most precise in their accounting, because, through most of World War II, American fighters were equipped with gun cameras, and no scores were recognized as "confirmed" without gun camera film footage as proof. American victory totals are often qualified by the mention of "probables" or "damaged" enemy aircraft, which are those which were "probably" shot down, but which cannot be "confirmed." These are often mentioned parenthetically, but are not included in official victory totals. In World War I, Americans had assigned whole numbers to several pilots participating in downing a single enemy, but this practice was not followed in World War II. Whereas the German practice was to simply not award any scores for "assists," the Americans developed a system during World War II for giving appropriate credit for "assists" by calling them "shared" victories.

The American system of "shared" victories that was used in World War II was much more precise and accurate than the system in place in the earlier conflict. It was also more complicated than the German system, it was certainly fairer, and it certainly encouraged teamwork. German "shared" victories were allocated to only one of the "sharees" or to nobody, but American "shared" victories were divided among the "sharees." If two Americans worked together to shoot down one enemy aircraft, then each American would have a half point added to his victory total. If three pilots were involved, then each pilot would officially have 0.33 added, and so on.

In World War II, Britain's Royal Air Force formally adopted the same method of counting "confirmed" and "shared" victories as the Americans, although, early in the war, shared victories were often counted with whole numbers, as had been the practice in the First World War. Like the Americans, the system the British used in World War I had been unofficial and tended to give credit for enemy aircraft "driven down" to a lower altitude or forced to land, even if it was behind their own lines. The counting of "probables" (and even "improbables") in the final totals definitely inflated scores in World War I. The practice was officially abandoned by the British relatively early in World War II.

Finland, where precise records were kept, also maintained the practice of using fractions to credit shared kills.

In World War II, the French Armée de l'Air counted everything in whole numbers. When France was invaded, desperate times probably led to desperate measures. In 1940, scores were credited for actually shooting down an enemy, but full scores were also given for "assists" and for "probables." Shared victories always got full scores and were often allocated to more than two or three pilots who were present at the time. This was almost certainly a propaganda measure designed to ensure that good news about the battle was reported in the French media. During World War II, the Italian Regia Aeronautica used the same method as the French Armée de l'Air, so the victory totals for most pilots of both air forces are drastically inflated.

In Eastern Europe, especially in Romania and Bulgaria, the tendency to officially inflate scores reached to the extreme. The Royal Romanian Air Force formally adhered to the practice of awarding multiple points depending on the type of aircraft shot down. This practice called for awarding three "victories" to a pilot that claimed a four-engine bomber, and two victories for downing a twin-engine aircraft. Shooting down a fighter in a dogfight, however, counted merely as one. As in France and Italy, the purpose of this practice was obviously for domestic consumption, to keep morale up.

Just the opposite was true a bit farther east in the Soviet Union, where the effort of the individual was officially subordinated to the collective effort. Early in the war, there was a deliberate and official practice of not recognizing individual scores, but the propaganda value of having aces as heroes of what the Soviet Union called the "Great Patriotic War" was soon recognized and the situation changed. Still, the unofficial nature of keeping the counts has led to some uncertainty about the exact numbers and regarding exactly how many aces there were.

With the Japanese, it was an official practice in the field to credit victories to the group or squadron rather than to the actual pilot. Such individual scores which do exist were kept informally and are not always accurate. Even for all of the important Japanese aces, there is a wide spread of numbers that are mentioned in the literature as their possible final score.

With Japan, as with the Soviet Union, the highest-scoring aces are well known, but the exact numbers for these men are not known for certain, although, with the Soviet aces, the numbers given for the major aces are probably more accurate. For both countries, the scores, and even the names of all the lesser aces will probably never be known for certain.

★
William Avery "Billy" Bishop, a Canadian with No. 50 Squadron, was the highest-scoring ace with Britain's Royal Flying Corps in World War I. He had 72 victories. *Author's Collection*

The highest-scoring ace of World War II was the German pilot, Erich Hartmann, who scored 352 well-documented aerial victories. Behind him, there were over 100 aces in the German Luftwaffe who scored more than 100 victories. No other country had any aces who are confirmed to have scored more than 100 victories. The highest number of confirmed victories outside the Luftwaffe is the score of 94.17 credited to Eino Ilmari Juutilainen of Finland. Next in line are the Japanese aces. Tetsuzo Iwamoto is credited with having scored 80 victories in World War II and 14 during the Sino-Japanese war for a total of 94. Hiroyoshi Nishizawa is credited with 87 in World War II alone. However, because of Japan's official record keeping practices—or the lack thereof—these totals are regarded as "best guesses."

The highest-scoring Soviet ace is known to have been Ivan Kozhedub, and his score of 62 is generally accepted by most sources. The highest-scoring British Commonwealth ace is known to have been Marmaduke "Pat" Pattle, but his exact score is not known. The reason is that the relevant records for his unit, Royal Air Force No. 33 Squadron were lost in the British evacuation of Greece in 1940, and Pattle himself was killed during this operation. His score is known to have been at least 40, which is enough to earn him the top slot, but it was almost certainly higher and may have been as high as 51. The highest-scoring American ace was Richard Ira "Dick" Bong. Well-kept records confirm that his score was exactly 40.

Just as they had the highest-scoring aces, the Luftwaffe also leads in the total number of aces. The number is at least 5,000, although many records are lost, and so perhaps are the

★
René Fonck, seen here with his Spad XIII, scored 75 victories to rank as the second highest-scoring ace of World War I and the top Allied ace. *Author's Collection*

names and numbers of some aces with smaller scores that would have been in the shadow of the well-known and widely reported scores of the aces with more than 100 victories. The number of Luftwaffe aces with more than 20 aerial victories is probably more than 950.

The combined total number of American aces in the USAAF, the US Navy and the US Marine Corps stands at about 1,280, but even with the Americans, names and numbers from the early part of the war are uncertain. The combined total number of aces for the British Commonwealth air services of Australia, Canada, New Zealand, South Africa, Britain itself and all others is also above 1,200. The Soviet Voenno-Vozdushnie Sily (VVS) may have had as many as 2,000 aces or as few as 300.

Italy and Japan are probably the only other countries with more than 100, but Italy's totals are inflated by an especially liberal count of shared victories and Japan's numbers are just the opposite. If some victories by leading aces could be overlooked, then all or most victories by less prominent aces were probably ignored.

The statistics, however, are really just a trivial part of the story. For fighter pilots to do battle, one on one, with other fighter pilots, was an act of courage and dedication that linked them with the timeless tradition of the classic warrior. Whatever can be said about the statistics, the variables, and the numbers, nothing can subtract from the skill, bravery and devotion to duty that is exemplified by those pilots who became aces in mankind's biggest global conflict.

★ (Above)
This is the view from inside the cockpit of a USAAF P-47 Thunderbolt as this pilot's wingman destroys a German Fw 190. This artwork was used in 1943 as part of an advertising campaign for a maker of pumps and hydraulic components for the aviation industry.
*Author's Collection*

★ (Below)
A US Marine Corps F4U Corsair heroically destroys a pair of Japanese A6M Zeros in this example of wartime advertising art.
*Author's Collection*

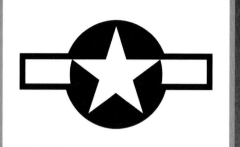

CHAPTER

01

# THE US ARMY AIR FORCES ACES

**W**HEN WORLD WAR II BEGAN IN 1939, the entity that evolved into today's US Army Air Force was the US Army Air Corps. In terms of men and aircraft, it was smaller than the Luftwaffe, Britain's Royal Air Force or the Soviet Union's VVS. However, thanks to the efforts of its chief, General Henry Harley "Hap" Arnold, the US Army Air Corps would become the autonomous US Army Air Forces (USAAF) and expand into the largest air force in history—in less than four years.

During World War I, the precursor to the Air Corps, the Air Service of the US Army's American Expeditionary Forces, had been in action for less than a year, but it managed to produce 21 aces with ten victories or more. Two of these, John Malone and Frederick Gillette, had scores of 20, while William Lambert had 22. America's Ace of Aces in World War I was the dashing former race car driver and future airline executive, Edward V. "Eddie" Rickenbacker. During the early years of American involvement in World War II, Rickenbacker's 26 victories became the Holy Grail of aspiring American fighter pilots.

Getting in the spirit of the times, Rickenbacker offered to buy a case of Scotch whiskey for the first Army pilot to top his score. Ironically, the first American to match Rickenbacker's score in World War II was not an Army pilot, but a Marine—Joe Foss.

In World War I, the Army Air Service fought in the skies over a small corner of France, but General Arnold realized that World War II would be a true global war, with American aircraft flying and fighting in the skies over every continent but Antarctica. For this task, he created a global force on a scale never previously imagined. Arnold organized the USAAF into numbered air forces, each one assigned a specific task in a specific theater. He started with seven, added six more in 1942, and ended the war with 16.

Among the overseas air forces involved in combat, the largest was the Eighth Air Force created in England in January 1942 for strategic operations against German-occupied Europe. The Ninth Air Force was created in England in December 1942 for tactical operations against German-occupied Europe, and the Twelfth Air Force was created in August 1942 for operations in the Mediterranean Theater. The Fifteenth Air Force was created in Italy in November 1943 for strategic operations against German-occupied Europe from bases in Italy. There were more USAAF aces among these air forces, especially the Eighth, than in any other region.

In the European Theater, the Eighth Air Force began its offensive against Germany in 1942 and in early 1943, the first escort fighter units became operational at bases in Britain. These included the 4th Fighter Group, 56th Fighter Group, and the 78th Fighter Group. Initially, these units were equipped with P 47 Thunderbolts, but by 1944, the more effective P-51 Mustang had arrived with its ability to escort the heavy bombers all the way to Berlin.

The top two USAAF aces in the European Theater were Francis "Gabby" Gabreski who scored 28 victories while flying with the 56th Fighter Group and Robert S. Johnson, who scored 27 with the 56th Fighter Group. Both men did so while flying the P 47 Thunderbolt.

Other top Thunderbolt aces in the European Theater were David C. Schilling, who scored 22.5 victories; Fred J. Christensen, with 21.5 victories; and Walker M. "Bud" Mahurin, with

★ (Above)
Captain Eddie Rickenbacker, America's "Ace of Aces" in World War I, became a household name and a folk hero to American military pilots going into World War II. Matching his score of 26 aerial victories was a "holy grail" for fighter pilots. *National Archives*

★ (Previous)
The North American Aviation P-51D Mustang was the quintessential USAAF fighter in the European Theater during World War II. *Ferocious Frankie* was the Mustang piloted by Major Wallace E. Hopkins and named for his wife. The aircraft carries five victory marks indicating that the pilot had just achieved "ace" status. Hopkins scored a total of eight aerial victories with the 374th Fighter Squadron, a component of the Eighth Air Force 361st Fighter Group, based at Bottisham, England. The black and white "Invasion Stripes" were added to Allied aircraft ahead of the June 1944 D-Day operations. *National Archives*

20.8 victories. All of these men flew with the 56th Fighter Group. Dominic "Don" Gentile, who scored 21.8 victories with the 4th Fighter Group, started out in the P-47, but scored many of his victories after the group transitioned to the P-51 Mustang.

The top European Theater Mustang aces were George Preddy, who scored 26.8 victories while flying with the 352th Fighter Group; John Meyer, with 24 victories while flying with the 352th Fighter Group; and Ray Wetmore, with 22.6 victories while flying with the 359th Fighter Group.

The Twelfth Air Force and Fifteenth Air Force pilots who flew in the Mediterranean Theater, found enemy aircraft strength to be significantly less than in northern Europe. The Germans abandoned North Africa in 1943 and the Italians surrendered in 1943. Unlike northern Europe, the Allies thoroughly outnumbered the Axis in the Mediterranean and southern Europe after the summer of 1943. There were many aces, but the scores were smaller. The two leading aces were John Voll, who claimed 21 victories while flying P-51s with the 31st Fighter Group and Herschel "Herky" Green, who scored 18 victories while flying P-47s with the 325th Fighter Group. Green was awarded the Distinguished Service Cross.

In the Pacific Theater, the formerly Philippines-based Far East Air Force (FEAF) became the Fifth Air Force, the formerly Hawaii-based Hawaiian Air Force became the Seventh Air Force, and the new Thirteenth Air Force was created in the Solomon Islands in December 1942. These were loosely united as the new Far East Air Forces (FEAF) under General George Kenney.

Units assigned to FEAF's Fifth Air Force, especially the 49th Fighter Group and 475th Fighter Group, carried the heaviest workload among USAAF fighter units during the 1942–1944

★
The North American Aviation P-51D Mustang is widely considered to have been the best USAAF fighter of World War II. More than 15,000 were built. The Mustangs pictured here were part of the US AAF Eighth Air Force's 361st Fighter Group, which was stationed at RAF Bottisham, and later at RAF Little Walden, in England during World War II. *National Archives*

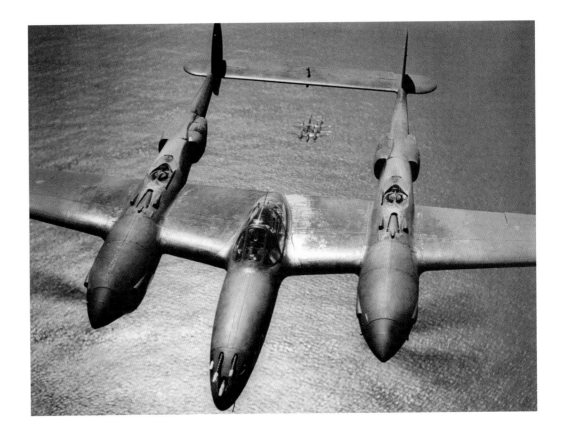

period when the Imperial Japanese Navy Air Force was at the apogee of its strength in the Solomons, New Guinea and the Netherlands East Indies (now Indonesia). As the P-51 Mustang would become the signature USAAF fighter in Europe, the P-38 Lightning was that aircraft for the FEAF in the Southwest Pacific.

The two leading American aces of the war were Richard Ira "Dick" Bong, who scored 40 victories while flying with the 49th Fighter Group, and Thomas "Tommy" McGuire, who had 38 victories while flying with the 475th "Satan's Angels" Fighter Group. Both men were recipients of the Medal of Honor, but neither would survive the war. Their story is told in the dual biography by this author, *Aces High: The Heroic Saga of the Two Top-Scoring American Aces of World War II*.

Other USAAF aces with scores of 20 or more in the Pacific Theater were Charles MacDonald, who scored 27 victories while flying with the 475th Fighter Group; Gerald R. Johnson, with 22 victories while flying with the 49th Fighter Group; Jay T. Robbins, with 22 victories while flying with the 8th Fighter Group; Robert Westbrook, with 20 victories while flying with the 18th Fighter Group (of the Seventh Air Force); and Thomas J. "Tommy" Lynch, who had 20 victories while flying with the 35th Fighter Group. MacDonald, Johnson and Robbins all were awarded the Distinguished Service Cross.

Also worth noting is a Texan, Lance Wade, who scored 25 victories while flying in North Africa with Britain's Royal Air Force (see Chapter 4). Unlike other men such as Don Gentile, who scored victories with the Royal Air Force as well as the USAAF, Wade never flew with the USAAF.

# BAUMLER AND TINKER:
## THE VOLUNTEERS

Albert T. "Ajax" Baumler in China in 1943 while assigned to the 76th Fighter Squadron of the USAAF Fourteenth Air Force. *US Air Force*

**THE SPANISH CIVIL WAR**, which raged from 1936 to 1939, pitted Spain's Republican government against the eventually-victorious Nationalist insurgents led by General Francisco Franco. The Spanish Civil War was seen at the time as a sort of dress rehearsal of the weapons and tactics that were used in World War II, particularly with regard to the use of air power. Germany and Italy sent fully organized "volunteer" air force contingents to help Franco, and the Soviet Union did the same to aid the Republicans.

Meanwhile, there were large numbers of actual volunteers who arrived in Spain to fight for one side or the other. Among these were many young Americans, who wanted to fight with the Republicans against the evils that they could see in the Fascist dictatorships of Hitler, Mussolini, and, potentially, Francisco Franco.

The Americans arrived in force in 1937 to join the Abraham Lincoln and George Washington battalions, which were part of the 15th International Brigade. This brigade also contained volunteers from Britain and Canada. Many American pilots also flew with the Republican air force and associated Soviet squadrons, where they were paid a base salary, plus $1,000—a considerable sum in the Depression era—for every Nationalist aircraft they shot down. The two most successful Americans in the Republican air force were Albert J. "Ajax" Baumler, who scored 13 victories in Spain, and Frank Glasgow Tinker, who claimed eight. They flew Polikarpov I-15s, and later I-16s, with the Soviet squadron, Escuadrilla Tarkhov, as well as with Escuadrilla Lacalle and 1 Escuadrilla de Caza. Tinker also flew with the Soviet Escuadrillas de Moscas.

Ajax Baumler arrived in Spain on December 27, 1936 and scored his first victory, an Italian Fiat CR.32, on March 16, 1937 while on a patrol near Madrid. On March 20, Baumler claimed another Fiat near Brihuega, when his unit broke up a bombing mission conducted by an Italian strike force with fighter escort. On April 17, while flying out of Sarrion, he scored one confirmed and one "probable" in an encounter with some Heinkel He 51 fighters of Germany's Condor Legion.

By the end of May, Baumler and Tinker were flying the Polikarpov I 16s, and Baumler scored his first victory in this type on June 2 near Segovia. His final victory in the Spanish Civil War came on July 8, when he destroyed a Fiat during a large battle in which his flight intercepted a bomber strike against Quejormas. Ajax Baumler went on to score one victory while flying with the American Volunteer Group in China, and 3.5 with the USAAF 75th Fighter Squadron during World War II.

# HILL: FLYING WITH THE TIGERS

**IF THE SPANISH CIVIL WAR PRESENTED A "DRESS REHEARSAL" FOR WORLD WAR II IN EUROPE,**
the Sino-Japanese War that began in 1937 was certainly a precursor to World War II in the Far
East. Indeed, when Japan went to war with the United States and Britain in 1941, the Sino-
Japanese War simply became the Asiatic Theater of World War II. Just as Germany, Italy and the
Soviet Union sent organized air forces of "volunteers" to fight one another in Spain, the United
States had sent a "volunteer" air force to China to help the Chinese fight Japan. The American
Volunteer Group (AVG) that fought in China was the brainchild of General Claire Chennault.

Chennault had quit his job as a Texas high school principal to become a flyer in World War
I, but the war ended before he earned his wings. He decided to remain in the Army after the
war and by 1925, he was commanding a pursuit squadron in Hawaii. Chennault became one of
the Air Corps' rising stars in the field of combat tactics for fighters and he was named to head

the Pursuit Section. In 1934, he organized an aerobatic team called Three Men on A Flying Trapeze to demonstrate his ideas.

Chennault retired from the Army in 1937, and was hired by China's first lady, Madame Chiang Kai-shek, to set up a school in China to train military pilots. China was then involved in a losing war with the Japanese, and Chennault watched the situation deteriorate from bad to worse. The Chinese air force was losing badly at the hands of the Japanese. In 1940, with the clandestine approval of the United States State Department, Chennault put together the American Volunteer Group. It was a fighter squadron composed of American civilian volunteer pilots who'd been trained in the US Army Air Corps, USW Navy, or the US Marine Corps.

Better known as the "Flying Tigers" because of the jagged teeth they painted on the cowlings of their Curtiss P-40 aircraft, the AVG pilots achieved amazing results against the Japanese because of the tactics they practiced. Chennault had studied Japanese aircraft and tactics and he taught the Tigers how to win. He instructed them not to get into a dogfight with the more maneuverable Japanese A6M Zero, but to use the P-40's speed to their advantage in fast, slashing attacks. The AVG was quite successful against the numerically superior Japanese, and their attacks on Japanese bombers are credited with keeping the Burma Road, China's critical overland supply route, from being destroyed or falling into Japanese hands, during the dark days before the United States and Britain entered the war against Japan.

Among the pilots who served with the Flying Tigers was Gregory "Pappy" Boyington, who may have scored six victories with the AVG, though that number is disputed. He later went back to the Marines during World War II, where he scored 22 victories and earned the Medal of Honor.

The highest-scoring ace with the AVG was David Lee "Tex" Hill, with 11.25 victories (some sources list 10.25). Born in 1914, the son of American missionaries in Korea, Hill was an aviator with the US Navy during the 1930s. He flew Douglas SBD Dauntless and Vought SBU scout bombers on aboard the USS *Yorktown*, USS *Ranger*, and USS *Saratoga*. Hill joined the AVG in April 1941, flying missions out of Toungoo, halfway between Rangoon and Mandalay in Burma. Here, the Flying Tigers operated from a crude landing strip and lived with insects and unbearable heat and humidity. However, for Hill it meant trading his $125 per month ensign's pay for a $750 monthly salary, plus a bonus of $500 for each Japanese aircraft destroyed.

On July 4, 1942, the American Volunteer Group was incorporated into the newly formed USAAF China Air Task Force as the 23rd Fighter Group. General Chennault was brought back into the USAAF to command the Task Force, which later became the Fourteenth Air Force. Robert Scott would become the commander of the 23rd Fighter Group and Tex Hill would command the 75th Fighter Squadron. During World War II, Hill added six victories to his score.

The story of Hill and the American Volunteer Group is told in great detail in this author's When Tigers Ruled the Sky: The Flying Tigers: American Outlaw Pilots over China in World War II.

# WAGNER:
# THE USAAF'S FIRST ACE

★
Boyd David "Buzz" Wagner was the first American ace of World War II, scoring his early victories in December 1941 while commanding the USAAF 17th Pursuit Squadron in the Philippines. *US Air Force*

**WORLD WAR II** began for the United States as a rude wake-up call on the morning of December 7, 1941. The primary target of the Japanese strike force was the US Navy base at Pearl Harbor in Hawaii, but the Japanese launched simultaneous attacks on American facilities in the United States Commonwealth of the Philippines. Since the Philippines are located across the International Dateline, it was already December 8 when the attacks came. The attack on Hawaii had been a hit and run, but the attack on the Philippines was the opening blow of a campaign. The Japanese meant to invade and occupy the Philippines. The American and Philippine forces fought back with all they had—which was not much, compared to the well-armed Japanese invaders.

One of the Americans' most potent weapons in the futile defense of the Philippines turned out to be a young USAAF pilot named Boyd D. "Buzz" Wagner.

He had studied aeronautical engineering at the University of Pittsburgh for three years before joining the Air Corps and completing flight training in June 1938. In December 1940, he was assigned to the 24th Pursuit Group, based at Clark Field, north of Manila in the Philippines. He was later assigned to command the group's 17th Pursuit Squadron, which was equipped with Curtiss P 40s.

When the Japanese struck, nearly half the USAAF strength in the Philippines was destroyed on the ground, and the remainder were badly outnumbered. On December 11, Buzz Wagner was on patrol toward the beaches on the northern part of the Philippine main island of Luzon, where the Japanese invasion forces were coming ashore. The Japanese had already begun landing troops and aircraft at Aparri, a base that they would use to support their ground attack on Manila and the rest of Luzon.

Lining up for a strafing attack on the airfield, Wagner came under fire from Japanese ships offshore and he was attacked by five Imperial Japanese Navy Air Force A6M Zeros. He managed to elude the attackers long enough to make two attacks on parked enemy aircraft. Having destroyed ten on the ground, Wagner shot down two of the Zeros that were after him. He thought he had shaken the rest, and he headed back to Clark. However, two of the Zeros tried to ambush him. He managed to down both. His score now stood at four.

On December 15, Wagner led an early morning, low-level, three-P-40 strike on another airfield at Vigan that the invaders were using. After a bomb run in which one P-40 was lost, Wagner attacked with his guns, destroying nine enemy aircraft before one Zero managed to get airborne. As the A6M came up behind him, Wagner chopped the throttle, let the pursuer overshoot, then shot him down. Buzz Wagner had his fifth and, a week after the attack on Pearl Harbor, America had its first ace. He would later be awarded the Distinguished Service Cross for this action.

A few days later, an anti-aircraft artillery shell exploded dangerously close to Wagner's aircraft, shattering his windshield and leaving glass fragments in his face and left eye. He was evacuated to Australia for medical attention. The Philippines were conquered by Japan before Wagner was able to fly again, but as soon as he was able, he was back in action, flying P-39 Airacobras in the campaign in New Guinea. The air battles over New Guinea in 1942 were some of the biggest of the Pacific Theater, and they were battles in which the Imperial Japanese Navy Air Force held the upper hand.

In his last air combat action, Wagner was involved in a huge fight in which Japanese aircraft jumped a flight of P-39s, destroying four of them. The remaining Americans fought back, destroying a like number of Japanese. Of this total, Wagner claimed three. His own final total was eight aerial victories.

In April 1942, the USAAF brought Buzz Wagner and his valuable experience back to the United States, where he would help to train future fighter pilots. Ironically, his last flight was a routine flight. En route from Eglin Field in Florida to Maxwell Field at Montgomery, Alabama November 29, 1942, Wagner suffered a mechanical failure and crashed to his death. Wagner High School at the postwar Clark Air Base was named for Buzz Wagner.

★
This rare color photo of First Lieutenant Buzz Wagner and Lieutenant Mark Muller was taken in Brisbane, Australia in January 1942. In April, Wagner became the youngest lieutenant colonel in the US Army and was reassigned to the 8th Fighter Group in New Guinea. *State Library of Queensland*

# BONG: AMERICA'S ACE OF ACES

**RICHARD IRA "DICK" BONG WAS THE HIGHEST-SCORING AMERICAN ACE OF WORLD WAR II,** and indeed of all time. He was born in Superior, Wisconsin on September 24, 1920, the first of nine children born to Swedish immigrant Carl Bong and Dora Bryce Bong. He grew up on the family farm in northwest Wisconsin, near Poplar, where he learned self-reliance, hard work, and—when predators came calling—good marksmanship. He entered the Superior State Teachers College in the autumn of 1938, but was anxious to learn to fly, so he joined the government sponsored Civilian Pilot Training Program at the college and earned his pilot's license in a Piper Cub.

In May 1941, Dick Bong enlisted in the Army Air Corps Aviation Cadet Program. After basic flight training at Gardner Field near Taft, California—where he soloed in a Vultee BT 13—Bong was assigned to Luke Army Air Field, Arizona for advanced pilot training in North American AT 6 Texans. His gunnery instructor at Luke was an officer named Barry Goldwater, later the long-time Arizona senator, who was the Republican candidate for President of the United States in 1964.

He earned his fighter pilot wings—along with high praise from his instructors—and was commissioned into the USAAF in January 1942, a month after the United States entered World War II. Ironically, the USAAF was reluctant to transfer him to an active combat unit because he was such a good instructor. In May, he was sent to Hamilton Field north of San Francisco, where he was assigned to the 49th Pursuit Squadron of the 14th Pursuit Group as a gunnery instructor in the Lockheed P 38.

Faced with the prospect of not getting into action, Bong engineered an infraction of rules so that he would be punished by an overseas assignment. Popular folklore holds that he looped an airplane around the center span of the Golden Gate Bridge in San Francisco and as a "penalty," he was sent to join the Fifth Air Force in Australia in September 1942. Actually, his commander at the time was General George Kenney, who was himself being reassigned to the Southwest Pacific Theater to command the Fifth Air Force. Kenney had been promised P-38s and he wanted pilots. He wanted Dick Bong.

When Bong reached Brisbane, he was assigned to the 9th Fighter Squadron of the 49th Fighter Group, but he was temporarily detailed to the 39th Fighter Squadron of the 35th Fighter Group. Kenney sent his best pilots where they could fly with experienced units and gain some combat experience themselves. The 35th Fighter Group was in the center of the action in the huge fighter battles that were raging over New Guinea between Allied units based at Port Moresby, and the Imperial Japanese Navy Air Force units based near Lae on the other side of the vast island.

The young pilot from Wisconsin got his New Guinea under-fire training and he scored his first two aerial victories in December 1942. By January 8, 1943, Bong had become an ace with

a Silver Star and the Distinguished Flying Cross—while still on temporary duty with the 39th Fighter Squadron. By March, he had scored nine, including one Mitsubishi A6M Zero and six Nakajima Ki-43 Oscars.

Reassigned to his "permanent" unit, the 49th Fighter Group, Bong became a double ace by April 14, 1943. Most of his scoring missions resulted in single or double victories, but he had a four victory mission on July 26, for which he was awarded the Distinguished Service Cross. By now he had equaled the best score in the Fifth Air Force, with 16, and he continued to work toward his goal of becoming the top USAAF ace in the Southwest Pacific Theater.

In the autumn of 1943, Bong returned home, where he was invited to appear at the Superior State Teachers College Homecoming. In the course of the festivities, Bong discovered that, since all of the men were away at war, there was no Homecoming King—so he was chosen to get the crown. As the story goes, the 1942 outgoing Homecoming Queen was supposed to crown the 1943 Homecoming Queen, but when 19-year-old Marjorie Vattendahl met the handsome young war hero in his uniform and medals, she was so awestruck that Bong had to crown the 1943 Queen.

It was love at first sight both ways. When Bong returned to the Southwest Pacific Theater, he renamed his P 38 "Marge" and mounted a large photo of Marjorie Vattendahl on the side. Soon Marge was one of the most recognized Lightnings in the 49th Fighter Group. On February 15, 1944 Dick and Marge scored their first victory together, a Kawasaki Ki-61 that went down in flames near Cape Hoskins, New Britain. Not all of their missions were triumphs, however. On March 8, Bong's friend, the 20-victory ace Thomas J. Lynch, was shot down by ground fire while the two men were on a strafing run.

199166

In April 1944, Bong hit the magic 27 victory count, becoming the first USAAF ace of World War II to surpass Eddie Rickenbacker's World War I score. General Kenney sent Bong a case of champagne, but General Arnold, knowing that Bong was not a drinker, sent two cases of Coca-Cola, accompanied by the message: "I understand you prefer this type of refreshment to others. You thoroughly deserve to have the kind you want. The Army Air Forces are proud of you and your splendid record. Congratulations!"

Rickenbacker himself sent a congratulatory telegram, telling Dick Bong: "Just received the good news that you are the first one to break my record in World War I by bringing down 27 planes in combat, as well as your promotion, so justly deserved. I hasten to offer my sincere congratulations with the hope that you will double or triple this number. But in trying, use the same calculating techniques that has brought you results to date, for we will need your kind back home after this war is over. My promise of a case of Scotch still holds. So be on the lookout for it."

Bong went back to the United States again in the summer of 1944. Now a celebrity, he was used on a war bond tour, but he also found time to attend the USAAF gunnery school to perfect his skills even further. When he returned to the Pacific in September, Bong was now officially a "gunnery instructor." His instructions from General Kenney were to avoid combat. The USAAF didn't want to lose the new Rickenbacker. However, gunnery instructor Bong did not stay out of the action. On October 10, General Kenney grounded Bong, whose score had now reached 30. By this time, the 49th Fighter Group had relocated to the Philippines, where American forces had just landed. Kenney needed all the help he could get from the 49th Fighter Group to support these operations, so he let Bong talk him into getting back into the air.

On November 15, Bong scored his 36th victory, prompting Kenney to recommend him for the Medal of Honor. In awarding the medal, General Douglas MacArthur, the theater commander and himself a Medal of Honor honoree, commented that Bong "has ruled the air from New Guinea to the Philippines."

The official Medal of Honor citation read: "For conspicuous gallantry and intrepidity in action above and beyond the call of duty in the Southwest Pacific area from 10 October to 15 November 1944. Though assigned to duty as gunnery instructor and neither required nor expected to perform combat duty, Major Bong voluntarily and at his own urgent request engaged in repeated combat missions, including unusually hazardous sorties over Balikpapan, Borneo, and in the Leyte area of the Philippines. His aggressiveness and daring resulted in his shooting down eight enemy airplanes during this period."

In the meanwhile, a competition had begun to develop between Bong and another Fifth Air Force P-38 pilot. Thomas McGuire had been in the Southwest Pacific since March 1943, he had topped the Rickenbacker number and was keeping pace with Bong. In November 1944, Bong and McGuire each scored three to bring their respective scores to 36 and 29.

On the third anniversary of Pearl Harbor, both men scored two victories, and on December 15 and 17, Bong shot down two more to bring his total to 40. Nearly half his victories had now come since he had completed a 158 mission combat tour, and was no longer required to fly such missions. Kenney finally decided to ground Bong again. He was America's top-scoring ace on any front and he had just been awarded the Medal of Honor personally by General Douglas MacArthur. Kenney sent him home for the last time.

When Dick Bong reached the United States on New Year's Eve, he was still America's top-scoring ace, but McGuire had shot down three Zeros on Christmas, and four more the next day to bring his score to 38. On January 7, 1945, however, McGuire lost his life in combat (see the following section), having scored no further victories.

Richard Bong and Marge Vattendahl were married February 10, 1945 at the Concordia Lutheran Church in Superior, Wisconsin, and after the honeymoon, the group reported for duty at the Flight Test Section of the USAAF Air Technical Services Command at Wright Field near Dayton, Ohio. America's Ace of Aces was earmarked to be part of the first generation of American jet fighter pilots. By this time, the USAAF was ready to start forming active jet fighter squadrons, using the Lockheed P-80 Shooting Star, the first American jet fighter to go into production. They were anxious to bring the best pilots up to speed in the new weapon, and Bong was the best of the best. At Wright Field, he was briefed on the technical aspects of the P-80, and in June, he was sent to Burbank, California, home of the Lockheed Aircraft Company. Having scored all of his 40 victories in a Lockheed fighter, Dick Bong would now test the newest Lockheed.

Beginning on July 7, Dick Bong logged four hours in 11 flights with the jet, and took off on his 12th on the afternoon of August 6, 1945. Just after the aircraft became airborne, the engine flamed out and the P-80 went down, killing Bong instantly. Ironically, Bong would die one day after the nuclear strike on Hiroshima that hastened the end of World War II (on August 6 in the United States, it is already August 7 across the International Dateline).

Out in the Pacific, General Kenney was on his way to General MacArthur's headquarters when he got the news. "I stopped thinking of the atom bomb which had wiped out Hiroshima that morning," he said. "I even stopped thinking of the capitulation of Japan which we all knew was about to take place in a few days. Wherever I landed, I found that the whole Fifth Air Force felt the same, that we had lost a loved one, someone we had been glad to see out of combat and on his way home eight months before. Major Richard I. Bong of Poplar was dead.... We not only loved him, we boasted about him, we were proud of him. That's why each of us got a lump in our throats when we read that telegram about his death. Major Bong, Ace of American Aces in all our wars, is destined to hold the title for all time. With the weapons we possess today, no war of the future will last long enough for any pilot to run up 40 victories again.

"His country and the Air Force must never forget their number one fighter pilot, who will inspire other fighter pilots and countless thousands of youngsters who will want to follow in his footsteps every time that any nation or coalition of nations dares to challenge our right to think, speak, and live as a free people."

Dick Bong and his wife Marge Vattendahl Bong in the cockpit of a P-38 Lightning at the Lockheed factory in Burbank, California. Bong had named each of the Lightnings that he flew after his wife. This picture was taken on March 9, 1945 just after her first flight in a P-38. Five months later, Dick was killed in a jet fighter crash near this airfield. *Author's Collection*

Eddie Rickenbacker commented that Bong was "An example of the tragic and terrible price we must pay to maintain principles of human rights, of greater value than life itself. This gallant Air Force hero will be remembered because he made his final contribution to aviation in the dangerous role of test pilot of an untried experimental plane, a deed that places him among the stout hearted pioneers who gave their lives in the conquest of sky and space."

Richard Ira Bong was buried in the Poplar Cemetery August 8. Marge remarried several years later and had two daughters. She did not speak publicly about her first husband for four decades, but after 1985, when she attended the dedication of the Richard Ira Bong Memorial Bridge in Minnesota, she has become active in veterans' affairs and in the efforts to build the Richard Ira Bong Heritage Center, located on the bay front in Superior, that honors all the Americans, especially from Wisconsin and Minnesota, who served in World War II. The centerpiece of the facility is a Lockheed P 38 that was restored by volunteers at the Minnesota Air National Guard in nearby Duluth and painted to be a replica of Bong's Marge, in which he scored his key 1944 victories.

In recalling her generation, the World War II generation, Marge is quoted to have said recently that "I feel that the people in that era were very unique…. There was such a sense of pride and patriotism. As far as Richard is concerned, he was one of the most visible heroes of the war. But he didn't feel like a hero. He expressed a sentiment that summed it up so well. He said he was just doing his job."

The story of Dick Bong and Tommy McGuire is told in great detail in this author's best-selling dual biography *Aces High: The Heroic Saga of the Two Top-Scoring American Aces of World War II.*

# MCGUIRE:
# HE DIED TRYING

★
The Lone Eagle and
the Ace: Legendary
aviator Charles
Lindbergh (left) with
Tommy McGuire at the
475th Fighter Group
base at Hollandia, New
Guinea in June 1944.
*US Air Force*

**THE SECOND HIGHEST-SCORING AMERICAN ACE OF WORLD WAR II,** Thomas Buchanan "Tommy" McGuire, Jr. was clearly one of the best combat pilots of World War II, but he spent the last year of his life racing to catch Richard "Dick" Ira Bong's score of 40. He never succeeded—though he reached 38—and he died trying.

Tommy McGuire was a tough and ambitious Irish-American from New Jersey who was a natural when it came to air combat. "Go in close," He would tell the younger combat pilots, echoing the words of legendary aces such as "Sailor" Malan and Erich Hartmann. "And when you think you're too close, go in closer."

He was born in Ridgewood, New Jersey on August 1, 1920, attended the Georgia Institute of Technology and later joined the USAAF as an aviation cadet at MacDill Field in Florida on July 12, 1941. McGuire trained at Randolph Field and Kelly Field in Texas and earned his pilot's wings in February 1942, two months after Pearl Harbor, and requested a combat assignment. At that time, United States strategic necessity dictated efforts to halt the Japanese advances in the South Pacific and the North Pacific. Lieutenant McGuire was assigned to the latter, as it was assumed that the Japanese were then headed for Alaska.

While they did capture several islands in the Aleutian chain southwest of Alaska, they never launched their invasion of mainland Alaska, and duty in Alaska became synonymous with boredom and inaction. After a year of seeing little action, McGuire asked to be reassigned to a theater where he could use his combat flying aptitude. Finally, in March 1943, he was reassigned to the 49th Fighter Group of the USAAF Fifth Air Force in the Southwest Pacific, where aerial combat was furious and constant.

In June 1943, he was transferred to the 475th "Satan's Angels" Fighter Group. Based at Dobodura on New Guinea, it was the first group in the Fifth Air Force to be composed entirely of Lockheed P-38 Lightnings, which were faster and had longer range than the Curtiss P-40s and Bell P-39s, which had previously comprised the backbone of the Fifth. At last in the air combat environment for which he had yearned, Tommy McGuire achieved his first three aerial victories over Dagua, New Guinea on August 18, and made ace by the end of the month. By October 17, he would reach "Lucky 13."

It was "Lucky 13" only in that he was lucky to be alive. On October 17, McGuire claimed three Mitsubishi A6M Zeros in one engagement, but as he banked away to help another pilot whose Lightning was damaged, he was bounced by three Zeros that shot up Pudgy—one of a series of P-38s that he flew, all named for his wife. As Pudgy nosed over and started to go down, and as it passed through 12,000 feet, McGuire tried to jump, but he was caught and couldn't get out. At 5,000 feet, he finally broke free, but discovered that the ripcord on his parachute had

ripped off. He finally got the parachute open just in time, but spent 40 minutes treading water in Oro Bay hoping that a US Navy patrol boat would reach him before the sharks or the Japanese.

By this time, Tommy McGuire and Dick Bong were the leading USAAF aces in the theater—with Bong eight victories ahead—so a competition naturally ensued. Both men eagerly sought the distinction of being the top-scoring USAAF ace in the Pacific. When Bong went home on leave, McGuire expected to make up the difference, but he wound up grounded by malaria until the end of December. The day after Christmas, he led a 475th Fighter Group force covering a US Navy convoy off Cape Gloucester on New Britain. The convoy came under attack, and McGuire led the counterattack. His formation destroyed 10 dive bombers and three fighters. To Tommy McGuire went three aerial victories and a Distinguished Service Cross for leadership and heroism.

Two of the top-scoring USAAF aces in the Southwest Pacific, Neel Kearby and Tommy Lynch, were shot down early in 1944, leaving Bong and McGuire at the apogee of acedom in the region. Bong pushed his score to 27 in April 1944—becoming the first USAAF ace of World War II to surpass Eddie Rickenbacker's World War I score—and was sent home to take part in a celebrity war bond tour.

While Bong was stateside, McGuire—now the commander of the 475th Fighter Group's 431st Fighter Squadron—was gaining on him. As an interesting footnote to the history of the 475th Fighter Group, it was in the summer of 1944 that the great aviation hero Charles A. Lindbergh joined the group—unofficially. He was serving as a civilian "consultant" with United Aircraft, makers of the Pratt & Whitney engines used in many American combat aircraft, albeit not in the P-38s, which had General Motors Allison engines. He was in the Pacific to observe, and he wound up teaching techniques for extending the range of the P-38. He did fly a number of combat missions and is known to have scored two aerial victories. These were never officially credited.

The competition between McGuire and Bong—which had reportedly become an obsession with McGuire—resumed when Bong came back into action by September 1944, and continued after the 475th Fighter Group relocated to Leyte in the Philippines after the October invasion. It was in October that the faster, longer range, P 38Ls were delivered to the 475th Fighter Group. McGuire's new aircraft—his fifth P-38—was promptly identified with his wife's nickname as *Pudgy V*.

On October 14, McGuire scored three more victories in his new aircraft, but the goal of reaching Bong's score still eluded him. According to the folklore, the two men were cordial to one another, and are often reported to have been friends. In any case, Bong—who was ahead with a comfortable margin—seems to have taken the competition less seriously than McGuire.

In November, Bong and McGuire scored three each to bring their respective scores to 36 and 29. On the third anniversary of Pearl Harbor, both men scored two victories, and on December 15 and 17, Bong shot down two more to bring his total to 40. With this, Fifth Air Force Commander General George Kenney decided to ground Bong. He was America's top-scoring ace on any front and he had just been awarded the Medal of Honor personally by General Douglas MacArthur. Kenney did not want to lose him, so he was grounded and sent home—permanently.

This left Tommy McGuire—the lanky 24-year-old who grew a black mustache to make himself look older—as the top-scoring USAAF ace still in combat. He was also now the commander of the 431st Fighter Squadron of the 475th Fighter Group.

When Dick Bong reached the United States, he was still America's top-scoring ace, but McGuire shot down three Zeros during a bomber escort mission on Christmas Day, and four more on December 26 to bring his score to 38—two short of Bong. In the latter engagement, he set his sights on one Zero that was attacking a B 24 and shot it down with a 45-degree deflection shot at a range of 400 yards. It was an impossible shot—but he did it.

Dick Bong was due to arrive in the United States on New Year's Eve, and there were plans for him to be greeted as "America's leading ace." General Kenney was under pressure from those who were choreographing the public relations aspect of Bong's arrival. They wanted to be sure that Bong really was "America's leading ace." He had been for months, and they wanted it to stay that way—at least until after the homecoming celebrations. With this in mind, Kenney grounded McGuire until January 6, 1945.

On January 7, 1945, McGuire took off before dawn from Marsten Field on Leyte, intending to add to his score and hoping to add three. He was not flying *Pudgy V*, but rather another P-38L that was assigned to fellow pilot Fred Champlin. He was accompanied by his usual wingman, Edwin Weaver, with a second element led by Jack Rittmayer with his wingman, Douglass Thropp. Each of the P 38's carried two 160 gallon external fuel tanks. The mission was to be a fighter sweep of Negros Island, which was known to have Japanese airfields. According to various sources, the mission was not officially authorized.

They made most of the flight at 10,000 feet, but at Negros, the weather forced them to descend to 6,000 feet, and then to 1,400 feet. After failing to engage the enemy over Fabrica, McGuire ordered the flight to proceed to another Japanese base. On the way, Rittmayer experienced engine trouble, and he became separated from the others while flying through a cloud.

Weaver then spotted a Japanese Nakajima Ki-43 fighter ahead and below the Americans heading in the opposite direction. The aircraft passed one another, and the Japanese pilot, Akira Sugimoto, turned to attack. He scored a hit on Thropp's P-38, but Rittmayer, who had caught up with the others, opened fire on Sugimoto.

Instead of breaking off his attack, Sugimoto slipped away from Rittmayer and opened fire on Weaver. There was now a serious dogfight going, and the pilots would obviously be inclined to jettison their drop tanks in order to be better able to maneuver. However, at some point early in the fight, McGuire specifically ordered that the tanks not be jettisoned. Dropping their extra fuel would greatly reduce the amount of time that they would have to spend over Negros before making the long flight back. It is theorized that McGuire gave the order because he was anxious to have as much time as possible to hunt for his three decisive kills.

When he came under attack, Weaver called for McGuire to help him. McGuire turned to go after Sugimoto, but his P-38 started to stall. Instead of backing off the tight turning maneuver, McGuire appeared to turn harder. His aircraft stalled, nosed over and started to go down. Since he was barely more than 1,000 feet above the jungle, McGuire had no time to recover control. The tight, fast turn at low altitude—with the heavy fuel tanks still in place—was what caused McGuire's P-38 to stall and spin. He was too low to recover and he crashed to his death in a ball of fire.

Weaver saw the explosion as McGuire crashed. Rittmayer and Thropp chased Sugimoto's damaged aircraft. Various versions of the story say that Sugimoto crash-landed and either died of bullet wounds suffered in the dogfight or was killed by Filipino guerrillas.

At this point, a second Japanese aircraft, a Nakajima Ki-84 piloted by Mirunori Fukuda, entered the fight. Weaver returned Fukuda's fire, but Fukuda then opened up on Rittmayer, who was trying to turn to get a shot. Rittmayer's P-38—also behaving sluggishly because of its fuel tanks—received a fatal burst from the Ki-84's guns and went down, crashing not far from where McGuire had crashed.

Fukuda then turned his attention toward Thropp, who escaped into a cloud bank with a damaged engine. Weaver then attempted to find Fukuda in the clouds. Failing that, he rendezvoused with Thropp and the two headed for home.

The news of McGuire's loss would not be released to the public for ten days. When he heard the news, Dick Bong is reported to have said sadly, "I was afraid of that."

Major Thomas Buchanan McGuire was posthumously awarded the Medal of Honor for his heroic actions on December 25 and 26, 1944. General George Kenney personally presented McGuire's Medal of Honor to his widow, Marilynn "Pudgy" McGuire, on May 8, 1946, at the City Hall in Paterson, New Jersey. Charles Lindbergh was reportedly in the crowd of family and friends.

Marilynn McGuire returned to her hometown of San Antonio, Texas, where she had met McGuire when he was at flight school there, and later remarried. In September 1949, the former Fort Dix Army Air Field near the New Jersey state capital of Trenton was reopened as a US Air Force facility and renamed McGuire Air Force Base in Tommy's honor. During that same year, McGuire's remains were identified and recovered from Negros Island and interred at Arlington National Cemetery near Washington, DC.

As noted above, the story of Tommy McGuire, Dick Bong and their rivalry is told in great detail in Bill Yenne's best-selling biography *Aces High: The Heroic Saga of the Two Top-Scoring American Aces of World War II*.

★
USAAF fighter pilot Thomas Buchanan McGuire, the second top-scoring USAAF ace of World War II, on a New Guinea flight line in 1942. This is as he appeared during his early days as a fighter pilot, before he grew his signature mustache. *US Air Force*

# KEARBY: TOP PACIFIC THUNDERBOLT ACE

Neel Kearby, who commanded the 348th Fighter Group of the USAAF Fifth Air Force, was the highest-scoring P-47 Thunderbolt ace in the Pacific. *US Air Force*

**THREE OF THE TOP TWO DOZEN USAAF ACES IN THE PACIFIC THEATER** would earn the Medal of Honor. Two were the top two aces—Dick Bong and Tommy McGuire—and the third was Neel Kearby, the number four USAAF ace in the theater. Kearby, like McGuire, had also figured in the Dick Bong story because, before his "ace race" with McGuire, Bong had been in a similar race with Kearby. In fact, in the months before Bong scored his magic 27th to top Rickenbacker, he and Kearby had been tied several times. This was something that McGuire had never been able to accomplish later in the war.

Kearby arrived on June 30, 1943, reaching Australia assigned to the 348th Fighter Group, the first unit in the area to be equipped with the P-47 Thunderbolt. For a year, the signature USAAF fighter in the region had been the P-38 Lightning and the P-38s showed little respect for the single-engine "Jug."

As the story goes, Kearby demonstrated the P-47's prowess in a mock dogfight with a P-38, but operationally, the Thunderbolts were hindered by their lack of range compared to the Lightnings, a situation that was exacerbated by the fact that the P-47s had no external fuel tanks until General George Kenney arranged for them to be manufactured locally.

From Australia, the 348th Fighter Group was forward-deployed to Port Moresby on New Guinea to bide its time until the drop tanks arrived. The unit finally got its first taste of combat on August 16, but Neel Kearby did not score his first aerial victories until September 4. He opened with a double—a fighter and a bomber—and he scored his third on September 15. He had openly stated that he planned to be the highest-scoring USAAF ace of World War II, and promised that he would not go home until he had scored 50 victories.

On October 11, Kearby was leading a four-Thunderbolt reconnaissance patrol near Wewak, northwest of Port Moresby, when he observed a Mitsubishi A6M below them. Kearby attacked, converting his altitude advantage to speed and destroyed the Japanese fighter. The four USAAF fighters had just resumed their patrol when they observed a huge armada of Japanese warplanes far below. There were a dozen bombers and three times that number of fighters, obviously headed for a raid on Allied positions.

Despite the enemy's numerical superiority, Kearby figured that surprise would convert to even odds, so he ordered an attack. In his first high-speed pass, Kearby claimed three, while Bill Dunham and John Moore each scored singles.

Kearby then ordered his patrol to break contact and return to base, but he observed the fourth American, Raymond Gallagher, under attack by a pair of Kawanishi Ki-61s. He dived into the fray and shot down both of the Japanese fighters. At that point, Dunham and Moore observed Kearby fighting six Ki-61s. He probably downed at least two of these, but his gun camera ran out of film, so his total for the day was six confirmed and one probable.

For setting an American record for victories scored in a single day, General George Kenney recommended Kearby for the Medal of Honor. At the time that General Douglas MacArthur personally awarded the decoration, Kearby was tied with Dick Bong as the highest-scoring aces in the USAAF, with 19 confirmed victories each.

Bong was to be the first to break the tie, increasing his score to 21. In turn, Kearby scored a double on January 9, 1944. The score was tied again. General Kenney, meanwhile, had become concerned about these young pilots becoming careless in their rush to pile up victories. He ordered Bong and Kearby to limit themselves to one kill per mission. If they scored, they were to then break off their attack. As it turned out, February came and went with neither man scoring victories. It was probably inevitable that the first man to get a kill in March would want to maintain the momentum and make up for lost time.

On March 5, Neel Kearby and Bill Dunham, along with Sam Blair, were on patrol to Wewak, the scene of Kearby's October triumph. Now, however, Kenney had forbidden Kearby to repeat the multiple victory action for which he had recommended him for the Medal of Honor. But the Thunderbolts ran into 15 Japanese aircraft.

Kearby claimed one almost immediately and turned back into the enemy formation for more. Suddenly, he was jumped by three Japanese fighters. Dunham and Blair quickly took out a pair of Zeros, but the third nailed Kearby from close range, and his P 47 augured into the hillside far below. At the time of his death, Kearby's score stood at 22.

★
Neel Kearby climbs out of his P-47, which is marked with 15 of his 22 aerial victories. On October 11, 1943, Kearby shot down six enemy planes to become the first P-47 ace of the Pacific Theater of Operations. This set a record for most victories in a single mission and earned Kearby the Medal of Honor. *US Army Air Forces*

# GABRESKI: THE USAAF TOP MAN IN EUROPE

**THE TOP-SCORING AMERICAN ACE IN THE EUROPEAN THEATER OF WORLD WAR II**, Francis Stanley "Gabby" Gabreski was also the top-scoring American ace to earn victories in two wars. To his 28 victories in Europe, Gabreski would add 6.5 in the Korean War.

Born and raised in Oil City, Pennsylvania, Gabby Gabreski was a medical student at the University of Notre Dame in Indiana, when he decided to take flying lessons. In 1941, Gabreski joined the USAAF and earned his fighter pilot's wings before the United States had entered World War II. He was then assigned to the 45th Pursuit Group, based at Wheeler Field in the Territory of Hawaii. It was here that Gabreski met Catherine Cochran, who later would become his wife, and it was here that Gabreski heard the wake-up call of war on the morning of December 7, 1941.

On that morning, Gabreski managed to get airborne in his Curtiss P-36, but not until after the attackers had escaped. His combat experience did not begin in the Pacific Theater, nor even with the USAAF, however. In early 1942, he was among a number of American pilots who were assigned to Royal Air Force units in Britain so that they could fly with, and learn from, combat-experienced pilots in combat situations. The American son of Polish immigrants, Gabreski had grown up speaking Polish, as well as English, so he was assigned to the No. 315 Squadron. Based at Northolt, No. 315 Squadron was a British squadron comprised of Polish pilots who had escaped to England when Poland was overrun by the German Blitzkrieg three years before.

After 20 scoreless missions flying a Spitfire with the Royal Air Force, Gabreski was reassigned to fly a Republic P-47 Thunderbolt with the USAAF 56th Fighter Group. The unit was then just forming, but it would eventually become one of the most famous in the USAAF Eighth Air Force, and one of the units most feared by the Luftwaffe. Commanded by the legendary Lieutenant Colonel Hubert "Hub" Zemke, the 56th would come to be known simply as "Zemke's Wolfpack," and it would set a record among USAAF units by shooting down a thousand Luftwaffe aircraft.

★
Francis Stanley "Gabby" Gabreski was the highest-scoring USAAF in the European Theater of World War II. He scored 28 aerial victories while flying P-47 Thunderbolts with the 56th Fighter Group of the USAAF Eighth Air Force. He also added 6.5 to his overall tally flying F-86 Sabre Jets, becoming one of only seven American combat pilots who were aces in two wars. *National Archives*

★
Gabby Gabreski and his crew chief, Sergeant Ralph Safford, prepare for a mission in June 1944 at the 56th Fighter Group base at Boxted, England. *National Archives*

Gabreski was assigned to the 61st Fighter Squadron of the 56th Fighter Group, which would also include several former Polish Air Force pilots, including Boleslaw "Mike" Gladych. The mission of the Wolfpack, as with most fighter groups within the Eighth Air Force, was to escort strategic bombers on their strikes into German-occupied Europe.

In June 1943, Gabreski became commander of the 61st Fighter Squadron, although he would not score his first aerial victory—against a Focke-Wulf Fw 190—until August 24. On November 26, he made ace on his 75th mission by shooting down a pair of Messerschmitt Bf 110s, and was awarded the Distinguished Service Cross.

On December 11, the 61st Fighter Squadron made their rendezvous with the B-17 bombers they were supposed to be escorting, only to find that the bombers were under attack by about 40 Bf 110s. In the course of the ensuing dogfight, Gabreski became separated from the other P-47s, but he attacked three Messerschmitts solo and downed one. Noticing that he was low on fuel, Gabreski turned for home. He ran into a Messerschmitt Bf 109, but had no fuel to get into a dogfight, so he decided to make a run for the British coast. He both outran and out-maneuvered the Messerschmitt, and managed to lose himself in a cloud when his turbo-supercharger played out. The engine failed just as he reached Britain.

In January 1944, Gabby Gabreski, now promoted to deputy executive officer of the 56th Fighter Group, scored his tenth victory. On May 22, Gabreski had the best day of his career, shooting down three Fw 190s. During Operation Overlord, the Allied invasion of Northern France on June 6, 1944, Gabreski led the 61st Fighter Squadron in air support missions over the beachhead, but soon the unit was back in action against the Luftwaffe. By July 5, Gabreski had exceeded the 26 victories scored by Captain Eddie Rickenbacker in World War I, making him the top scoring USAAF ace in the European Theater.

On July 20, having completed 193 missions, Gabreski was about to be rotated home, when he chose to fly one more mission, a mission that he did not have to fly. One version of the story tells that he was actually on the field with his bags packed, waiting for the transport that would take him home.

The fateful flight took Gabreski and the 61st Fighter Squadron on a strafing attack against various targets in western Germany, including an air base near Coblenz. Gabreski made one low pass over the field, scoring many good hits on German aircraft. However, capriciousness overcame good sense and he went back for another pass. This time, he was too low and the angle of attack was too high. His tracers were going over the tops of the targets. He nosed down slightly, and as he did so, the tips of his propeller blades clipped the runway and bent. The resulting vibration almost literally shook the plane apart, and it was starting to tear the engine apart. Oil gushed from the Pratt & Whitney R-2800 Double Wasp and splashed over the windscreen.

Gabreski couldn't fly and was too low to bail out, so he decided to try a crash landing. He brought the Thunderbolt down in a wheat field just as German ground troops began shooting at him. Another P-47 attacked the Germans and Gabreski managed to escape into the woods. For five days, with the help of a Polish laborer that he met, he alluded German patrols. Imported

★
Gabby Gabreski
rolls across the
ramp at Boxted in
his big Republic
P-47 Thunderbolt.
*National Archives*

from Poland to work as a slave for the Germans, the man was a prisoner himself, but he risked himself to try to help Gabreski to avoid becoming a prisoner.

Finally, however, Gabreski was captured and sent to Stalag Luft I, a prisoner of war camp holding Allied air officers that would also be Hub Zemke's home after he was shot down in October 1944. Gabreski, as one of the senior officers in the camp, was one of the leaders who oversaw operations of a clandestine radio receiver and several tunnel-digging projects, all of which went unnoticed by the guards. After enduring a bitterly cold winter in captivity, Gabreski, Zemke and their 8,496 fellow prisoners were liberated by the Russians in March 1945, and repatriated.

Back in the United States, Gabby Gabreski and Catherine Cochran were finally married, and Gabby was assigned to the Air Logistics Command Engineering Flight School at Wright Field, Ohio, where he became a test pilot. He left the service in 1946, however, for the greener pastures of private industry and he spent a year doing promotional work for the Douglas Aircraft Company, while studying for a degree in Political Science at Columbia University.

In September 1947, the USAAF was divorced from the US Army to become the independent US Air Force and Gabreski was lured back into uniform as commander of his World War II unit, the 56th Fighter Group. The 56th Fighter Group was now based at Selfridge Field, Michigan and making the transition to jets.

In 1951, a year after the start of the Korean War, Gabreski was assigned to command the 4th Fighter Interceptor Group. Flying North American Aviation F-86A Sabre Jets, the group was sent to the Korean War under the command of John Meyer who, like Gabreski, had been an ace in the Eighth Air Force in England during World War II.

In July 1951, Gabreski shot down a MiG-15 to score his first jet-to-jet aerial victory. In December 1951, after two more MiGs, he was placed in command of the 51st Fighter Interceptor Group, which had just become operational at Suwon Air Base with the newer F-86E aircraft. The specific mission of the 51st was to escort B-29 bombers on strikes against targets in North Korea.

Gabreski would continue flying combat missions, becoming a jet ace early in 1953 and ending the Korean War with a score of 6.5 to add to his 28 scored in World War II. With the 34.5 total victories, Gabreski was the third highest-scoring American ace of all time—after Richard "Dick" Bong with 40 and Thomas "Tommy" McGuire with 38. With his 28 in World War II, he had been in third place among USAAF pilots in World War II, but he was behind the highest-scoring US Navy ace David McCampbell, who had 34 in World War II, and tied with top US Marine Corps ace Gregory "Pappy" Boyington.

Gabby Gabreski also ended the Korean War with a Distinguished Service Medal and a ticker tape parade. In 1955, after serving as Director of Safety Air Operations and Chief of Combat Operations and finally Chief of Special Projects at Norton Air Force Base in California, Gabreski completed a course at the Command and Staff School, and was named Deputy Chief of Staff Operations in the Ninth Air Force.

In 1960, Gabreski received his penultimate operational command as commander of the 18th Tactical Fighter Wing at Kadena Air Base, Okinawa. In 1962, he became the director of the Secretariat for the Commander in Chief of the Pacific Air Forces (PACAF) at Hickam Air Force Base, Hawaii, and later he served as PACAF Inspector General. In 1964, Colonel Gabreski accepted his last US Air Force assignment, as commander of the 52nd Fighter Wing on Long Island, New York.

After his retirement in 1967, Gabreski worked in Public Relations and Customer Relations at the Grumman Corporation, and later as president of the Long Island Railroad. He also wrote his autobiography, Gabby, A Fighter Pilot's Life. Gabreski's son Donald Gabreski followed in his father's footsteps, graduating from the US Air Force Academy in 1966 and later serving as a fighter pilot. Gabreski Airport at Southampton Beach on Long Island, New York is named for Gabby Gabreski.

★
The famous photo of Lieutenant Colonel Gabby Gabreski in the cockpit of his P-47 Thunderbolt with his markings of 28 victories over the Luftwaffe. Gabreski scored his 28th victory on July 5, 1944 and was scheduled to rotate back to the states when he decided to fly "one last mission" on July 20. He was shot down and captured, but survived as a prisoner and received a belated hero's welcome. *National Archives*

# JOHNSON:
## THE COUNTRY BOY ACE

★
Robert Samuel Johnson
was the second highest-
scoring USAAF ace in
the European Theater,
achieving 27 victories
during the conflict
while flying various
P-47 Thunderbolts with
the 56th Fighter Group
of the USAAF Eighth
Air Force. Here he is
greeted by his crew
chief, Staff Sergeant
Ernest D. Gould, after
Johnson's return from
a three-victory mission.
*National Archives*

**THE USAAF'S NUMBER TWO ACE IN EUROPE,** like its number one ace, was a pilot with the legendary 56th Fighter Group, "Zemke's Wolfpack." The wolf in this case was a baby-faced country boy who was born in Lawton, Oklahoma on February 21, 1920. Robert Samuel "Bob" Johnson had studied aeronautical engineering at Cameron College, and boxed in the amateur 112 to 149-pound class in his spare time. Interested in flying since his childhood, he took lessons and joined the US Army Air Forces in 1941. The USAAF trained him as a bomber pilot but reassigned him to fighters.

Trained in the Republic P-47 Thunderbolt, Bob Johnson went to England in January 1943 and was assigned to the 56th Fighter Group. Johnson entered combat in April, escorting bombers across the English Channel or the North Sea. Johnson scored his first victory, a Focke-Wulf Fw 190, on June 13. In October, he became an ace. Though Johnson wouldn't know it for half a century, his fifth victory was one of the Luftwaffe's finest, Oberstleutnant Hans Philipp, the commander of Jagdgeschwader 1, who had scored 177 victories on the Eastern Front and another 29 in the West.

In the engagement that made him an ace, Johnson had observed four Fw 190s attacking some USAAF bombers over France and dove 5,000 feet to attack the lead ship. Just as he destroyed Philipp's Focke-Wulf, Johnson himself was hit and he lost his rudder. Using his trim tabs to compensate for lost rudder control, he managed to escape the remaining Luftwaffe fighters and rendezvous with the P-47s of the 62nd Fighter Squadron, who escorted him back to England. When they reached Boxsted, the 62nd pilots wanted the crippled Johnson to land first but, in a gentlemanly gesture, he let them go first because if he crashed on landing, it would block the runway.

By the end of 1943, the P-47s had proven themselves to be so effective against the Luftwaffe that the Germans pulled their defensive line back to the limit of the Thunderbolt's operational range, which meant that they withdrew from the French and Netherlands coastlines, to the area roughly between Kiel and Hanover.

It was here that a number of massive aerial battles occurred, including those on March 6, 8, and 15, 1944, when Bob Johnson led a handful of Thunderbolts against more than 100 Luftwaffe fighters sent up to attack American bombers. There were 34 bombers lost on March 8, but on March 15, Johnson used his radio to vector a large number of American fighters into the battle when the Germans attacked, and no bombers were lost to interceptors.

The Country Boy Ace would fly 91 missions and score 27 victories, with the final two—a Bf 109G and an Fw 190—coming on the 91st mission on May 8, 1944. Some lists credit him with 28 victories, but the 28th was one that was actually scored by Ralph Johnson on the same day and later officially corrected. Bob Johnson was the second-highest scoring American pilot in the European Theater, with one fewer victory than Gabby Gabreski, who scored his 28th after Johnson left the theater.

Bob Johnson returned to the United States in June 1944, just after the invasion of Europe and was assigned to go on a publicity tour to help sell war bonds. It was during this tour that he met Richard "Dick" Bong, who was the top-scoring USAAF ace in the Pacific Theater, at that time with 27 victories, the same as Johnson.

While Bong would return to combat and push his total to 40, Johnson left the service—though he remained in the Air Force Reserve—to go to work for Republic Aviation, the makers of the aircraft that he had flown in combat. Johnson's first task with Republic was to redesign the P-47 cockpit to make it more user friendly for the pilots by clustering the instruments so that they could be seen at a glance.

Johnson traveled to Korea in December 1951 at the height of the Korean War, as a representative of Republic, whose F-84 Thunderjet was in combat there. Two years later, in the uniform of a US Air Force Reserve lieutenant colonel, he was present at the armistice talks at Panmunjom. He was with Republic for 18 years before going into the insurance business. His book, *Thunderbolt! Flying the P-47 with the Fabulous 56th Fighter Group in World War II* was published in 1997. Robert Johnson died on December 27, 1998.

★
Robert S. Johnson was the first USAAF fighter pilot in the European theater to surpass Eddie Rickenbacker's World War I score of 26 victories. This US Army photograph was released on May 26, 1945. *National Archives*

Colonel Charles Henry "Mac" MacDonald was the third highest-scoring USAAF ace in the Pacific Theater and also served as commander of the 475th Fighter Group of the USAAF Fifth Air Force. *US Air Force*

# MACDONALD:
# WITH LINDBERGH
# IN THE PACIFIC

**TIED WITH BOB JOHNSON FOR THE NUMBER FOUR SPOT AMONG ALL USAAF ACES OF WORLD WAR II,** Charles H. "Mac" MacDonald scored his 27 victories in the Pacific Theater, and had the distinction of being the highest-scoring of the great P-38 aces to survive the war. Dick Bong and Tommy McGuire are the best remembered, and indeed, they were the two highest-scoring American aces, but MacDonald not only survived the war, he was there when it started. Like Gabby Gabreski, he was at Wheeler Field on December 7, 1941.

During the late 1930s, MacDonald had taken his civilian pilot training while he was studying philosophy at Louisiana State University, and he joined the USAAF after having graduated with his degree and pilot's license. Assigned to 20th Pursuit Group at Wheeler Field on the fateful Sunday morning, MacDonald was among those who chased the Japanese but got no hits.

MacDonald remained in Hawaii until early 1943, when he came back to the continental United States to be trained in the P-38 Lightning. He was then assigned to command the newly-formed 340th Fighter Squadron of the 348th Fighter Group, which was destined to be sent out to New Guinea, which was where the most intense confrontations between the USAAF and the Imperial Japanese Navy Air Force were taking place.

Though the 348th Fighter Group moved to New Guinea in June 1943, MacDonald would see no action until October, when he was re-assigned as executive officer of the 475th "Satan's Angels" Fighter Group—Tommy McGuire's unit—at Dobodura.

Shortly after arriving with the 475th Fighter Group, MacDonald was on a patrol that intercepted a Japanese bomber strike force that had been attacking Allied ships. MacDonald dove to attack and claimed his first two aerial victories in a matter of minutes. As he maneuvered to attack a third, his P-38 started taking hits from behind. The Japanese fighter on his tail managed to knock out one of his two engines and damaged his hydraulic and electrical systems. The enemy then broke off, probably assuming that he was a goner. Somehow, MacDonald managed to coax the Lightning back to base.

Later in the month, MacDonald earned his first of two Distinguished Service Crosses on a bomber escort mission to the huge Japanese base at Rabaul, New Britain. The escort team included four flights of P-38s, but the one that MacDonald commanded was the only one that managed to stay with the B-24s when the weather became exceptionally ugly. As it was, they were desperately needed when the Imperial Japanese Navy Air Force fighters came after the bombers. In the ensuing dogfight, MacDonald claimed one of the attacking A6M Zeros himself.

★
Colonel Charles
MacDonald and
Al Nelson in
the Pacific with
MacDonald's P-38J
Lightning *Putt Putt
Maru*. US Air Force

In November 1943, MacDonald was promoted to command the 475th Fighter Group when George Prentice, the previous commander, was rotated back to the United States. Over the course of the next few months, MacDonald raised his score to 10.

On June 26, 1944, MacDonald was playing checkers with his deputy commander in the operations shack at Hollandia, New Guinea, when someone walked in. MacDonald glanced up, saw a man in a naval uniform without insignia of rank—or pilot's wings. The man said he was there to see Colonel MacDonald, but MacDonald told him to wait and went back to the game. When the game was over, MacDonald asked him what his name was and what he wanted.

"Charles Lindbergh." Came the reply, and he went on to explain that he was a civilian consultant with United Aircraft, makers of the Pratt & Whitney engines used in many American combat aircraft.

MacDonald, who was preoccupied with his checkers and hadn't caught the name, asked the man if he was a pilot. The way that he said "yes" made MacDonald look up again. It was in fact, the legendary "Lone Eagle." MacDonald dropped everything, and the two men talked flying for hours. It turned out that the great aviator already had a few hours in the P-38, so MacDonald invited him to fly as part of a four-ship patrol the following day. Lindbergh not only flew with

used the Focke-Wulf's own contrail to mask his attack. He came up from below and behind and fired from close range. Awarded a second Distinguished Service Cross, Meyer became deputy commander of the 352nd Fighter Group.

During late December 1944 and early January 1945, the Luftwaffe launched their huge Operation Bodenplatte (Base Plate) offensive, the biggest air attack on Western Europe in over four years. The 352nd Fighter Group had by this time started sending advance units to air fields in recently-liberated areas of continental Europe, in preparation for the group's eventual relocation to a base at Chievres in Belgium.

On New Year's Day, Meyer was with the advanced units in Belgium—assigned to the IX Tactical Air Command—during one phase of the Luftwaffe offensive. He was leading a dozen Mustangs that were preparing to take off, when a large number of German aircraft attacked the field. The attack caught Meyer just as his Mustang lifted off the runway. He opened fire and claimed an Fw 190 before he had even got his landing gear up.

The American fighters got off and attacked the Germans. Over the course of 45 minutes, the 352nd Fighter Group shot down 23 Luftwaffe aircraft, including a second Fw 190 for Meyer, his 24th victory.

Eight days later, while he was en route to Paris in a US Army vehicle, the icy roads did to Meyer what the Luftwaffe never did. His injuries would keep him out of the air for the remainder of World War II, but they did not keep him down.

After the war ended, Meyer remained in staff jobs as the USAAF went through the metamorphosis to become the US Air Force in September 1947. He was assigned to the office of the Secretary of the Air Force in Washington, DC and, in 1948, he became the US Air Force liaison with the United States House of Representatives.

In August 1950, two months after the start of the Korean War, Meyer returned to a tactical flying unit when he assumed command of the 4th Fighter Interceptor Group, then located at New Castle Airport in Delaware. When the Chinese and Soviet pilots entered the war, operating Mikoyan-Gurevich MiG-15 jet fighters, they had routed the United Nations forces. Desperate measures were needed to gain control of the situation. The US Air Force had the aircraft to do the job, the North American F-86 Sabre Jet. The 4th Fighter Interceptor Group was the unit to fly them, and John Meyer would command them.

In November, Meyer took the unit overseas to Johnson AB in Japan in preparation for operations over Korea. The 4th Fighter Interceptor Group and its F-86 Sabre Jets were responsible for taking back control of the Korean skies. By March 1951, the 4th Fighter Interceptor Group was able to move to a base at Suwon in Korea. From here, daily patrols into "MiG Alley," the air space near the Chinese border, systematically compelled the MiG pilots to get into a fight which, nine times out of ten, was won by a 4th Fighter Interceptor Group pilot. During the war, 792 MiG-15s were lost, for 78 F-86s.

John Meyer remained in command of the 4th Fighter Interceptor Group through May 1951, and the worst of the battle for air supremacy. During that time he had the opportunity to lead several patrols personally, during which he claimed a pair of MiG-15s. One of the subsequent commanders of the 4th Fighter Interceptor Group was Gabby Gabreski, who scored 6.5 victories in Korea.

Back in the United States, Meyer served as director of operations for the Air Defense Command and the Continental Air Defense Command. After graduating from the Air War

Wartime ace John Meyer is seen here as a postwar four-star general. In 1972, he became the commander-in-chief of the US Air Force Strategic Air Command. *US Air Force*

College at Maxwell AFB in Alabama in 1956, he remained as an instructor. His next post was with the Strategic Air Command, for whom he commanded two air divisions in the Northeastern United States. The World War II fighter commander was now in the bomber business. In June 1962, he moved to Strategic Air Command headquarters at Offutt AFB in Nebraska as deputy director for planning. While there, he also served as the Strategic Air Command representative to the Joint Strategic Target Planning Staff.

In November 1963, General Meyer made the move from the Strategic Air Command to the Tactical Air Command, returning to fighters as commander of the Twelfth Air Force in Texas, where he coordinated ground support for the US Army. In February 1966, he moved back to Washington, DC to serve on the staff of the Joint Chiefs of Staff, first as deputy director and later as vice director. In May 1967, he moved across the hall as director of operations for the joint staff under Chief of Staff General John P. McConnell. Between August 1969 and April 1972, now wearing his fourth star, he served as Vice Chief of Staff, the number two job in the US Air Force, under Chief of Staff General John Dale Ryan.

On May 1, 1972, General Meyer went back to bombers, and back to Offutt AFB to command the Strategic Air Command as its Chief of Staff. While there, he oversaw the Linebacker II operations against North Vietnam in December 1972 that helped end the War in Southeast Asia. John Meyer retired from the US Air Force at the end of July in 1974. The seventh ranked all time USAAF/US Air Force ace, and a three-time recipient of the Distinguished Service Cross, died of a heart attack on December 2, 1975.

# PREDDY: THE TOP MUSTANG ACE

★
Major George Earl Preddy was the highest-scoring USAAF flying P-51 Mustangs, and the eighth highest-scoring American ace in history. He served with the 49th Pursuit Group in the Pacific before joining the 352nd Fighter Group of the USAAF Eighth Air Force in the European Theater. *US Air Force*

**BORN IN 1920**, George Preddy began his World War II combat career at age 21 in the Pacific Theater, but moved to the European Theater to become the highest-scoring ace to fly the USAAF's premier air superiority fighter, the P-51D Mustang. Personally, he was recalled as a man who genuinely cared about those who served under him, and who hated to kill, but viewed combat as a game. As a flight leader, he lost his first wingman, and vowed successfully, "not again."

He spent the early months of 1942 flying patrol missions along Australia's northern coastline at a time when a Japanese invasion was not only feared but considered probable. When his 25th Northern Australian mission ended ignominiously in a mid-air collision on July 12, 1942, Preddy was sent back to the United States to recuperate and prepare for his next assignment. In January 1943, he posted to the 34th Fighter Squadron, a part of the 352nd Fighter Group that was to be assigned to the Eighth Air Force. They were based at Republic Field on Long Island and taught to fly P-47 Thunderbolts. In July 1943, Preddy finally went overseas a second time, as the 352nd was shipped out to Britain, specifically to a base at Bodney.

Preddy began flying missions with the 34th Fighter Squadron, which was redesignated as the 487th Fighter Squadron, shortly after the base opened for business on July 7. He did not score his first victory until December 1, but he would get his second before Christmas. He and Richard Grow, another P-47 pilot, were escorting a B-24 strike force, when they observed six Messerschmitt Me 210 "bomber destroyer" aircraft escorted by 10 Bf 109s that were attacking a stray bomber that couldn't keep up with the main formation.

As the two P-47s attacked, Grow was shot down almost immediately, but Preddy succeeded in disrupting the attack, and in downing one of the Me 210s. For this action, he was awarded the Silver Star.

Preddy scored two more victories flying the Thunderbolt, but in April 1944, the 352nd Fighter Group began transitioning to the P-51D, and he scored his fifth in a Mustang on May 13. Now an ace, Preddy racked up additional scores in his new aircraft, which he dubbed Cripes a'Mighty. Soon he was the number three USAAF in the European Theater behind Francis "Gabby" Gabreski and Robert Johnson. In June, just after the Normandy Invasion, Johnson, who had 27, went home, and on July 20, Gabreski, who had 28, went down and was captured. This left Preddy, with 18.83, as the number one by default. However, he was determined to be number one, period, but he had a ways to go. He had served his 200 hours and had put in for enough extensions to double the time that he could fly in combat.

Colonel John Meyer, the 352nd Fighter Group commander, tasked Preddy with leading a group-strength escort mission on August 6. On August 5, when bad weather forced a cancellation, a party was scheduled. By the time that the weather cleared late that night, and the mission was reinstated, Preddy had imbibed to the point where it took some doing to make him fit to fly by the time that the mission had to be launched.

Preddy did fly that day, and he would see the kind of action that he craved—although he had never imagined getting the wish while his head was held in the vise-like grip of a hangover. When the Luftwaffe intercepted the B-17 heavy bombers that the 352nd Fighter Group was escorting, Preddy was the first to act, diving into the Bf 109s with the other Mustang pilots following. He quickly downed three German fighters and added two more as the dogfight ensued. Finally, one Messerschmitt dived to 5,000 feet to get away. Preddy followed and claimed him as his sixth kill for the day. For his mission fought with a hangover, Preddy was awarded the Distinguished Service Cross and a chance for a leave in the United States. Nevertheless, he was anxious to get back to Bodney and back into the air war over Europe.

In October 1944, George Preddy was in action again, with a new assignment as commander of the 328th Fighter Squadron of the 352nd Fighter Group. Preddy saw little of the desired combat until December, when the Germans launched their winter offensive that would result in the Battle of the Bulge. Overhead, the Luftwaffe contributed Operation Bodenplatte (Base Plate), the most massive air offensive that they had launched in continental Western Europe since the Battle of France in 1940.

Much of the Allied air response to the German attack was hampered by bad weather, but December 25, Christmas Day, dawned bright and sunny across northern Europe and Preddy led elements of the 328th Fighter Squadron into action over southern Belgium, where the Germans were thrusting through the Allied lines. During the fight, P-51Ds were chasing German fighters at low level all over the rolling hills of Belgium. Preddy managed to down two more Bf 109s to bring his score to 26.83, less than a point from topping Bob Johnson's score. One clean kill would make him number two. Two would make him the top USAAF ace in the European Theater.

As such a thought was probably racing through Preddy's mind, he and his wingman, James Cartee, were then vectored to attack a schwarm of German fighters near the city of Liege. Preddy was observed diving on a Focke-Wulf Fw 190, when suddenly the air was filled with the ugly black puffs of anti-aircraft fire—it was American anti-aircraft fire. The Focke-Wulf slipped away, but George Preddy did not. He died a victim of friendly fire.

# GENTILE: AN AMERICAN ACE IN TWO AIR FORCES

**THE HIGHEST-RANKING ACE** having victories with both the Royal Air Force and the USAAF, Dominic Salvatore "Don" Gentile had scored two victories with the Royal Air Force before going on to raise his overall total to 21.83 while flying with the USAAF Eighth Air Force. Lance Wade, the American who scored 25 victories with the Royal Air Force, never flew with the USAAF (see Chapter 4).

Gentile was born on December 6, 1920 in Piqua, Ohio to Italian-American parents. Dominic Gentile was one of those people who grew up obsessed with flying and who also turned out to be an excellent pilot. Indeed, he was already flying his own biplane when he was in high school. By 1941, with World War II raging in Europe, he had started calling himself "Don" rather than "Dom" because the latter sounded Italian (which it was) and Italy was part of the Axis.

With the war going, Gentile was anxious to get into action and do some combat flying. In 1941, the US Army Air Corps required two years of college to get into flight training, but British Empire air forces did not, so Gentile crossed the border to join the Royal Canadian Air Force. After finishing an eight-week training program in two weeks, he was sent to England. Early in 1942, Gentile, now a Royal Air Force pilot officer, was assigned to the Royal Air Force No. 133 Squadron, one of several "Eagle" squadrons comprised of American pilots who had volunteered to fly with Britain against the Germans.

While flying a Spitfire with No. 133 Squadron, Don Gentile shot down a Focke-Wulf Fw 190 and a Junkers Ju 88 in the space of ten minutes on August 1, 1942. For this he was awarded the British Distinguished Flying Cross. By this time, the United States had entered the war and USAAF fighter units were forming in Britain under the organizational umbrella of the Eighth Air Force. As this occurred, the Eagle Squadron pilots were being transferred from the Royal Air Force to the USAAF's 4th Fighter Group.

As part of this administrative transfer, Don Gentile was assigned, in September 1942, to the 336th Fighter Squadron of the 4th Fighter Group based at Debden. The unit was ultimately so successful that Hermann Göring referred to them as the "Debden Gangsters." Within the group a competition soon ensued between Gentile and Duane Beeson over who would ultimately be the highest-scoring ace among the former Eagles. Gentile would win, but Beeson was second with 19.3.

By the autumn of 1942, Gentile and his wingman, another ex-Eagle named John T. Godfrey (who ended up with 18 victories), were soon recognized as a remarkably potent combat team. In a typical lead-and-wingman situation there is a designated leader, and the leader has a wingman. Gentile and Godfrey decided that whichever man first spotted a target, or whoever was in the best position to take a shot, would take the lead, while the other covered him. They were

★
Dominic Salvatore "Don" Gentile was an American who joined the Royal Canadian Air Force and scored two aerial victories before transferring to the USAAF 4th Fighter Group in September 1942. *National Archives*

General Dwight D. Eisenhower awarding the Distinguished Service Cross to Don Gentile (center) and Donald Blakeslee on April 11, 1944. Both men were aces, Gentile with 21.83 victories and Blakeslee with 14.5. From January to November 1944, Blakeslee commanded the 4th Fighter Group of the USAAF Eighth Air Force. On March 6, 1944, Blakeslee flew the first P-51 Mustang mission over Berlin. *US Air Force*

together for more than six months and nearly 100 missions, during which time Hermann Göring is said to have actually established a "bounty" for their capture.

Gentile, who was the 4th Fighter Group's leading ace, had some very good days with Godfrey at his wing. On March 8, 1944, he claimed 4.25 German aircraft. On March 29, and again in his last combat action on April 8, 1944, Don Gentile shot down three Luftwaffe aircraft. This would bring his overall score to 19.83 with the 4th Fighter Group, plus the two he had scored with 133 Squadron. He also had seven "ground kills," which the Eighth Air Force assessment board mentioned at that time because they wanted to encourage pilots to destroy enemy aircraft on the ground. He was also awarded the Distinguished Service Cross, the Silver Star, the Distinguished Flying Cross and the Air Medal, in addition to his British Distinguished Flying Cross.

Don Gentile was rotated back to the United States, and in June 1944, he was assigned to the Air Logistics Command test center at Wright Field, Ohio, where he worked as a test pilot with Lockheed P-80s until his discharge from the USAAF in April 1946. He rejoined in December 1946 and served as a plans and training officer in the Fighter Gunnery Program until September 1948 when he went to the Air Tactical School.

In June 1949, he enrolled at the University of Maryland to earn his undergraduate degree in military science. On January 28, 1951, he took off from Andrews Air Force Base for a short flight in a Lockheed T-33 jet trainer. The aircraft crashed near Forestville, Maryland and both Gentile and a passenger were killed. The Defense Electronics Supply Center at Kettering, Ohio, which was established in 1962, was named Gentile Air Force Station in his honor. It provided electrical and electronics logistical support to various branches of the United States armed services until it was closed in 1993 as part of a Defense Department cost-cutting exercise.

# ZEMKE: FROM WOLFPACK TO STALAG

**THE MOST SUCCESSFUL USAAF GROUP COMMANDER IN WORLD WAR II**, Colonel Hubert "Hub" Zemke is also remembered for serving as commander of 8,498 caged Americans in the prisoner of war camp known as Stalag Luft I. For two years he commanded the 56th Fighter Group, which came to be known as "Zemke's Wolfpack," as it racked up 665 aerial victories as the top-scoring fighter group in the European Theater. Zemke himself scored 17.75 confirmed victories in 154 combat missions, while building a reputation as one of the leading tacticians in the Eighth Air Force.

A USAAF officer and a fighter pilot before the United States entered World War II, he spent the early part of the war on liaison missions to the British Royal Air Force and the Soviet Voenno-Vozdushnie Sily—learning from the British and teaching the Soviets to operate American Lend Lease equipment. By mid-1942, he was among the officers who traveled to England to begin setting up the framework around which the USAAF would construct its largest numbered air force—the "Mighty Eighth." The purpose of the Eighth Air Force was to be the strategic bombardment of the German Reich, so the centerpiece of its organization would be the Bombardment Groups with their eventual thousands of Boeing B-17 Flying Fortresses and Consolidated B-24 Liberators. However, the bombers would need escorts and the escorting fighters would ultimately be tasked with nothing short of achieving air superiority over Germany itself. Men like Ira Eaker and Carl "Tooey" Spaatz would create the bomber force, but men like Hub Zemke would create a force of fighters that would take them to the heartland of the Fatherland.

Colonel Hub Zemke took command of the 56th Fighter Group in September 1942. The 56th Fighter Group was created as the 56th Pursuit Group at the end of 1940 as an air defense unit, and it was based at various locations throughout the Southeast during 1941, moving from Savannah to Charleston to Charlotte. After Pearl Harbor, however, the USAAF decided to make the 56th Fighter Group into one of its first line operational units for combat action overseas. In July 1942, the 56th was moved to Bridgeport, Connecticut, equipped with P-47 Thunderbolts and told to prepare for war. Zemke took over the 56th Fighter Group in September and he took it to Britain in January 1943.

First based at King's Cliffe, the 56th Fighter Group would move to Horsham St. Faith in April 1943, to Halesworth in July 1943, and finally to Boxted in April 1944 in anticipation of operations related to the Normandy Invasion.

★
Colonel Hubert "Hub" Zemke was an example of a brilliant tactician and a group commander who led from the front. During more than 20 months in 1942–1944, when he commanded the 56th Fighter Group of the USAAF Eighth Air Force, it came to be known as "Zemke's Wolf Pack." *US Air Force*

Tactically, the 56th Fighter Group evolved gradually with Zemke constantly defining and redefining tactics. In 1944, after dozens of missions escorting the Eighth Air Force heavy bombers into Europe, Zemke challenged established Eighth Air Force policy. The idea of having the escort fighters stay close to the bombers throughout the mission had never been officially questioned before Zemke. He theorized that if part of the fighter force fanned out ahead of the bombers, they could hit and kill or disrupt the interceptors before the bombers arrived.

Zemke successfully convinced his boss, General William Kepner, commander of VIII Fighter Command (the Eighth Air Force's fighter component), to go along, and the "Zemke Fan" was born. The tactic was first implemented on May 12, 1944, with less than auspicious results. Zemke led a four-ship patrol ahead of the bomber stream, but one aborted and the remaining three were attacked by seven Messerschmitt Bf 109s, led by the legendary Luftwaffe ace, Günther Rall. Rall attacked, downing two of the P-47s and leaving Zemke alone. By putting his Thunderbolt into a steep dive, Zemke was able to get away, but the Zemke Fan had gotten off to a bad start.

Eventually, however, as it was perfected, Zemke's idea greatly reduced bomber losses, while increasing the scores for the aces of the 56th Fighter Group—which was now known universally as "Zemke's Wolfpack."

During 1944, there was a running competition between the Wolfpack with its P-47s and Don Blakeslee's 4th Fighter Group, which had converted to P-51s. When the war ended, the 56th Fighter Group was ahead in aerial victories.

In August 1944, after commanding the Wolfpack for two years, Zemke volunteered to take over the morale-challenged 479th Fighter Group. At the time, the Wattisham-based group was in the process of transitioning from Lockheed P-38 Lightnings to P-51s, and Eighth Air Force leadership felt that it needed a new boss to get it into line. Zemke was the man.

By the end of October, Zemke was given orders that would move him upstairs to become the Chief of Staff at the headquarters of the 65th Fighter Wing at Saffron Walden, England. Flying his last mission before taking the desk job, Zemke ran into severe turbulence over Germany and was forced to ditch over the Reich.

★
Some of the leading figures of the Eighth Air Force fighter establishment, circa 1944. Standing, left to right: Group commanders Edwin Chickering (357th Fighter Group), Hub Zemke (56th Fighter Group), James Stone (78th Fighter Group), Don Blakeslee (4th Fighter Group) and Glen Duncan (353rd Fighter Group). Seated are two Eighth Air Force fighter wing commanders, Ed Anderson and Murray Woodbury. Zemke, Blakeslee and Duncan were all aces, with 17.75, 14.5 and 19.5 aerial victories respectively. Duncan was the highest-scoring ace of the group that he commanded.
*US Air Force*

Once on the ground, he was captured and sent to Stalag Luft I, located on the Baltic Sea at Barth, Germany. At the prisoner of war camp, Zemke became reunited with Gabby Gabreski, the Eighth Air Force's leading ace, who had been shot down two months before, also on what might have been his last mission before leaving combat.

At Stalag Luft I, Zemke was the senior officer among more than 8,000 Allied airmen in a stark and miserable prison camp. By the end of 1944, living conditions in Germany had deteriorated. Food was scarce and luxuries nonexistent. In the prisoner of war camp, things were that much worse. The camp was filthy, with poor rations, inadequate sanitation and virtually no medical attention. Morale and discipline were naturally at a very low ebb.

Gradually, Zemke was able to work with prisoners to restore discipline and morale and to work with the camp commandant to improve conditions. He helped the men get through the last bitter winter of World War II. As it became obvious that Germany would lose the war, the Germans became more cooperative, and Zemke was able to negotiate a quiet surrender. On April 30, 1945 with the Soviet armies approaching, the German commandant ordered

★
This Republic P-47D
Thunderbolt is painted
in the markings
of the 56th Fighter
Group aircraft flown
by Hub Zemke in
1944. It is displayed
at the American Air
Museum, part of the
Imperial War Museum
complex at Duxford in
England. *Alan Wilson
licensed under Creative
Commons*

Zemke to get the prisoners ready to be moved, but Zemke convinced the Germans to just walk away and leave the prisoners in charge of the compound.

The following day, with the Germans gone, Zemke assumed responsibility for maintaining order in the camp, and sent out contact parties to meet with advancing Soviet troops. These forces, the 65th Army of the 2nd Byelorussian Front, under Colonel General Pavel Batov, showed little interest in the needs of the former prisoners for food and water, nor did they cooperate with Allied authorities in arranging an evacuation of the camp. Finally, on May 12, the USAAF started sending transport aircraft to airlift the men to the West.

According to the documentation compiled at the time, 8,498 prisoners—1,415 British and 7,083 American personnel—were released and repatriated in the airlift, which was completed on May 15. Rumors persisted of several hundred that remained in Soviet custody, but no proof ever surfaced.

Hub Zemke remained in the USAAF as it made the transition to the independent US Air Force in 1947, and retired in 1966. He eventually moved to Oroville, California, in the foothills of the Sierra Nevada, where he lived until his death on August 30, 1994.

CHAPTER

02

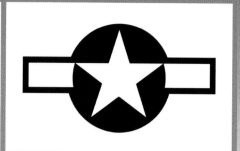

# THE US NAVY & MARINE CORPS

**T**HE UNITED STATES was unique among the major powers in World War II in that it had not one but three air forces, and each of them had aces. The US Army technically controlled the USAAF—forerunner to the independent US Air Force—though it was autonomous after 1941. The other two "air forces" were the aviation components of the US Navy and the US Marine Corps—both of which operate under the US Department of the Navy.

Naval aviation in World War II involved both shore-based operations and aircraft carrier-based operations. The former involved patrol aircraft—both seaplanes and landplanes based at facilities with runways. Carrier operations included fighters, patrol aircraft and attack bombers (including torpedo bombers). The US Navy's carriers typically had a Carrier Air Wing with homogenous squadrons of fighters and of various classifications of bombers.

The US Navy has always viewed its carrier bomber squadrons as the core of the carrier's offensive role, while fighters are a defensive component. Fighters have always existed aboard carriers for the primary purpose of protecting the carrier and the ships of the carrier's battle group from enemy bombers, whether they be shore-based or carrier based. The secondary role of carrier fighters is escorting the carrier-based bombers on their missions.

During World War II, the naval aviators who became aces were members of carrier-based fighter squadrons, which were designated by numbers (which originally corresponded to the number of the carrier) accompanied by the prefix "VF." The majority of US Navy air combat operations during World War II were in the Pacific Theater, where the great carrier battles took place, and where all of the US Navy's top aces became aces.

The leading US Navy ace was David McCampbell, who scored 34 victories while flying F6F Hellcats with VF 15. He is followed by Cecil Harris of VF-9 with 24 victories, and Eugene Valencia of VF 18 with 23. Three aviators are tied for third with 19 apiece. They are Alexander Vraciu, who flew with VF 6 and with VF 16; Cornelius Nooy of VF 31; and Patrick Fleming of VF 80. Douglas Baker of VF 20 scored 16.3, and Ira Cassius "Ike" Kepford had 16 with VF 17.

Like McCampbell, all of these men scored their victories in the Grumman F6F Hellcat, except Kepford, who scored his while flying a Vought F4U Corsair. For all, their highest decoration was the Navy Cross, except Baker who was awarded the Silver Star, and McCampbell who earned the Medal of Honor, America's highest award for bravery under fire.

The US Marine Corps was conceived as being the US Navy's "ground forces" or "sea soldiers." As such, their role has generally been to go into action in conjunction with US Navy ships. In World War II, this involved the many amphibious operations that were undertaken in capturing islands from the Japanese. US Marine Corps aviation exists primarily to support ground and amphibious operations, either by directly attacking the enemy on the ground, or intercepting enemy aircraft before they attack the marines on land or sea. US Marine Corps squadrons use a designation system similar to that used by the US Navy, but with the letter "M" inserted after the "V" which denotes aviation. Hence, Marine fighter squadrons are indicated with the prefix "VMF."

★ [Previous]
When the war began, the standard front line fighter in service with the US Navy and Marine Corps was the Grumman F4F Wildcat. It was technically inferior to the Japanese Zero, but a number of skilled pilots achieved ace status in the Wildcat. The F4F-3 variant pictured here in early 1942 wears the prewar US insignia with the red "meatball" in the center. This was soon deleted from the insignia to avoid confusion with the Japanese insignia *US Navy*

In World War II, US Marine Corps air operations were concentrated in the Southwest Pacific, in the skies over the hundreds of islands that make up such groups as the Bismarck Archipelago, the New Hebrides and the Solomons. Guadalcanal in the Solomons became one of the most important battlegrounds of World War II, when the Marines landed there in 1942 to stop the tide of Japanese aggression. It was in the Solomons and neighboring islands that the great US Marine Corps aces had their finest hours during World War II.

During the difficult days of 1942 and 1943, Marine aviators fought under difficult conditions against a determined and powerful enemy. Among them, the top four US Marine Corps aces of World War II would all receive the Medal of Honor. The leading Marine aces were Joseph Foss, who scored 26 victories while flying with VMF 121; Robert Hanson, who scored 25 victories with VMF 215; Gregory "Pappy" Boyington, who scored 22 victories with VMF 214 and Kenneth Walsh, who scored 21 victories while flying with VMF 124. Boyington had also claimed six victories while flying with the American Volunteer Group in China before the war, so his total of 28 made him the highest-scoring Marine, although Foss and Hanson scored more while actually flying with the US Marine Corps.

Other World War II Marine aces of note were Donald Aldrich, who scored 20 victories while flying with VMF 215; John Smith, who scored 19 victories—and earned a Medal of Honor—while flying with VMF 223; Marion Carl, who scored 18.5 victories while flying with VMF 223; and Wilbur J. Thomas who scored 18.5 victories while flying with VMF 213.

★
The Grumman F6F Hellcat was an immense improvement over the earlier Wildcat. Entering combat in September 1943 as the standard US Navy carrier-based fighter, the F6F outperformed the Zero and allowed the US Navy to achieve and maintain air superiority over the Pacific Theater. The bars added to the US insignia in mid-1943 were outlined in red for just a couple of months. *US Navy*

★
When the Vought F4U Corsair entered service in early 1943, it was found to be less well suited for carrier operations than the Hellcat. However, the Marines, operating from land bases on South Pacific islands found that its performance, much better than that of the aging Wildcat, allowed them to achieve air superiority in their contests with the Japanese. *US Navy*

# McCAMPBELL:
## THE NAVY'S TOP ACE

★
Captain David McCampbell was the US Navy's "ace of aces" and a Medal of Honor recipient. On October 24, 1944, he became the only American ace to down nine enemy aircraft in a single day. He flew both the F6F-3 and F6F-5 Hellcat, and is seen here in the Hellcat that he dubbed Minsi III. The aircraft carries the victory marks of 25 of his 34 aerial victories.
*US Navy*

**DAVID S. McCAMPBELL**, the US Navy's "Ace of Aces," was the third highest-scoring American ace of World War II, with 34 victories. On October 24, 1944, during the Battle of Leyte Gulf, McCampbell shot down nine Japanese aircraft in a single day. This, in part, led to his being awarded the Medal of Honor.

McCampbell was born on January 16, 1910 in Bessemer, Alabama and attended Staunton Military Academy in Virginia and Georgia Tech in Atlanta. Appointed to the US Naval Academy at Annapolis in 1929 by Senator Park Trammell of Florida, McCampbell joined the swim team and distinguished himself as AAU diving champion in 1931 and Eastern Intercollegiate champion a year later. In 1933, he graduated with a degree in marine engineering. Because regular officer commissions were limited, McCampbell was shunted into the Naval Reserve, and spent the next year working at various civilian jobs.

In June 1934, he finally got an active assignment in the US Navy, aboard the cruiser USS *Portland*. After three years as an aircraft gunnery observer and a year of flight training, McCampbell became a naval aviator in 1938. For two years, he was assigned to the carrier USS *Ranger* and was later transferred to the USS *Wasp* as a landing signal officer (LSO), which is where he was based when the United States entered World War II. When the USS *Wasp* was sunk by a Japanese submarine off Guadalcanal in September 1942, McCampbell was rescued and sent to Florida as an LSO instructor.

In August 1943, McCampbell returned to combat in the Pacific Theater, first as commander of VF-15, and from February 1944, of Carrier Air Group 15—later known as the "Fabled Fifteen"—aboard the USS *Essex*. McCampbell flew his first combat mission in this role on May 19, 1944, during a fighter sweep over Marcus Island and he scored his first aerial victory less than a month later, on June 11, during the American assault on Saipan.

Eight days later, during the Battle of the Philippine Sea, McCampbell led the fighters flying to intercept a vast Japanese bomber armada headed to attack the United States Fleet. In this aerial battle, known to Hellcat pilots as the "Great Marianas Turkey Shoot," the enemy force was completely destroyed and McCampbell personally shot down seven enemy aircraft, as well as two "probables." These seven included five on the morning patrol, one during the afternoon patrol and one that he scored while returning to the USS *Essex* from the afternoon patrol. He and George Duncan, another VF 15 aviator, observed a pair of A6M Zeros attacking a seaplane that was trying to rescue a downed pilot. They attacked and each claimed a Zero.

By October 1944, when Allied forces moved into position for the recapture of the Philippines, McCampbell's score of enemy aircraft destroyed in battle was already an

★
Grumman F6F-3
Hellcats of Carrier
Air Group 5 aboard
the aircraft carrier
USS *Yorktown* (CV-10)
during the Marcus
Island raid of August
1943. *US Navy*

impressive 19. The end of that month would see the largest air and surface naval battle of the Pacific Theater of World War II, and probably the last great naval battle in history—the Battle of Leyte Gulf.

On October 24, during the Battle of Leyte Gulf, McCampbell and his wingman, Roy Rushing, intercepted and attacked a force of approximately 40 enemy fighters. On this day, Carrier Air Group 15 was tasked with launching two strike missions. McCampbell was to lead the fighters escorting the second strike. However, after the first group went out, a Japanese strike force was detected as coming toward the USS *Essex*. McCampbell immediately took off, leading the only seven Hellcats that were available.

The Japanese were encountered, now just 22 miles from the USS *Essex*. McCampbell ordered five Hellcats to attack the bombers, while he and Rushing intercepted their fighter escort. They each downed one of the A6M Zeros on their first pass, and McCampbell got a second. The Japanese then went into a defensive circle rather than striking back, and finally turned away and started back toward their base in the Philippines. The Hellcats attacked again, and again both aviators scored.

The Americans chased the Japanese until their fuel ran low. By the time that they turned back, McCampbell had shot down nine—plus two "probables"—while Rushing had claimed six. Equally important, they and the other Hellcat pilots had forced the Japanese force into retreat without a single one of them reaching an American ship.

The next day, McCampbell coordinated an air strike by three carrier air groups against Japanese targets in which they sank an enemy aircraft carrier, a light cruiser and two destroyers. McCampbell's "Fabled Fifteen" continued to serve through November 1944, when the USS *Essex* concluded her cruise, establishing a record unmatched in the history of carrier warfare. They had shot down 318 enemy aircraft (11 percent of these by McCampbell himself) and had sunk 296,500 tons of enemy shipping, including the battleship Musashi, three carriers and a heavy cruiser.

McCampbell is quoted as having said that "Aggressiveness was a fundamental to success in air to air combat and if you ever caught a fighter pilot in a defensive mood you had him licked before you started shooting."

David McCampbell was awarded the Navy Cross as well as the Silver Star, Legion of Merit and the Distinguished Flying Cross for his part in the seven-month cruise of the Fabled Fifteen. On January 10, 1945, President Franklin D. Roosevelt personally awarded him the Medal of Honor for his actions on June 19 and October 24, 1944.

His Medal of Honor citation read: "For conspicuous gallantry and intrepidity at the risk of his life above and beyond the call of duty as Commander, Air Group 15, during combat against enemy Japanese aerial forces in the First and Second Battles of the Philippine Sea. An inspiring leader, fighting boldly in the face of terrific odds, Commander McCampbell led his fighter planes against a force of 80 Japanese carrier based aircraft bearing down on our fleet on 19 June 1944. Striking fiercely in valiant defense of our surface force, he personally destroyed seven hostile planes during this single engagement in which the outnumbering attack force was utterly routed and virtually annihilated.

"During a major fleet engagement with the enemy on 24 October, Commander McCampbell, assisted by but one plane, intercepted and daringly attacked a formation of 60 hostile land based craft approaching our forces. Fighting desperately but with superb skill against such overwhelming airpower, he shot down nine Japanese planes and, completely disorganizing the enemy group, forced the remainder to abandon the attack before a single aircraft could reach the fleet. His great personal valor and indomitable spirit of aggression under extremely perilous combat conditions reflect the highest credit upon Commander McCampbell and the US Naval Service."

He would see no more combat action after November 1944, but his career in the Navy and in naval aviation would continue until his retirement in 1964. He would serve two years as chief of staff to commander fleet air and as commander of carrier air groups before being assigned to the Armed Forces Staff College in 1947. Between 1948 and 1951, he was the senior naval aviation advisor to the Argentine Navy, and in 1951 he returned to carrier duty as executive officer of the USS *Franklin D. Roosevelt*. After a stint as flight test coordinator at the Naval Air Test Center in Patuxent River, Maryland, he sailed as commander of the USS *Severn*, and later in command of the USS *Bon Homme Richard*. In 1960, he took a staff job at the Pentagon in Washington, DC with the Joint Chiefs of Staff, and in 1962, he accepted his final assignment, as assistant deputy chief of staff for operations to the commander in chief of the Continental Air Defense Command.

After his retirement in 1964, David McCampbell moved to Palm Beach County, Florida. In 1988, Palm Beach International Airport officially dedicated its David McCampbell Terminal. McCampbell died at his home in Florida on June 30, 1996 after a long illness.

# O'HARE: THE MOST DARING SINGLE ACTION

Butch O'Hare smiles from the cockpit of his F4F Wildcat, which is painted with five victory marks. On February 20, 1942, he single-handedly attacked a formation of nine Japanese bombers approaching his aircraft carrier, the USS *Lexington*. He downed five to become an ace in one day, earning the Medal of Honor. *US Navy*

**IN 1942**, the course of World War II was not going well for the United States and the Allies. The United States needed something positive. A hero was needed, and a hero was found in Edward H. "Butch" O'Hare. He was the US Navy ace responsible for what was referred to in 1942 as "the most daring single action in the history of combat aviation."

O'Hare was born in St. Louis, Missouri on March 13, 1914, but he grew up in Chicago. He considered it to be his hometown when he joined the US Navy, and it was "the Windy City" that paid him his most lasting tribute.

Already a naval aviator at the time that the United States was drawn into the conflict, O'Hare was a fighter pilot with VF-3, commanded by Lieutenant Commander John Thach, aboard the USS *Lexington*. Only two months had passed since the Japanese attack on Pearl Harbor, as the USS *Lexington's* task force—including cruisers and destroyers—was steaming west toward the Gilbert Islands in February 1942. The objective was to interrupt Japanese shipping in and around the huge Imperial Japanese Navy base at Rabaul on the island of New Britain.

The force was 400 miles from this objective at dawn on February 20, when it was discovered by a Japanese patrol bomber. Thach took off with a force of Grumman F4F-3

Wildcats. They shot down the intruder, but not before the position of the task force was revealed to the Japanese forces at Rabaul. Late in the day, Thach and five other VF-3 pilots—aided by surface fire from the warships—managed to destroy a wave of nine land-based Mitsubishi G4M1 "Betty" bombers. However, a second wave of bombers was detected.

Butch O'Hare was one of the six pilots who went up to confront the second wave, which the Japanese timed to arrive 30 minutes after the first. The Wildcats split up to search for the incoming bombers and, as it turned out, only O'Hare and his wingman were in a position to intercept the enemy when they arrived on the scene. Then the wingman's guns jammed, and O'Hare was forced to face the enemy alone.

Braving defensive fire from the bombers, O'Hare attacked from the right rear of their "vee" formation. He managed to shoot down two of the bombers in rapid succession and switched to the opposite side. He ultimately succeeded in shooting down six of the nine Japanese bombers and disrupting the bombing accuracy of the remaining three, so that no bombs fell on the carrier. It was observed from below that there seemed to have been three of the bombers falling in flames simultaneously.

The US Navy Department official communiqué of March 3, 1942 observed that "Only three enemy planes of the first formation reached their bomb release point over the aircraft carrier, which avoided all bomb hits by split second maneuvering. The leading bomber of this group attempted a crash landing on the carrier and was shot down by heavy close range antiaircraft fire when barely 100 yards from its objective. In the second attack only five bombers of the enemy formation reached the bomb release point. In this instance the salvo of enemy bombs was closer to the carrier than in the first attack, but again no hits were obtained. Sixteen of the 18 attacking enemy bombers were shot down in this action. There was no damage to our surface forces. Lieutenant (j. g.) Edward H. O'Hare, US Navy, fighter pilot, personally accounted for six bombers of the enemy. In the two attacks only two of our fighter planes were lost. The pilot of one was recovered. The next of kin of the lost pilot has been notified. There is nothing to report from other areas."

An after-action examination of O'Hare's guns indicated that he had used a mere 60 rounds for each of the kills. Scoring six victories in his first combat action, O'Hare was recommended for, and received, the Medal of Honor as well as a promotion to the rank of lieutenant commander. He was also the US Navy's first ace of World War II. He would later be awarded the Navy Cross and the Distinguished Flying Cross with one gold star.

His Medal of Honor citation read: "For conspicuous gallantry and intrepidity in aerial combat, at grave risk of his life above and beyond the call of duty, as section leader and pilot of Fighting Squadron 3 on 20 February 1942. Having lost the assistance of his teammates, Lieutenant O'Hare interposed his plane between his ship and an advancing enemy formation of nine attacking twin engine heavy bombers. Without hesitation, alone and unaided, he repeatedly attacked this enemy formation, at close range in the face of intense combined machine gun and cannon fire. Despite this concentrated opposition, Lieutenant O'Hare, by his gallant and courageous action, his extremely skillful marksmanship in making the most of

★
Edward Henry "Butch" O'Hare, seen here at Norfolk, Virginia in May 1942, would become the US Navy's first ace. *US Navy*

every shot of his limited amount of ammunition, shot down 5 enemy bombers and severely damaged a sixth before they reached the bomb release point. As a result of his gallant action—one of the most daring, if not the most daring, single action in the history of combat aviation—he undoubtedly saved his carrier from serious damage."

In November 1943, during operations related to the invasion of Tarawa, O'Hare was in charge of the first attempts at intercepting enemy aircraft at night from carriers. This involved a team of two Hellcats and one radar equipped Grumman TBF Avenger operating from the USS *Enterprise*, led by O'Hare. In operation, the fighters flew wing on the Avenger and after being vectored to the vicinity of the enemy aircraft by the ship's fighter director, they relied on the Avenger's radar to get within visual range. On the first occasion, no intercepts were made, but on the second, the enemy was engaged. It was the first aerial battle of its type, and it so disrupted the attack, that the flight was credited with saving the task group from damage. On the third mission, Butch O'Hare was accidentally shot down.

Meanwhile back in Chicago, suburban Orchard Place Airport was the site of the factory which produced the Douglas C 54 transport in what is said to have been the largest wooden roofed building in the world. After the war, in 1946, the Chicago City Council authorized the acquisition of 1,080 acres of this property from the War Assets Administration in order to build a second major airport facility in Chicago to supplement the heavily used Chicago Municipal Airport, later called Midway Airport. Commercial aviation was growing so rapidly at the time that another airport would clearly be needed.

In 1949, as expansion of the Orchard Place Airport got underway, there was a search for an appropriate name for the new facility. Various politicians were considered, but in the end, it was named for Chicago's favorite war hero. Today, Chicago O'Hare International Airport ranks as one of the busiest airports in the world.

# HARRIS: SECOND PLACE NAVAL ACE

**THE NUMBER TWO ACE IN THE HISTORY OF THE US NAVY,** Cecil E. Harris, was the only top naval ace to fly combat missions in both the Atlantic and the Pacific. He flew both the F4F Wildcat and the F6F Hellcat, although he scored all of his aerial victories in the Hellcat.

Born in 1919 in South Dakota—the home state of top US Marine Corps ace, Joe Foss—Harris was at Northern State Teachers' College in 1939 when World War II began, and he made the decision to join the US Navy before the United States entered the war in December 1941. After earning his wings as naval aviator at NAS Corpus Christi, he was assigned to VF-27, aboard the small escort carrier USS *Suwanee* in April 1942.

On November 8, 1942, Allied forces launched Operation Torch, landing troops in northwest Africa to gain a foothold for the eventual defeat of German and Italian forces in North Africa. The USS *Suwanee* was part of the armada of warships that supported the invasion. The defenders against the Operation Torch landings were primarily Vichy French forces that put up little resistance. There was some limited air combat, but Harris saw none during the missions that he flew over North Africa.

Early in 1943, the USS *Suwanee* was redeployed to the Southwest Pacific to support operations in the Solomons. To conserve deck space aboard the small carrier, VF-27 was relocated ashore. Harris scored his first two victories here, but was later reassigned to the new, full-sized carrier USS *Intrepid*, which was commissioned in August 1943. He became an ace while flying F6Fs with the USS *Intrepid's* VF-18, and on September 13, 1944, he downed four Imperial Japanese Navy Air Force aircraft in a single day.

In October 1944, the USS *Intrepid* was part of the massive US Navy force that was involved in the invasion of the Philippines. The ship was assigned to Fast Carrier Task Force 38 that was given the job of attacking Imperial Japanese Navy Air Force facilities, especially bomber bases, on the Japanese held island of Formosa (now called Taiwan). The plan called for three days of attacks, beginning on October 12. A 16-plane force from VF-18 was tasked with flying the initial fighter sweeps over northeast Formosa early in the morning of the first day.

Cecil Harris was in the third of four flights of Hellcats as the attack began. They reached a Japanese base just as five bombers were taking off. In a fast attack, four of these were shot down, two of them by Harris. Then the Zero fighters were observed high above and diving to attack. One Hellcat went down, but another Hellcat attacked his killer. A second Zero wormed into the fight and Harris went after him. Out of the four aircraft involved in this dogfight, both Hellcats scored. As they headed back to the USS *Intrepid*, Harris encountered a stray Zero and shot him down, making it four in one day.

★
Lieutenant Cecil Harris was the US Navy's second highest-scoring ace. On January 17, 1945, Vice Admiral Marc Mitscher presented Harris with the Navy Cross and Silver Star, as well as a gold star to the Distinguished Flying Cross that he was previously awarded.
*US Navy*

During his mission over Formosa on October 14, Harris claimed three Yokosuka D4Y Suisei "Judy" dive bombers. On October 29, VF-18 was on patrol over the main Philippine island of Luzon, when a large mass of Imperial Japanese Navy Air Force fighters was observed, stalking a US Navy strike force of bombers and torpedo bombers. Harris led the attack on the enemy aircraft. The attack was disrupted and Harris claimed four victories. For this action, he was awarded the Navy Cross.

On November 25 off Luzon, the USS *Intrepid* was badly damaged in a kamikaze attack, ending her cruise. As she limped home for repairs, Cecil Harris also headed home. He had ended his combat career with 24 confirmed victories. In addition to his Navy Cross, he was also awarded the Distinguished Flying Cross, a Silver Star, and two Gold Stars. When World War II ended, Harris left the US Navy to pursue his teaching career in South Dakota.

★
The Navy's two top-scoring aces had 58 aerial victories between them. On January 10, 1945, Lieutenant Cecil Harris (left) and Commander David McCampbell (right) sat down with Assistant Secretary of the Navy Artemus Gates in Washington, DC to pass around a model of a Hellcat and tell some war stories. *US Navy*

# VALENCIA:
# KAMIKAZE KILLER

**THE THIRD HIGHEST-SCORING US NAVY ACE OF WORLD WAR II**, Eugene Valencia was born in San Francisco in 1921, joined the US Navy in 1941 and earned his wings in April 1942. Like many of the best student pilots in 1942, he was retained by the Air Operational Training Command (predecessor of the Naval Air Training Command) as an instructor, but like most naval aviators retained as instructors in 1942, he was anxious to get into action. He finally got his wish, shipping out aboard the new USS *Essex* in February 1943, as she departed on her first cruise after being commissioned on the last day of 1942.

Sailing for the Southeast Pacific, the USS *Essex* was sent into action off New Britain, and it was over the big Imperial Japanese Navy base at Rabaul on the island, that Valencia scored his first three kills. On November 20, the USS *Essex* was part of the task force involved in the invasion of the island of Tarawa, and here Valencia scored his fourth.

Early in 1944, the USS Essex was involved in launching strikes against the Imperial Japanese Navy base on the heavily-fortified island of Truk. On February 16, Valencia was on patrol over Truk when he became separated from his wingman, Bill Bonneau. Valencia, flying alone, was jumped by A6M Zeros. He managed to outmaneuver them without taking any hits, so he turned to the attack, assuming the enemy not to be good marksmen. He was right, and he claimed three.

Now an ace, Valencia completed his time aboard the USS *Essex*, and was sent to NAS Pasco in Washington State to develop and train an elite fighter unit. The idea was to start with experienced pilots and allow them the opportunity for extensive training and practice of proven air combat techniques. The technique that they developed, known as the "Mowing Machine," would prove very effective in the final months of the war.

In February 1945, Valencia's handpicked division, known as "Valencia's Flying Circus," was assigned to VF-9, which shipped out aboard the USS *Lexington*. On February 16, VF-9 led the first carrier-based air strike against Tokyo since the Doolittle raid in 1942. They experienced rain and snow over the Japanese capital, but Valencia observed a Nakajima Ki-44 Shoki "Tojo," which was shot down by Harris Mitchell, another Circus pilot. In all, the Circus would claim six confirmed kills on their first mission.

The Circus transferred to the new fast carrier USS *Yorktown* in March, as part of Task Force 58, which was organized for operations against Okinawa. It was at Okinawa that the Japanese launched the most massive of their desperate Kamikaze ("Divine Wind") suicide attack operations against the United States Fleet. Strong Japanese air opposition developed on April 6 in the first wave of a series of mass suicide attacks involving some 400 aircraft. In seven mass raids—and many smaller ones—between April 6 and May 23, the Japanese

★
Eugene Anthony Valencia was the US Navy's third highest-scoring ace. He flew Grumman F6F Hellcats from the USS *Essex* in 1943 and 1944. He returned to the Pacific in 1945 with VF-9 aboard the USS *Lexington* and USS *Yorktown*. On April 17, 1945, he shot down six enemy aircraft in one day. *US Navy*

expended some 1,500 aircraft, principally against naval forces supporting the campaign. In the three-month struggle against the Kamikaze force, the US Navy took the heaviest punishment in its history. Although Task Force 58 lost no ship during the campaign, eight heavy carriers and one light carrier were hit. On April 16 alone, over 100 kamikaze attacks were launched, sinking the destroyer USS *Pringle*, and hitting 11 other ships. Among the badly damaged was the USS *Intrepid*, with a 12 by 14 foot hole in the flight deck, 40 planes destroyed, and 9 men killed.

On the following day, April 17, VF 9 was on patrol, watching for Kamikazes or other enemy action against US Navy ships, when the radar operator aboard the USS *Yorktown* vectored them against a Japanese force of at least 35 aircraft. The force was composed primarily of bomb-laden Nakajima Ki-84 Hayate "Frank" fighters, although there were some A6M Zeros included as well. They were all kamikazes.

The Circus attacked in pairs, but the Japanese aircraft did not vary from their course to fight them. Rather they continued on their suicide run toward the United States fleet offshore. The Circus destroyed nine of the attackers, including three by Valencia, when the Japanese finally broke formation. Valencia and Mitchell had each claimed a Ki-84, when the Japanese began to strike back. Valencia got one more and then attacked another one that had jumped a Hellcat. He downed this one, bringing his tally for the day to six.

At this point, with fuel running low, the Circus broke off to return to the USS *Yorktown*. Valencia spotted a lone Japanese fighter and attempted to attack, only to discover that he was out of ammunition. Valencia would not score his seventh, but the Circus bagged 17. It was their best one-day score ever, although their "Mowing Machine" would clip 11 Kamikazes on May 4 and 10 during the May 11 suicide attack.

When the war finally ended, Valencia's Flying Circus had destroyed 50 Japanese aircraft and had lost none of their own. Eugene Valencia ended the war with 23 victories.

After the war he commanded VF(AW) 3, a naval air defense fighter unit equipped with Douglas F4D Skyray jet fighters. It was the only US Navy unit to be assigned to the North American Air (later Aerospace) Defense Command (NORAD). Nevertheless, under Valencia's leadership the lone US Navy unit twice won NORAD's highest honors for efficiency and readiness, winning over the other squadrons assigned to NORAD, all of which were US Air Force or Royal Canadian Air Force units.

★
An F6F-3 Hellcat from VF-5 rolls toward a takeoff from the USS *Yorktown* (CV-10), as condensation forms rings around its spinning prop. *US Navy*

# FOSS: A MARINE MATCHES RICKENBACKER

DURING THE EARLY DAYS OF WORLD WAR II, when aerial combat was discussed, whether it was on a street corner in Seattle or on an American airstrip in some remote land, talk always turned to speculation about who, if anyone, would be the first fighter pilot to equal the 26 victories that were the World War I score of the great Eddie Rickenbacker. The answer came on January 13, 1943.

In addition to being the first ace to reach the magic 26, Joseph Jacob "Joe" Foss was one of the US Marine Corps' first aces, and one of a handful of Marine aviators to be awarded the Medal of Honor.

Born in Sioux Falls, South Dakota on April 17, 1915, Joe Foss took an interest in aviation at the age of 12 when he saw Charles Lindbergh perform during one of the Lone Eagle's barnstorming trips through the Dakotas. Foss enrolled at the University of South Dakota in 1934, but it was the trough of the Great Depression, and among the hardest hit Depression victims were Dakota farmers—and this included the Foss family. Joe Foss left school to help at home, but returned, and finally graduated with a business administration degree in 1940.

Foss had learned to fly during his years at the University of South Dakota, and he even went so far as to help establish a civilian pilot training program at the university. After graduation, he joined the US Marine Corps Reserve as an aviation cadet. He received his wings and officer's commission in 1941 and was working as a flight instructor when the United States entered World War II.

Initially assigned to a reconnaissance squadron, Foss requested a transfer to a fighter squadron. Because of his advanced age—he was 26—the request was denied. Foss lobbied hard and was finally sent to a training squadron to learn to fly the F4F Wildcat. After logging 150 hours in the F4F during June and July 1942, he was finally sent overseas with VMF-121, aboard the escort carrier USS *Copahee*, bound for the Solomon Islands, where the Allies were digging in to halt the Japanese advance against Australia.

The ship arrived off Guadalcanal, and on October 9, Joe Foss made his first and only carrier take-off, landing at Henderson Field, a rugged landing strip hacked out of the Guadalcanal jungle. At this time the Marines had captured only part of the island, so Japanese snipers were still active, and Japanese air attacks against Henderson Field were also frequent. This, combined with primitive living conditions, rounded out the difficult situation that the men of VMF-121 found themselves in.

Foss was assigned as executive officer of VFM-121 and flew his first mission on October 13. He scored his first victory and was almost shot down. He was attacked by Japanese A6M Zeros, but as one overshot him, he opened fire, destroying it. In turn, other Zeros shot him

★
USMC Captain Joseph Jacob "Joe" Foss was the first American ace to match the record of 26 aerial victories scored by America's leading World War I ace, Eddie Rickenbacker. *US Marine Corps*

up and he was forced to make a dead stick landing at Henderson Field. Having scored his first victory on his first mission, he went on to get his second the following day.

Over the next few days, the Imperial Japanese Navy Air Force launched a major offensive aimed at destroying Henderson Field. On the ground, the damage was tremendous. Offshore, a barge carrying aviation fuel was destroyed, so VMF-121 was forced to drain fuel from wrecked aircraft in order to keep flying. The Marine aviators on Guadalcanal were flying obsolescent Grumman F4F Wildcats against a Japanese force equipped with the superior Mitsubishi A6M Zero, but they nevertheless achieved impressive results.

On October 18, Foss had an impressive day himself. His flight engaged a flight of Zeros, and in the ensuing dogfight, he managed to jump three from above, destroying two quickly and pursuing the third into a twisting, turning fight that ended with the Zero's engine aflame.

Having waded through three of the enemy fighters, Foss turned to the bombers that they were escorting. He attacked a flight of Mitsubishi G4M1 Betty bombers, diving on one and pulling up to destroy a second from below.

In just nine days, Foss had become an ace, but he would follow this up with three sets of double victories by October 25. On November 4, Foss shot down two enemy aircraft while participating in an American attack on Japanese ships that were shelling American shore positions. Returning to base, however, Foss' Wildcat went down at sea when its engine failed.

He swam part of the five miles to Guadalcanal, but he was finally picked up by some local islanders and an Australian mill operator and taken to another island. The next day, he was collected by a US Navy flying boat and returned to Guadalcanal. By now, Foss' reputation had spread, and for his actions thus far, he was awarded the Distinguished Flying Cross. It was awarded personally by Admiral William "Bull" Halsey, who paid a visit to Henderson Field.

During the latter days of 1942, VMF-121 came to be called "Joe's Flying Circus" in honor of Joe Foss. It would, in fact become a squadron of aces, with five in addition to Foss, and a combined score of 72 kills against the Imperial Japanese Navy Air Force. For example, on November 12, they destroyed 21 out of 22 bombers in a Japanese strike force.

After a bout with malaria in December, Foss returned to action and, on January 13, 1943, he shot down three Japanese aircraft. This brought his total score to 26, making him the first American ace to match the 26 aerial victories officially credited to Rickenbacker in World War I.

After matching Rickenbacker's record, Foss was shipped home. The Navy Department wanted the publicity value of a live hero rather than risking the chance that he might be unlucky one day as he ran up further aerial victories in the Pacific. Back home, Foss was tasked with participating in a publicity and war bond-selling tour. Now a high-profile celebrity, Foss made radio broadcasts, toured the Grumman factory on Long Island, New York and made appearances at the US Naval Academy and other bases.

On May 18, 1943, President Franklin D. Roosevelt presented him the Medal of Honor. The citation read: "For outstanding heroism and courage above and beyond the call of duty as executive officer of Marine Fighting Squadron 121, 1st Marine Aircraft Wing, at Guadalcanal. Engaging in almost daily combat with the enemy from 9 October to 19 November 1942, Captain Foss personally shot down 23 Japanese planes and damaged others so severely that their destruction was extremely probable. In addition, during this period, he successfully led a large number of escort missions, skillfully covering reconnaissance, bombing, and photographic planes as well as surface craft.

★
On May 18, 1943, Joe Foss received the Medal of Honor from President Franklin Delano Roosevelt personally in a White House ceremony. The medal is cropped out of this official USMC photo said to have been taken on the occasion.
*US Marine Corps*

"On 15 January 1943, he added three more enemy planes to his already brilliant successes for a record of aerial combat achievement unsurpassed in this war. Boldly searching out an approaching enemy force on 25 January, Captain Foss led his eight F4F Marine planes and four Army P 38s into action and, undaunted by tremendously superior numbers, intercepted and struck with such force that 4 Japanese fighters were shot down and the bombers were turned back without releasing a single bomb. His remarkable flying skill, inspiring leadership, and indomitable fighting spirit were distinctive factors in the defense of strategic American positions on Guadalcanal."

★

A Grumman F4F-4 Wildcat takes off from Henderson Field on Guadalcanal in 1942. Joe Foss scored his early victories flying Wildcats from Henderson. *US Navy*

Joe Foss would eventually go back to active duty in the South Pacific as commander of VFM-115, but his celebrity status precluded further combat flying, so his official score remained at 26.

After the war, Foss returned to South Dakota as his home state's premier war hero and was promptly elected to the state house of representatives. He was also instrumental in organizing the South Dakota Air National Guard, and he served as a colonel in the US Air Force during the Korean War. In 1952, he became the chief of staff of the South Dakota Air National Guard with the rank of brigadier general. He later served as a director of the US Air Force Academy.

In 1954, Foss was elected governor of South Dakota, and he was subsequently reelected to a second term. He also served as a commissioner of the American Football League (AFL) and he hosted two weekly television programs, American Sportsman and The Outdoorsman: Joe Foss.

He continued his interest in aviation, serving for six years as the director of public relations for Royal Dutch Airlines (KLM). In 1980, he was awarded the Outstanding American Award by the Los Angeles Philanthropic Foundation.

In 2002, at the age of 86, Foss was detained at the Phoenix Airport by the TSA while on his way to a speaking engagement at the United States Military Academy at West Point. The metal detector had discovered he was carrying his Medal of Honor!

"I wasn't upset for me," he said at the time. "I was upset for the Medal of Honor, that they just didn't know what it even was. It represents all of the guys who lost their lives—the guys who never came back. Everyone who put their lives on the line for their country. You're supposed to know what the Medal of Honor is."

When the news got out, a tide of public opinion rallied to his support.

★
Debriefing after
a mission, Pappy
Boyington (center)
enjoys a moment of
revelry with members
of his Black Sheep
Squadron (VMF-214) at
the Turtle Bay Fighter
Strip. *US Navy*

# BOYINGTON:
## THE BLACK SHEEP

**ONE OF THE BEST-LOVED ARCHETYPES AMONG WARRIORS** is that of the swashbuckling hero who breaks all the rules off the battlefield while being both brave and effective in battle. Among the aces of World War II, no ace exemplified this ideal better than Gregory "Pappy" Boyington. In the air, he was an extraordinary pilot and a skilled squadron leader with an almost uncanny knack for aerial combat. On the ground, however, he drank heavily and, indeed, broke all the rules. He had an almost unnatural proclivity for fistfights.

Pappy Boyington was the "Bad Boy" fighter pilot who became the highest-scoring ace to fly with the US Marine Corps, but he scored only 22 of his 28 total victories while flying with a Marine unit. This left Joe Foss, who scored 26 victories as a Marine aviator, with the record for the most victories while flying as a Marine.

Boyington's image is that of a man who enjoyed success and the pursuit of the good life, but his own real life was nothing short of tragic. Afflicted with emphysema, alcoholism and attention deficit disorder (ADD), Boyington lived a difficult life, was never able to make a career for himself after the war, and failed at nearly everything he attempted. Everything, that is, except flying fighter aircraft.

Born on December 4, 1912 in Coeur d'Alene, Idaho, Boyington grew up in the rugged mountains of the Idaho panhandle and eventually settled with his parents on an apple farm in Okanagan, Washington. Like many others of his generation, he joined the armed services during the depths of the Great Depression because there were simply no other opportunities available. He earned his wings in 1935, and by 1941, Boyington was a US Marine Corps instructor pilot at Naval Air Station Pensacola in Florida.

A divorced father of three with a well-chronicled mean streak, he was hovering on the edge of a dishonorable discharge for habitual disorderly conduct when he was suddenly offered a chance to change his life and to channel his wild side into combat flying. The United States had not yet entered World War II, but a former US Army Air Corps fighter commander named Claire Chennault was putting together a clandestine air force—with the support of the United States State Department—to help the Nationalist Chinese side in the long-running Sino-Japanese War.

Many US Navy and Marine aviators, as well as pilots from the Air Corps, were recruited to fly with Chennault's American Volunteer Group (AVG), and Boyington was one of them. Operating the shark-face-painted Curtiss P-40 Warhawks that earned them the name "Flying Tigers," the AVG flew combat missions against the Japanese from bases in Burma and southern China. This would continue for a year, lasting for seven months after the United States entered the war. During this time, Boyington may have become one of the AVG's aces. He claimed to have shot down six Japanese aircraft, though official records showed him with only two. In a disagreement over this and other issues, he resigned from the AVG in April 1942 and hitchhiked home on a series of air transport flights.

In September 1942, he rejoined the Marine Corps, but he did not go overseas again until April 1943. In May 1943, he became commander of Marine Fighter Squadron VMF-222 on Guadalcanal, but the unit saw little actual combat and Boyington became restless. After suffering a minor broken bone in a scuffle with some squadron-mates, Boyington was sent to New Zealand for recuperation.

When he returned to Espiritu Santo in the central Solomon Islands combat zone in September 1943, Boyington lacked a squadron assignment, so he set up a squadron of his own. Utilizing the unused designation VMF-214, he assembled his unit from unassigned Vought F4U Corsair fighters and unassigned pilots like himself. Some of the aviators—though not all—were facing disciplinary action for various minor infractions, and this tended to feed the folklore of VMF-214 being a band of misfits and outcasts, which they would always insist they were not. Nevertheless, they called themselves "The Black Sheep Squadron." Major Boyington was given the nickname "Pappy" because, at 31, he was almost ten years older than most of his pilots.

What followed for the ensuing twelve weeks was the stuff from which legends are made. Indeed, it was the stuff from which a Hollywood movie and a television series would be made. These were also the best weeks of Boyington's career. In less than four months, the Black Sheep of VMF-214 literally made that legend for themselves, shooting down 94 Japanese aircraft—mostly fighters—and damaging or destroying on the ground more than 100 more. Boyington himself would shoot down 19 of this total through the end of 1943, including five on one day.

★
Gregory "Pappy" Boyington had the highest score of aerial victories of any USMC ace when his claims while flying with the Flying Tigers were included in the total. He became famous as commander of VMF-214, the "Black Sheep" Squadron. *US Marine Corps*

As 1944 began, Boyington had 25 aerial victories (if the six claimed with the AVG are included) to his credit, one short of the 26 scored by Eddie Rickenbacker. There was a great deal of interest—including intense speculation by the media back in the United States—as to when Boyington would match or exceed the "magic 26."

For Boyington it naturally became something of an obsession. This was especially underscored by the fact that VMF-214's combat tour would end in a matter of days.

On January 3, 1944, Pappy Boyington and his Black Sheep took off on a mission to the Japanese base at Kahili on the island of New Britain. They were intercepted by an overwhelming number of Imperial Japanese Navy Air Force fighters, but Boyington managed to shoot down three, exceeding the Rickenbacker number, as well as that of Joe Foss, who had earlier achieved a total score of 26. However, the day was not to be a day of triumph for Boyington. He was set upon by a Zero of the 253rd Kokutai and shot down.

It was not observed whether Boyington had survived, and a massive search for him came up empty handed. When he was not found, and nothing was heard through international channels regarding his having been captured, he was officially declared missing in action.

Assumed to be dead, and a fallen hero at that, Boyington was posthumously awarded the Medal of Honor and the Navy Cross. The "posthumous" citation for his Medal of Honor read: "For extraordinary heroism and valiant devotion to duty as commanding officer of Marine Fighting Squadron 214 in action against enemy Japanese forces in the Central Solomons area from 12 September 1943 to 3 January 1944. Consistently outnumbered throughout successive hazardous flights over heavily defended hostile territory, Major Boyington struck at the enemy with daring and courageous persistence, leading his squadron into combat with devastating results to Japanese shipping, shore installations, and aerial forces. Resolute in his efforts to inflict crippling damage on the enemy, Major Boyington led a formation of 24 fighters over Kahili on 17 October and, persistently circling the airdrome where 60 hostile aircraft were grounded, boldly challenged the Japanese to send up planes. Under his

★ (Left)
An F4U Corsair being prepared for flight at the Marine airstrip on Cape Torokina on the western coast of the island of Bougainville. The 3rd Marine Division captured the area in November 1943 and Boyington's Black Sheep moved in shortly thereafter. *US Navy*

★ (Right)
Members of the Black Sheep Squadron (VMF-214) receiving final instructions before a mission from Boyington (center) at the Turtle Bay Fighter Strip on Espiritu Santo on September 11, 1943. *US Navy*

brilliant command, our fighters shot down 20 enemy craft in the ensuing action without the loss of a single ship. A superb airman and determined fighter against overwhelming odds, Major Boyington personally destroyed 26 [actually 22] of the many Japanese planes shot down by his squadron and, by his forceful leadership, developed the combat readiness in his command which was a distinctive factor in the Allied aerial achievements in this vitally strategic area."

The incorrigible "Bad Boy" ace, who had become a media celebrity at the end of 1943, had now become a dead hero.

However, Boyington had survived the crash, and was picked up by a Japanese submarine and taken to New Britain. Over the next 20 months, Boyington would be held captive, mainly in Ofuna, Japan. He and a number of others were held as "special prisoners," rather than as prisoners of war, meaning that they did not receive full rations, and their names were not part of the prisoner of war rosters supplied to the Red Cross, and ultimately to the families of prisoners.

Boyington had survived the war and was repatriated shortly after the occupation of Japan in September 1945. As a colorful Medal of Honor hero and 28-victory air ace who had just "returned from the dead," Boyington became the object of intense media attention as soon as he arrived in the United States.

The Marine Corps used Boyington—now promoted to lieutenant colonel—in a campaign to sell bonds, but on the last night of a nationwide speaking tour, he appeared in public very drunk and very incorrigible. Having embarrassed himself and the Marine Corps, much of the glory of his triumphal return quickly faded.

Discharged as a colonel in 1947, Boyington spent most of the next decade battling alcoholism and drifting from job to job, which included being a draft beer salesman and a referee for wrestling matches. His life began to turn around by the late 1950s, though, as he got a job flying for a charter airline out of Burbank, California. He also completed his autobiography, *Baa Baa, Black Sheep*, which was published in 1957.

This popular book became the basis for a made-for-television movie of the same name that was first aired in 1976, and which evolved into a weekly series that continued on the NBC network until 1978. These programs, which starred Robert Conrad as Boyington, glorified the "misfit" aspect of VMF-214, and were derided as inaccurate in nearly every respect except that the fictitious Black Sheep flew F4U Corsairs, as had the real Black Sheep. But they did serve to keep the Pappy Boyington legend alive in the minds of the public.

Meanwhile, a former IJNAF pilot named Masajiro Kawato was suggested as having been the person who shot him down, but this was never confirmed. Kawato had moved to the United States and the two met in the 1970s.

Gregory "Pappy" Boyington finally pieced his life together and lived out his last years in Fresno, California, where he died on January 11, 1988. He is buried at Arlington National Cemetery near Washington, DC.

★
A US Marine Corps Vought F4U-1 Corsair aircraft from Boyington's Marine Fighter Squadron VMF-214 taking off from the Turtle Bay Fighter Strip on the island of Espiritu Santo in the New Hebrides in September 1943. *US Navy*

# HANSON:
## TOP CORSAIR ACE

★
In the pantheon of USMC aces, Robert Murray Hanson was a close third to Foss and Boyington with 25 aerial victories. Like them, he received the Medal of Honor. He went missing on February 3, 1944, one month after Boyington disappeared. But unlike Boyington, Hanson was never seen again. *US Marine Corps*

**ROBERT M. HANSON** scored more victories in the Vought F4U Corsair than any other pilot and he was in the top tier of US Marine Corps aces, with 25 victories. All of Hanson's kills were scored between August 1943 and February 1944, and 20 of his 25 were scored in a single 13-day period. Hanson was also the youngest Marine Corsair pilot to receive the Medal of Honor.

Robert Hanson was born on February 4, 1920 at Lucknow in India, the son of American missionaries and became the heavyweight wrestling champion of India's United Provinces during the mid-1930s. He later set out to tour Europe by bicycle, and as the story goes, the teenager was bicycling through Austria in 1938 when it was absorbed into Nazi Germany.

Joining the US Marine Corps after the United States entered World War II, Hanson earned his wings and was assigned to VMF 215 in 1943. By the time that Hanson had reached the Southwest Pacific, the American forces had developed an unstoppable momentum, gradually retaking the islands that the Imperial Japanese forces had previously occupied and fortified. Advancing up the Solomons chain since February in a series of amphibious operations, the US Navy and Marine Corps had moved from Guadalcanal toward the Japanese naval base at Rabaul. Beginning with the unopposed landing in the Russells, these forces leapfrogged through the islands establishing bases and airfields as they went. Moving into Segi of the New Georgia Group in June, through Rendova, Onaivisi, Wickham Anchorage, Kiriwini and Treasury Islands by October. They reached Bougainville in November, where landings on Cape Torokina were supported by Marine air strikes.

One of Hanson's initial tasks was helping to cover the Bougainville landings. On November 1, 1943, he shot down a pair of A6M Zeros, plus a Nakajima B5N "Kate" attack bomber. These victories, scored over Empress Augusta Bay, would make Bob Hanson an ace. During the 1943 and 1944 period, VMF 215 was home to many other aces, including Harold Spears, who eventually scored 15 victories, and Donald Aldrich, who ended the war with 20.

By the end of 1943, Hanson had achieved a momentum analogous to that of the Marine Corps as a whole during 1943. He very quickly became known as the Marine Corps' master of multiples. On January 14, 1944 he downed five A6M Zeros. Only ten days later, he would destroy another four. On January 26, he scored three for the day, all Zeros. On January 30, the multiple contained a pair of Zeros and a Nakajima Ki-44 Shoki.

On February 3, a day before Hanson would have turned 24, VMF-215 conducted a strafing run and hunt for targets of opportunity over Japanese-held New Ireland. For Hanson, one of the targets was a lighthouse at Cape St. George that the Japanese used as an anti-aircraft platform. His fellow VMF-215 aviators observed Hanson's F4U taking hits and starting to disintegrate. He seemed alive just before the Corsair hit the water, but it came apart in an explosion of debris. They circled and saw no sign of life in the shark-infested water.

Hanson's Medal of Honor citation read: "For conspicuous gallantry and intrepidity at the risk of his life and above and beyond the call of duty as fighter pilot attached to Marine Fighting Squadron 215 in action against enemy Japanese forces at Bougainville Island, 1 November 1943; and New Britain Island, 24 January 1944. Undeterred by fierce opposition, and fearless in the face of overwhelming odds, 1st Lieutenant Hanson fought the Japanese boldly and with daring aggressiveness. On 1 November, while flying cover for our landing operations at Empress Augusta Bay, he dauntlessly attacked six enemy torpedo bombers, forcing them to jettison their bombs and destroying one Japanese plane during the action. Cut off from his division while deep in enemy territory during a high cover flight over Simpson Harbor on 24 January, 1st Lieutenant Hanson waged a lone and gallant battle against hostile interceptors as they were orbiting to attack our bombers and, striking with devastating fury, brought down four Zeroes and probably a fifth. Handling his plane superbly in both pursuit and attack measures, he was a master of individual air combat, accounting for a total of 25 Japanese aircraft in this theater of war. His great personal valor and invincible fighting spirit were in keeping with the highest traditions of the US Naval Service."

★
A USMC F4U Corsair at the airfield on Green Island (now Nissan Island) off the coast of Bougainville. The island was captured by the 3rd Marine Division in February 1944. *US Marine Corps*

CHAPTER

03

GERMANY

**O**F ALL THE COUNTRIES THAT FOUGHT IN WORLD WAR II, none was better prepared militarily—on the ground and in the air—than Germany. The German armed forces, known as the Wehrmacht, had designed their weapons for the blitzkrieg (lightning war), a fast, aggressive type of warfare that coordinated air and ground forces to overwhelm an enemy with fast movement and ease of maneuver. This devastated all opponents that Germany faced on land or in the air in the first two years of the war. Britain was an exception, because the over-water crossing of the English Channel had never been properly planned.

The German air force, the Luftwaffe, was the most well-oiled component of the well-oiled machine of the Wehrmacht. Within the structure of the Luftwaffe, the basic building block for fighter operations was the fighter wing, or "Jagdgeschwader," which is abbreviated as "JG." This prefix is used throughout this chapter to identify specific wings. Within these Luftwaffe wings were fighter squadrons, known as "Jagdstaffeln."

The Luftwaffe had a better than four-to-one superiority over every foe that it would meet during 1939 and 1940, and in most cases, it was able to bring a ten-to-one superiority to bear. With the possible exception of the Royal Air Force (which was outnumbered), the Luftwaffe was the best air superiority and ground attack force in the world in the early years of World War II. When the Soviet Union was invaded in 1941, the Luftwaffe was so superior to the Soviet air force, the Voenno-Vozdushnie Sily, that it was able to destroy a sizable proportion of Soviet front line air power within a few weeks. On the first day, over 300 Soviet aircraft were shot down, and nearly 1,500 were destroyed on the ground. By the end of the first week, 5,000 Soviet aircraft had been erased—more than the entire air forces of most countries—but Luftwaffe losses were fewer than 200.

With the exception of certain British aircraft, the Luftwaffe also had far better equipment than any enemy that it would face between 1939 and 1942. In terms of training, only Britain's Royal Air Force had pilots that were on a par with those of the Luftwaffe during the first three years of the war, but these were much fewer in number. Part of the reason for this was that the Luftwaffe had been created from scratch between 1935 and 1939. Under the Treaty of Versailles that ended World War I, Germany had not been allowed to have an air force. The new Luftwaffe had been designed from the ground up for the blitzkrieg under the direction of Hermann Göring, a World War I ace with high standing in the Nazi Party, and Erhardt Milch, a brilliant planner and tactician.

During the Spanish Civil War of 1936–1939, Germany supported the Nationalists militarily and the Luftwaffe sent its Condor Legion, an organization of "volunteers." This allowed Germany's air arm to test both weapons and tactics against the types of aircraft that were expected to be faced in the future war. It also gave many Luftwaffe pilots the air-to-air combat experience that they would need.

Having described it as a well-oiled war machine, it can certainly be added that Germany's military might had serious shortcomings in its overconfidence and short sightedness. Adolf Hitler had insisted on preparing for just 18 months of war. For all of their preparedness, the

★ [Previous] Germany's Luftwaffe was the only air force to use jet fighters in combat in World War II, and the Messerschmitt Me 262 was the first such aircraft to see action. First introduced in April 1944, the Me 262 achieved its greatest fame as a fighter, though Adolf Hitler originally insisted that it be used as a bomber. [Note that this Me 262 is armed with a pair of bombs.] Jet fighter pilots downed more than 500 Allied aircraft, and 28 pilots achieved ace status while flying the Me 262. *Author's Collection*

★ The Messerschmitt Bf 109 was Germany's principal fighter throughout World War II. It was flown on all fronts and by all the top Luftwaffe aces. Between 1935 and 1945, more than 37,000 were produced in more than two dozen variants. Of these, 71 percent were subvariants of the ubiquitous Bf 109G "Gustav." Seen in these two images is a Bf 109G-6 of Jagdgeschwader 2, photographed in 1943 as it was preparing for a mission. *Author's Collection*

Germans failed to have a mechanism in place to replace pilots and aircraft that were lost beyond that time. When the war lasted longer than expected, pilot training and increased aircraft production had to be organized and expanded under wartime conditions and the well-oiled machine became sloppy. By 1944 and 1945, the thoroughly-trained pilots were being replaced by the hastily-trained novices. The Luftwaffe planners never developed long-range strategic bombers, as the British and Americans did, and which proved to be decisive.

Germany also had a technological edge. German engineers and aircraft designers created the most advanced weapons and aircraft in the world during World War II. However, because Hitler wanted to plan for a war that he arrogantly thought he could win in 18 months, Luftwaffe planners were never able to develop a method to adequately test and mass produce the leading edge "secret weapons" that had been developed. Until very late in the war, when it was much too late, the Reichluftfahrtministerium (the German Air Ministry) refused to give adequate funding or priority to the advanced aircraft projects that would have given German pilots the technological edge. The projects and machines existed, but most would never get close to becoming operational. The Luftwaffe was, however, the only air force in the world to have turbojet aircraft in squadron service and air-to-air combat during World War II.

The first German ace of World War II was Hannes Gentzen, a Bf 109D pilot, who shot down two Polish fighters and a bomber on September 3, 1939, then four attack bombers the following day. During the Battle of France, he would add ten victories flying Bf 110s, before being killed in a crash on May 26, 1940. At the time, he was the highest-scoring ace—of any nation—in World War II, but he would soon have his record eclipsed by Luftwaffe aces who scored by the dozen, and who would eventually push their scores beyond 100.

To say that the German aces of World War II outscored the aces of any other air arm is a huge understatement. The Luftwaffe had over 100 aces who outscored the top ace of every other nation involved in the war. While other nations assigned "ace" status with a fifth victory, the Luftwaffe maintained the World War I practice of considering a pilot to be an ace only after he had scored ten victories. In the Luftwaffe, the word for ace was experte. In the Luftwaffe, there were 105 such individuals who exceeded 100 confirmed victories and 15 Luftwaffe experten who exceeded 200 confirmed. Two passed the 300 milestone—Gerhard Barkhorn with 301 and Erich Hartmann with 352.

The Luftwaffe was disbanded after World War II, but when the government of the German Federal Republic established its postwar air force, the Bundesluftwaffe, in 1955, many of the wartime aces including Barkhorn and Hartmann joined the new service.

★
The Focke-Wulf Fw 190 was second only to the Bf 109 in importance as a Luftwaffe fighter aircraft. It entered service in August 1941, two years into World War II, and quickly proved its effectiveness in the hands of German aces. More than 20,000 were built. Seen here is a Fw 190A-8 variant belonging to Jagdgeschwader 4 that was captured in January 1945. *US Army Air Forces*

# HARTMANN:
## THERE IS ONLY ONE NUMBER ONE

**ERICH ALFRED HARTMANN** was the leading ace of all time. Flying exclusively with Jagdgeschwader 52 (JG 52) on the Eastern Front, he scored 352 aerial victories, including seven USAAF P 51s that he downed in operations over Romania. He flew 1,425 missions between October 1942 and May 1945, and he was one of the select nine Luftwaffe aces to be awarded the Knight's Cross with Oak Leaves, Swords, and Diamonds.

In Germany, he came to be known as "the Blonde Knight," but to the Soviet pilots, he was called "the Black Devil," because the cowlings of the Messerschmitt Bf 109s that he flew were painted with a sinister-looking black, tulip-shaped pattern. To his friends and comrades, though, he was simply "Bubi," an affectionate term implying that he was just a baby-faced boy.

Despite the heroics for which he was awarded his decorations, Hartmann's greatest triumph was probably surviving the Soviet gulag archipelago, where he was held, in violation of international law, for more than ten years after the war ended. He is remembered for never having been broken, despite the cruelty that he suffered, and for being an inspiration to fellow prisoners.

Erich Hartmann was born on April 19, 1922 in Weissach, near Stuttgart, in the German state of Wurttemberg. His father, Dr. Alfred Erich Hartmann, had served as a physician during World War I. By 1925, because economic conditions in Germany had deteriorated so much, Dr. Hartmann decided to accept a job in Changsa, China. The family remained here until 1929, when a rash of violence against Europeans forced Dr. Hartmann to send his family home. Erich, his younger brother and their mother returned to Germany by train, traveling across the Soviet Union, a place where Erich was destined to spend much more of his life than he could have imagined in 1929. Later in the year, Dr. Hartmann also came home to stay.

Back in Germany, Erich's mother, Elisabeth Wilhelmine Machtholf Hartmann, became an accomplished glider pilot, eventually making the transition to powered aircraft. By the time he was 14, Erich too was flying. He graduated from the gymnasium (high school) at Korntal in April 1940 and had dreams of studying medicine to follow in his father's footsteps. But war—and compulsory military service—intervened. Eventually, his brother Alfred would become a doctor and take up their father's practice, but Erich would follow another track.

Erich's other dream was flying. Early in World War II, the air aces of the Luftwaffe, such as Werner Mölders and Adolf Galland, were the heroes of the German media, and they inspired excitement in impressionable teenagers like Erich Hartmann, who already held a pilot's license. He joined the Luftwaffe in October 1940 and was assigned to the 10th Flying Regiment at Neukuhren in East Prussia near Konigsberg.

★
Erich Alfred Hartmann scored 352 aerial victories, making him the highest-scoring Luftwaffe ace of World War II and the highest-scoring ace of any nation for all time. All but two victories against the USAAF were against the Soviet Red Air Force. *Author's Collection*

Hartmann would spend the better part of his first two years in the Luftwaffe learning how to fly high-performance fighter aircraft, and gaining an intimate understanding of the Messerschmitt Bf 109, the aircraft that would serve him so well in the years to come. The exhaustive training that he received in 1940–1942 was in stark contrast to the brief time which was available to pilots who were mustered into the Luftwaffe during the later years of World War II. Hartmann was finally sent to a front line unit in October 1942.

Assigned to JG 52, based deep inside the Soviet Union, on the southern part of the Eastern Front, Hartmann would fly with such great aces as Günther Rall (275 victories) and Walter Krupinski (197 victories). One of his first assignments was as Krupinski's wingman. Another JG 52 experte was Gerhard Barkhorn, who scored 301 victories to become the only experte, other than Hartmann, to exceed 300. In all, JG 52 was the highest-scoring unit in history, credited with the confirmed destruction of more than 10,000 Voenno-Vozdushnie Sily aircraft in less than four years of war.

Hartmann's first aerial victory, an Ilyushin Il-2 Sturmovik, came on November 5, 1942, but he would not score his second until January. His inclination, like that of every other novice fighter pilot, was to shoot at his enemies from too far away. Krupinski would spend several months yelling "Get in closer, Bubi!"

When Bubi finally did learn to get in close, he would become lethal. His second on January 27, 1943 was followed by a third on February 9 and a fourth the next day. He scored his fifth on March 24, enough to make him an ace in any air force but the Luftwaffe, but by the end of April, he had exceeded ten. In May, he became commander of JG 52's 7 Staffel.

By this time, Hartmann had developed his four-step method of aerial combat: "See, decide, attach, reverse." In other words, when the enemy was spotted, the hunter would decide whether to pounce, and if so, the attack came quickly and was followed by breaking off before the enemy formation knew what had hit them. As Hartmann would later instruct novice pilots, "Once committed to an attack, fly in at full speed. After scoring crippling or disabling hits, I would clear myself and then repeat the process. I never pursued the enemy, once he had eluded me. Better to break off and set up again for a new assault."

The baby-faced boy who took two months to score his second victory quickly became an accomplished hunter. He scored four on July 5, seven on July 7 and four more on July 8. During August, he scored 46 aerial victories, including five on August 4 and seven on August 7. On August 17, he matched Baron von Richthofen's score of 80 from World War I.

On August 20, however, after bringing his score to 90, Hartmann went down behind Soviet lines. He had been hit by ground fire while he was chasing an Il-2 that was attacking German ground forces. He was captured by the enemy almost immediately but he feigned injury until he had an opportunity to make a break. He eluded capture and managed to walk to German lines.

Back in the air, Hartmann continued to run up his score. On October 29, he scored 150 victories, making him second only to Krupinski, who had achieved 150 on the first day of the month. Of course, Krupinski had been in action since 1939. Hartmann had scored all but two of his kills in eight months. For this, he was awarded the Knight's Cross. Hartmann had developed an intuitive aggressiveness in combat. No longer timid, he knew that the only way to score a certain kill was to be aggressive and not shoot until he could not miss. "The key to the approach was simple," he later said. "Get in as close to the enemy as possible. Your windscreen had to be black with image."

★
Standing next to his Messerschmitt, Erich Hartman celebrates another aerial victory, somewhere on the Eastern Front. The bleeding heart insignia is that of the 9th Staffel (squadron) of Jagdgeschwader 52. The unit was known as the "Karaya Staffel" after the hit song "Karaya" by popular singer Mimi Thoma. *Author's Collection*

Despite the cold and bad weather, Hartmann scored 50 victories during January and February 1944. To this, he would add ten in one day on March 2. His total was now 202. For this, he was sent home to Germany to have the Oak Leaves attached to his Knight's Cross in a ceremony at Berchtesgaden.

By the time that Hartmann returned to JG 52 in late March, German forces were being pushed back, and the geschwader had to relocate itself farther and farther to the west on a weekly basis. The weather was wet and the airfields were crowded with equipment and muddy. By now, Hartmann was starting to face the reality of combat with pilots who truly knew their stuff. The opposition still contained novices, but it wasn't like the situation in 1941–1942. The VVS pilots were aggressive and, like the Luftwaffe aces, hunters. "If I was taken by surprise," Hartmann wrote of reacting to Soviet attackers, "I would do one or the other automatically, depending on conditions. If I had time, and saw my attacker coming in, I would wait to see how close he would come before opening up. If he began firing at long range, I could always turn into him. If he held his fire, I got ready for a real battle. If your attacker held his fire until he was really close, you knew you were in with someone who had a great deal of experience."

In April and May, JG 52 started operating from bases within Romania. It was in late June that Hartmann scored his victories against the Americans. Units of JG 52 were assigned as part of the air defense net for the huge oil refinery complex in and around Ploesti, Romania that was an important target for the B-17 and B-24 heavy bombers of the USAAF Fifteenth Air Force, based in Italy. During the course of these actions, Hartmann tangled with the North American P-51 Mustang, arguably the best piston-engine fighter of World War II. He would shoot down seven. In July, after recording his 239th victory, Erich Hartmann was awarded the Swords for his Knight's Cross, becoming one of 75 persons to receive the award.

Back with JG 52, Hartmann finally surpassed Gerd Barkhorn on August 22, to become the highest-scoring experte in the Luftwaffe. Two days later, he shot down 11 Soviet aircraft in one day. This brought his total to 301, making him the first experte to exceed 300. For this, he would become the 17th man to have Germany's ultimate decoration, the Diamonds, attached to his Knight's Cross.

The awarding of his Diamonds, by Adolf Hitler himself, took place at the Führer's "Wolf's Lair" headquarters in East Prussia. Only a few weeks had elapsed since Hitler had been severely wounded in the Wolf's Lair bomb attack that nearly killed him. It was a surreal environment. Damage was evident and Hitler was obviously still traumatized by the assassination attempt. Security was so tight as to border on paranoid. Hartmann was ordered to surrender his sidearm, but he refused, saying that he did not wish to receive the Diamonds from a leader who did not trust him. He kept his pistol during the ceremony and a subsequent chat with Hitler, who did not notice, nor seem to care.

Having exceeded 300 victories, Hartmann was given an extended leave, during which he married his childhood sweetheart, Ursula "Usch" Paetsch on September 9. Gerd Barkhorn was his best man. After a brief honeymoon, Hartmann returned to JG 52, where he succeeded in raising his victory total to 331 by November 24. He then was given a well-earned Christmas leave, the last he would have for 11 years.

In the early months of 1945, General Adolf Galland, the Luftwaffe's former commander of fighter units, put a great deal of pressure on Hartmann to join his "Jagdverband 44." Galland was personally assembling all the top Luftwaffe aces to fly in a special super geschwader that was equipped with the new Messerschmitt Me 262 jet fighter. During March, Hartmann took leave from JG 52 to fly the jet. However, when it finally came time to officially join JV 44, Hartmann told Galland that he felt he had a moral obligation to continue to fly with his comrades in JG 52. It seemed to him like the right thing to do at the time, but it would be the most regretted decision of his life.

Hartmann had scored 14 victories with JG 52 in February, and he scored five more in April to bring his total to 351. However, by now the Eastern Front was collapsing and German forces were spending all of their time withdrawing. By early May, Germany was in full retreat, and JG 52 was at its last base, Deutsche Brod in Czechoslovakia.

On May 8, Hartmann took off on a reconnaissance patrol directed at identifying how close the Soviet ground forces were to the field JG 52 was using. In the course of this mission, Hartmann encountered a large number of Soviet fighters. He attacked quickly and shot down a Yak-7, his 352nd and final victory. After he broke off, he noticed a formation of USAAF fighters arrive on the scene. He then watched the surreal spectacle of Americans attacking Soviet aircraft, each side thinking the other to be German.

Hartmann landed back at Deutsche Brod, where he was informed that the war was over. He and his superior, Hermann Graf—a "Diamonds" awardee and an experte with 212 victories— were ordered to fly to Dortmund to surrender to British forces, but they chose to remain with the rest of JG 52, which would attempt to travel overland and surrender to American ground forces before the Soviet armies caught up with them. This was another huge mistake.

The men from JG 52 managed to surrender to an American unit, but because they were in an area that Soviet forces were scheduled to occupy, they had to be turned over to the Soviets. Had they gone to Dortmund as ordered, Hartmann and Graf would probably have been back with their families within two months. Instead, the passage of those two months found them deep in the Soviet Union, at a forced labor camp near Gryazovets. By this time, they realized that they would not soon be released.

The large number of German prisoners incarcerated at Gryazovets were starved, kept in primitive conditions and tormented psychologically. Weeks gave way to months, and the prisoners endured the harsh winter under barbaric conditions. Hartmann's wife did not find out that he survived the war until January 1946, and he did not find out until May 1946 that his son had been born on May 21, 1945, while he was in a cattle car crossing the steppes.

The prisoners were in the custody of the dreaded NKVD, the Narodny Kommisariat Vnutrennikh Del (People's Commissariat for Internal Affairs), the brutal internal security police that Josef Stalin used to keep his iron fist on the pulse of the Soviet Union. One of the projects that the NKVD undertook was to try to get the former German officers to come over to the Soviet cause. The idea was that they would become pawns the Soviet Union could use to help run their sector of occupied Germany. Many would succumb to the pressure, but Hartmann, who was apolitical, never did.

Being the so-called "Black Devil," however, Hartmann was singled out for especially harsh treatment. The NKVD tried hard to break Hartmann. They starved him, and they intercepted and held his mail. In 1947, he was transferred to Kuteynikovo, a mile from where he had been stationed with JG 52 in 1943. It was here that he endured the first of many months spent in solitary confinement. It was also in 1947 that Hartmann was declared not a prisoner of war but a war criminal, and sentenced to 25 years of hard labor.

When Hartmann was transferred to Shakhty to begin working in a coal mine, he refused because under the Geneva Convention, officers are not required to work. This touched off a prisoner revolt in which Hartmann himself prevented the Germans from killing the Soviet guards. He then stared down a force of Soviet troops that came to restore order. Instead of going to the coal mine, Hartmann went back into solitary confinement at Novochgerkassk.

Hartmann almost never received his mail. He would not know until 1948 that the son he had never seen died in 1947 at age two. He did not know about his father's death in 1952 for over a year. Months gave way to years. Except for about a year at Diaterka prison camp in 1953–1954, Hartmann would remain in Novochgerkassk until October 1955. Hermann Graf, who signed a "confession" to being a war criminal, was released in 1950.

Hartmann's release came as part of an effort toward mending relations between the Soviet Union and the new Federal Republic of Germany. Stalin had died in 1953, and West German Chancellor Konrad Adenauer asked for the release of German prisoners as one of the conditions of a new trade relationship that the Soviet Union wanted. Suddenly, Hartmann was on a train to Germany to be reunited with friends and family after more than a decade in captivity.

Meanwhile, many of Hartmann's former Luftwaffe comrades, including Barkhorn, Krupinski and Rall, had joined the new West German air force, the Bundesluftwaffe. They invited him to join as well, and, since the only trade he had ever known was flying aircraft, he did so. Hartmann resumed flying in 1956 at Landsberg, and he also trained at the facility that the Bundesluftwaffe established in Arizona, which has much better flying weather than Germany. Hartmann's wife, Ursula, recalled the Arizona experience as being one of the most pleasant of her life with Bubi Hartmann.

Back in West Germany, Hartmann was assigned as commander of the newly-formed geschwader, JG 51, which was equipped with the new Lockheed F-104 Starfighter that was to prove so problematic for the Bundesluftwaffe in the early 1960s. Though he did an exceptional job of turning JG 71 into a first rate unit, Hartmann's lack of political skills caused him to be overlooked for promotions in the peacetime military, and he resigned to take a job with Germany's civilian aviation authority. He died in 1993.

# MÖLDERS: FIRST TO TOP THE RED BARON

**LIKE HANS-JOACHIM MARSEILLE,** Werner Mölders died early in his career after having achieved an amazing record. The highest-scoring German ace in the Spanish Civil War, he became the first to exceed von Richthofen and the first ace to top 100. Mölders was born at Gelsenkirchen on March 18, 1913 and grew up in Brandenburg, where his father was posted with the 35th Fusilier Regiment. In April 1931, he joined the army and was assigned to an infantry regiment in East Prussia. Two years later, after becoming an officer, he joined the Luftwaffe at Cottbus.

Mölders began his combat career in 1938, as one of the Luftwaffe pilots that joined the German Condor Legion to fight on the side of Francisco Franco's Nationalists during the Spanish Civil War. In Spain, he flew both Heinkel He 51 biplanes and Messerschmitt Bf 109Cs, scoring 14 victories to become leading scorer in the Condor Legion. His last two victories, a pair of Polikarpov I-16s, came on October 15, 1938.

When World War II began, Mölders was assigned to Jagdgeschwader 53 (JG 53) on the Western Front, and had scored four kills by the end of 1939. He quickly racked up an impressive roster of kills during the Battle of France and was the top scoring ace of the war—with 25—when he was shot down on June 5, 1940. After two weeks as a prisoner of war, France capitulated and he was assigned to JG 51 for the Battle of Britain.

During the Battle of Britain, Mölders vied with Helmut Wick for being the highest-scoring ace in that pivotal campaign. Mölders would reach 40 (excluding his 14 scored in Spain) on September 20, followed by Adolf Galland four days later and Wick on October 6. Early on November 28, Wick downed a Spitfire, his 55th victory, to surpass Mölders. However, late in the day, Wick went into dogfight with John Dundas, a 13.5-victory ace with the Royal Air Force No. 609 Squadron over the Isle of Wight. Dundas managed to down Wick's Messerschmitt Bf 109, but was himself downed by Wick's wingman.

By this time, Mölders had received the Oak Leaves for his Knight's Cross. He was also already being credited as a tactical genius and had developed the types of tactics with which many younger pilots would become great aces. Indeed, he was known for setting up a kill, and then letting a newer man take the shot and get the score. One of his most important contributions to Luftwaffe tactics was the development of the two-ship rotte formation as a basic fighting unit.

In 1940, Mölders had earned the nickname "Vati," meaning "Daddy," for being the "father" of German fighter tactics, for being a mentor to newer pilots, and for his relatively advanced age. He was 27.

Early in 1941, JG 51 made the transition to the Bf 109F, and on February 26, Mölders scored his 60th victory of World War II. In May, JG 51 moved east in preparation for Operation

★
Oberstleutnant Werner Mölders is seen here in a press release photo, circa November 1940, wearing Knight's Cross of the Iron Cross with Oak Leaves. He was the first ace in World War II to top the World War I score of Baron Manfred von Richthofen, the "Red Baron." He was also the first ace to top 100 aerial victories. *Public Domain image from the Bundesarchiv, colorized by Ruffneck'88 and licensed under Creative Commons*

Barbarossa, the invasion of the Soviet Union. Mölders scored four victories on June 22, the first day of the operation, and surpassed von Richthofen's 80 a few days later. For this, the Swords were attached to his Knight's Cross. By July 15, his score stood at 99 for World War II. On that date, he scored his final two victories, exceeding 100 for World War II, and raising his final score for both wars to 115.

On July 16, Mölders became the first man to be awarded Diamonds for his Knight's Cross, and he was promoted to be the youngest colonel (oberst) in the Luftwaffe. However, the Luftwaffe high command forbade him to fly further combat missions. The Propaganda Ministry did not want to lose the man who topped the Red Baron to a stray Soviet bullet.

On August 7, Mölders was promoted to the temporary rank of general in order for him to become Inspekteur General der Jagdflieger (Inspector General of Fighters), with duties at the Reichluftfahrtministerium overseeing the management of all fighter units within the Luftwaffe. In November 1941, Mölders was on an inspection tour of JG 77 on the Eastern Front when he was summoned to Berlin for the funeral of Ernst Udet.

Udet had been the second highest-scoring German ace of World War I, with 62 victories. He had gone on to a career as an aerobatic pilot and he had even flown in several motion pictures. When the Luftwaffe reformed, he joined and was assigned as Inspector General of Ground Attack aircraft, where he helped develop the Junkers Ju 87 Stuka dive bomber. On November 17, 1941, he committed suicide under questionable circumstances after a disagreement with Hermann Göring.

Since no transport aircraft was available, Mölders decided to fly to Berlin in a Heinkel He 111 bomber on November 22. The aircraft suffered an engine failure near Breslau (now Wroclaw,

Poland) en route to Berlin, and on final approach into Breslau Hundsfeld airfield, the second engine failed. Mölders, who was on the flight deck, was killed in the crash, but his aide survived. In his honor, his old unit, JG 51, added his name to their designation, officially renaming the geschwader, "JG 51 Mölders."

Recently, it has come to light that Mölders had found out about the super-secret Nazi T-4 project and had been so enraged that he threatened to return his Knight's Cross with Diamonds if T-4 was not stopped. T-4 was the code name for the Reich Work Group on Sanatoriums and Nursing Homes (Reichsarbeitsgemeinschaft Heil und Pflegeanstalten). It was a grisly project that used mentally disabled people as guinea pigs for gruesome—and typically fatal—medical experiments. T-4 was also responsible for developing the means for killing large numbers of people under controlled circumstances, such as in concentration camps. The organization operated from the Reich Chancellery in Berlin, specifically located at Tiergarten 4, hence the T-4 name. Early in 1941, T-4 agreed to permit Shutzstaffel (SS) boss Heinrich Himmler to use its personnel and facilities to rid the concentration camps of "excess prisoners," such as those most seriously ill physically and mentally. This was called "prisoner euthanasia."

As people outside the T-4 inner circle started to find out about it, there was a groundswell of condemnation. It was denounced by the clergy and by many in government, including Mölders. Himmler, meanwhile, was more upset that the secret had gotten out. He is reported to have said "If operation T-4 had been entrusted to the SS, things would have happened differently, because when the Führer entrusts us with a job, we know how to deal with it correctly."

It is not known whether Mölders' death was an aspect of "dealing with it correctly'" but Himmler would not have shied away from such a "job."

On November 28, Mölders was interred near Udet at the Invalidenfriedhof in Berlin, close to the tomb of Manfred von Richthofen. The site was disrupted during the building of the Berlin Wall, and again during construction of other installations in 1975. The area was repaired in 1992 after the Wall came down.

★
Werner Mölders (left) meets with top German leaders on July 25, 1941 at Hitler's Wolfsschanze (Wolf's Lair) headquarters in Rastenburg, East Prussia. Mölders had just achieved his 100th aerial victory and had been awarded the Knight's Cross of the Iron Cross with Oak Leaves, Swords and Diamonds. The others are Wehrmacht commander-in-chief Field Marshal Wilhelm Keitel, Adolf Hitler and Reichsmarschall Hermann Göring, commander of the Luftwaffe. *Wikimedia Commons*

# GALLAND:
## THE GENERAL WAS AN ACE

**WHEN ONE LOOKS AT THE CAREERS OF WORLD WAR II FIGHTER ACES,** few stand out as having had such an amazing career, both during the war and after, as Adolf Galland—the dashing young man with the movie star presence, jet black hair and pencil-thin mustache. One of the leading aces of the Battle of Britain, Galland became a geschwader commander, and was second only to Mölders to become a recipient of the Knight's Cross with Diamonds. Galland also would succeed him as Inspekteur General der Jagdflieger (Inspector General of Fighters). After having held that post longer than anyone, he went back into combat as commander of Jagdverband (JV) 44, the Luftwaffe's last all-jet geschwader. He then became an ace again, a jet ace. After the war, he wrote his memoirs—entitled The First and the Last—and became one of the leading spokesmen for German fighter pilots at reunions and air shows.

Adolf Galland was born on March 19, 1912 at Westerholt in Westfalia, the second of Adolf and Anne Galland's four sons. An avid glider pilot, he established a local soaring record of more than two hours aloft in February 1932. In February 1934, having joined the army, he was assigned to an infantry regiment in Dresden for basic training, but in March 1935, he transferred to the Luftwaffe's JG 1 in Doberitz.

In May 1937, Galland arrived in Spain as part of the Condor Legion, and was placed in command of Jagdstaffel 88, which was known as the "Mickey Mouse Squadron" because of the insignia that the cigar-smoking Galland designed—a cigar-smoking Mickey Mouse holding an axe and a pistol. Unlike his friend Werner Mölders, Galland did not become an ace in the Spanish Civil War, although his staffel contained all the Condor Legion aces. For his work as a commander, he was awarded the Spanish Cross in Gold with Diamonds on June 6, 1939. It had been awarded only 12 times in Spanish history. One of his unique innovations had been to base his unit aboard a train. The aircraft were mobile and could land in fields anywhere. With Galland's plan, the train brought the base to wherever the aircraft landed after a mission, rather than having them be compelled to fly back to a fixed base.

When World War II began in September 1939, Galland flew ground attack missions against Polish ground forces in a Henschel Hs 123, and was awarded the Iron Cross on October 1, 1939. He was then reassigned as a fighter pilot, flying Messerschmitt Bf 109s with JG 27, which went into action in the Battle of France in May 1940. He claimed his long-awaited first aerial victories on May 12, downing two Royal Air Force Hawker Hurricanes in two missions.

Prior to the Battle of Britain, Galland was reassigned to JG 26. This geschwader was known informally as "the Abbeville Boys" because they were based at Abbeville, which is in the Pas de Calais region of northern France, just across the Channel from Britain. This placed him in the thick of the action—he shot down two aircraft on his first day with JG 26. For his 17th victory, scored on

August 22, 1940, Galland was awarded the Knights Cross and made Kommodore of JG 26.

Galland was a colorful character, the kind of swaggering knight of the air that one would expect to encounter only in the movies. He was often seen in the company of glamorous women—after all, he could drive to Paris in only a few hours. He served gourmet food in his officers' mess, he liked good wine—as well as fine cigars. Galland even had a cigar lighter installed in the cockpit of his Messerschmitt Bf 109.

For him, his days with the Abbeville boys were among the greatest moments of his life, filled with virtually nothing but combat and parties, the two activities that he enjoyed most. One of the wildest tales from Abbeville folklore concerns the day that he combined both, by accident. He was flying solo, en route to a party hosted by General Theo Osterkamp (ultimately a 32-victory ace)—carrying lobster and champagne for the party in his Bf 109. Suddenly, he was jumped by three Spitfires. Galland succeeded in outmaneuvering the attackers and shooting down all three. Coincidently, the entire exchange was overheard on the two-way radio at the party. When he landed at the site of the party, the lobster and champagne were shaken but undamaged, and Galland was neither damaged nor shaken.

Through the end of 1940, Galland scored 52 victories, half of his eventual final tally. More combat and additional victories would come the way of JG 26 during early 1941, but the urgency of the Battle of Britain had subsided. Both sides knew that there would be no cross-channel invasion in 1941—in either direction.

It was not all glory for Galland, however. On June 21, 1941 he was shot down twice. In the morning, the Abbeville Boys attacked a force of Royal Air Force bombers, but were jumped by Spitfires and Galland's Bf 109 was badly damaged. He managed to limp back to base and crash-land. After lunch, he took off again, but was not so lucky. He was bounced by Spitfires after scoring against one, and barely managed to force his way through a jammed canopy before his

★
In another scene from the table at Theodor Osterkamp's birthday party on April 15, 1941, Adolf Galland took a turn describing one of his own recent aerial combat experiences as Werner Mölders (center) looked on.
*Wikimedia Commons*

Adolf Galland meets
with Dr. Albert Speer,
the Reich minister
for armaments and
war production at
the Luftwaffe testing
and development at
Rechlin, about 60
miles north of Berlin
in September 1943.
*Wikimedia Commons*

Messerschmitt crashed. As the story goes, Galland was smoking a cigar on the operating table as doctors were sewing and patching him up. In one day, Galland was responsible for downing five aircraft—two British and two piloted by himself.

One of the most interesting stories in World War II fighter ace folklore is of the that of the friendship between Galland and the legless British ace, Douglas Bader (also see Chapter 4). Like Galland, Bader was a colorful character with a media following and a relatively high score of enemy aircraft. On August 9, 1941, Bader was shot down by JG 26 over northern France. When Galland found out, he invited him to dinner. One of Bader's artificial legs was lost and the other damaged when his parachute brought him down. Galland made a request through the International Red Cross for replacements, guaranteeing safe passage for a Royal Air Force aircraft to parachute them to the JG 26 base. However, the British plane that dropped them also bombed the base.

Bader got the legs and was sent to a series of prisoner of war camps from which he subsequently made a series of unsuccessful escape attempts. The two met again after the war and remained friends until Bader's death in 1982.

Meanwhile, on August 7, Werner Mölders was promoted to temporary rank of Inspekteur General der Jagdflieger, to manage fighter units within the Luftwaffe. When he died in a plane crash on November 22 en route to Ernst Udet's funeral, Galland was named to succeed him as Inspekteur General. As the story goes, Hermann Göring pulled Galland aside at the funeral and gave him the job on the spot.

On January 28, 1942, when Galland arrived in Berlin to assume his new duties, he was awarded the Diamonds for his Knight's Cross by Adolf Hitler himself. One of his first tasks at his new desk job was to organize and plan the air cover for the German navy's famous "Channel Dash," in which the battle cruisers Scharnhorst and Gneisenau, and the heavy cruiser Prinz Eugen slipped through the English Channel from France to Germany. Between February 11 and 13, the three ships made their way, covered by a rotation of various fighter wings that provided an "air umbrella" to protect them from British air attacks. It was successful. Not a single major hit was made on the warships.

By the end of 1942, the 30-year-old Galland had been promoted to general major (the equivalent of an American brigadier general), and in November 1944 he became a general leutnant (the equivalent of an American major general)—but through it all, he missed flying fighters in combat.

It was during 1942 that Galland first inspected the Messerschmitt Me 262 jet fighter, which was still in development. He immediately recognized its potential. Galland became a convert to jet fighters with his first introduction to the new aircraft. In 1943, after he'd had a chance to fly the aircraft, Galland said that piloting it was like "being pushed by an angel."

In his official capacity, Galland recommended to Göring and Hitler that the Me 262 should go into production as soon as possible. He advocated that all production resources for fighters—except those building Fw 190s—should be devoted only to jets. He also recommended the deployment of a massive jet fighter force. Any fighter pilot who flew the Me 262 recognized that such a force would completely reshape the nature of aerial warfare in Germany's favor.

When Hitler saw the Me 262, he was impressed, but insisted that it become a bomber. This was a task for which it was utterly unsuited, but it would take until late 1944 to get Hitler to change his mind. Galland was convinced that a force of Me 262s deployed to France in June 1944 could have probably stopped the Normandy Invasion by removing its air cover. Certainly, when Me 262s attacked the Allied bomber formations, they were deadly and unstoppable—while in the air.

In July 1944, a month after the invasion, Galland finally decided to prove to Hitler what the Me 262 could do as a fighter. He chose Walter Nowotny, a Knight's Cross holder with over 200 victories to head a demonstration unit, to be based at Achmer, that was called Kommando Nowotny. In combat, especially against bombers, the Me 262 proved to be a potent weapon, although it was found to be vulnerable to Allied fighters during takeoffs and landings. On November 8, Galland happened to be at Achmer when Nowotny himself was shot down by a USAAF P-51 while on final approach after a mission.

By the end of 1944, a deep chasm had opened between the Luftwaffe's flying officers and its desk-bound officers at the Reichluftfahrtministerium—and Galland was caught in the middle. Luftwaffe Chief Göring was ignoring the tactical recommendations made by Galland and the Luftwaffe field commanders, and was ordering operations that were not only ineffective but costing lives unnecessarily. The lack of initiative in getting the Me 262s into production was only the tip of the iceberg. Göring had lost the confidence of the flying officers who demanded more effective leadership.

It all came to a head in January 1945. The leading commanders came to Galland, who set up a meeting with Göring. The leader of the revolt was Günther Josten, a geschwader kommodore and an experte with 178 victories. Also present was Johannes Steinhoff, a commander and an experte who would ultimately claim 176 victories, and well as Günther Lutzow, a Luftwaffe officer who was the son of the great World War I admiral. The meeting was not pleasant. Göring was unreceptive, and flatly refused to modify policies that the officers felt were damaging to

Germany. The officers finally demanded that Göring resign. He became enraged and demoted everyone present, including Galland, who was not.

Hitler overruled Göring on Galland's demotion. He was allowed to keep his rank, but he lost his job as Inspekteur General. His new job was, however, much more to his liking. Galland was tasked with finally creating an all-jet jagdgeschwader. It was designated as "Jagdverband 44," the only such unit ever created, although if Galland had had his way, there would have been ten of them 18 months earlier. He brought in Johannes Steinhoff, who in turn recruited Heinrich Bär, Gerhard Barkhorn, Walter Krupinski, Erich Hohagen, Günther Lutzow, Wilhelm Herget and Erich Rudorffer—all Knight's Cross-holders with high scores in conventional aircraft. Erich Hartmann was invited but chose to continue with JG 52 on the Eastern Front.

Though JV 44 did not get into action until March 1945—less than two months before the war ended—the impact was dramatic. By now, the new Me 262A 1a/U1 was available, with a withering complement of guns, including two 20mm MG151s, two 30mm MK103s and two 30mm MK108s. Using high-velocity air-to-air rockets as well as guns, the Me 262s were extremely effective. It was as though technology of the future had suddenly arrived aboard a time machine, but it was too late to effect the outcome of the war. Nevertheless, JV 44 ran up a very impressive tally. Many of the pilots—including Galland, Steinhoff, Bär and Rudorffer—became aces all over again in the jets.

Galland's last mission came on April 26. He had shot down a pair of USAAF Martin B 26 Marauders, his 103rd and 104th victories, but as he banked to turn back into the bomber formation, fire from another Marauder poured into his cockpit, wounding him and damaging the Me 262. As he limped back to base, he found that it was under attack by a large number of P-47s. As he struggled up from a missed approach, he was bounced by a Thunderbolt piloted by James Finnegan. Galland survived but was badly injured. The war would end before he could recuperate. Bär took over JV 44 for the last ten days of World War II.

Because of his role as Inspekteur General, Galland was arrested by the Allies on May 14, 1945 and remained a prisoner of war until 1947. When he was released, he was forbidden to be a pilot in occupied Germany, so he held various odd jobs before being invited to Argentina to help build the postwar Argentine air force. President Juan Peron, an ardent nationalist who was often compared to Hitler and Mussolini, was anxious to build a powerful military, and he was able to find many capable advisors among the ranks of Germany's former military officers.

Adolf Galland established Argentina's air force training and operations school, and he helped to develop the tactical training program. Many of the tactical doctrines instilled by Galland were used successfully by Argentina in the 1982 Falklands War. Galland also played an important role in the development of the Pulqui, Argentina's first indigenously-produced fighter aircraft. Most important for him, he was able to fly again.

In 1954, Galland married Countess Sylvina von Donhoff, and early in 1955, he left Argentina to relocate to Germany. Later that year, his application to serve as head of the newly constituted West German Bundesluftwaffe was rejected by the Defense Ministry in favor of General Josef Kammhuber, who had headed the Luftwaffe's night fighter operations during World War II.

Over the ensuing years, Galland operated a successful aerospace consulting business in Bonn and was an active participant at fighter pilot reunions in Germany, as well as in Britain and the United States. He died on February 9, 1996 of a heart ailment at the age of 83.

# BARKHORN:
# ALSO OVER 300

**THE ONLY EXPERTE OTHER THAN ERICH HARTMANN TO SCORE MORE THAN 300 VICTORIES,** Gerhard "Gerd" Barkhorn flew most of his missions with Hartmann's unit, JG 52, on the Eastern Front. In April 1945, he was one of the pilots tapped by Adolf Galland and Johannes Steinhoff to fly Me 262 jet fighters with the all-jet geschwader, Jagdverband 44.

Barkhorn was born in Konigsberg in East Prussia on March 20, 1919 and joined the Luftwaffe in 1939. In August 1940, during the Battle of Britain, he was assigned to JG 52—which was then based in France—but he did not score any kills during the campaign. In preparation for Operation Barbarossa, the invasion of the Soviet Union, JG 52 was transferred to the Eastern Front. On July 2, 1941, ten days after the invasion, Barkhorn scored his first victory.

On August 23, 1942, with 59 victories to his credit, Barkhorn was awarded the Knight's Cross. By the middle of December, he had pushed his score to 100, and on January 12, 1943, he received the Oak Leaves to mark his 120th kill. In June he became a commander of II Staffel within JG 52, and on November 30 reached 200 victories. By now, Barkhorn had become one of the most effective fighter pilots on the Eastern Front. With his 250th kill on February 13, 1944, he joined a pantheon that only five Luftwaffe aces would reach, and on March 2, he became the 52nd man to have the Swords added to his Knight's Cross.

In January 1945, having surpassed 300, Barkhorn was transferred to JG 6 on the Western Front, although it was soon after that he was picked to transition into the Me 262. On April 21, just six days after he joined JV 44, Barkhorn was badly injured in the crash of his Me 262. He would not recover in time to fly again, and the Luftwaffe's second-place ace would add no jet fighter victories to his tally of 301 that he'd scored in piston-engine aircraft.

In 1955, when the postwar Federal Republic of Germany created the new Bundesluftwaffe, Barkhorn was one of the former Luftwaffe aces to be called upon to serve as one of its general officers. He died in 1983.

★ [Left]
Gerhard Barkhorn in his Messerschmitt Bf 109G near the Russian city of Anapa on the northern coast of the Black Sea in the fall of 1943. At the time he was a squadron commander within Jagdgeschwader 52. *Wikimedia Commons*

★ [Right]
Gerhard Barkhorn received the Knight's Cross of the Iron Cross with Oak Leaves and Swords in March 1944 for achieving 250 aerial victories, but he went on to top 300, scoring his 301st and final one on January 5, 1945. He was the Luftwaffe's second highest-scoring ace and the only ace other than Erich Hartman to exceed 300. Both men served with Jagdgeschwader 52. *Author's Collection*

# NOWOTNY:
# THE AUSTRIAN EXPERT

**THE LUFTWAFFE'S FIFTH HIGHEST-SCORING EXPERTE,** and the first officer from any nation to command a jet fighter unit, Walter Nowotny was born on December 7, 1920 in Gmund. At that time, as it is today, Gmund was located in Austria. However, in 1938, when Nowotny was 17 years old, Austria was absorbed into the German Reich in the Anschluss, and Nowotny became a German. The following year, he joined the Luftwaffe and applied for training as a fighter pilot.

In the spring of 1941, he was posted to JG 54, which was assigned to the northern (Baltic) part of the Eastern Front for Operation Barbarossa, the German invasion of the Soviet Union on June 22, 1941. Nowotny's first aerial victories came on July 19. Off to an auspicious beginning, he downed three Soviet aircraft that day. However, his luck quickly unraveled when his Messerschmitt Bf 109 was shot down by a Polikarpov I 153 over the Riga Bay off Latvia. After three days and nights adrift in the Baltic, Nowotny finally reached the shore and was picked up by German troops. As the story goes, the superstitious Nowotny was so glad to have survived that he would fly all his future missions wearing the same pair of pants that he had on during this ordeal.

Through the course of his first winter on the Eastern Front, Nowotny would rack up 48 victories, a good showing, but nothing like what was to come. The second phase of Nowotny's career as a fighter pilot began on August 4, 1942. On that day, JG 54 was on a bomber escort mission over Leningrad when Soviet fighters jumped the bombers. No sooner had Nowotny nailed one of the enemy fighters than he had a second in his sights. The sky was so filled with Polikarpovs that this happened again and again, until Nowotny had claimed six. As he banked to turn for home, it happened again and he scored his seventh for the day. Nowotny was awarded the Knight's Cross on September 14, 1942, and on October 25 he was given command of 9 Staffel of JG 54.

Nowotny would reach 100 victories on March 25, 1943, and nine days later, he shot down 10 enemy aircraft in one day. Shortly after, he was placed in command of I Gruppe of JG 54. His successes as a fighter pilot became legendary. During March, he scored 41, only to top this record with 49 in August. The August total included nine on August 13 and seven on August 21, to bring his tally to 157.

On the first day of September, Nowotny had his second run of ten in one day, and on September 4, the Oak Leaves were added to his Knight's Cross to honor him for 189 victories. Five days later, he

★
On October 19, 1943, Walter Nowotny was awarded the Knight's Cross of the Iron Cross with Oak Leaves, Swords and Diamonds by Adolf Hitler personally. *Wikimedia Commons*

★
This model on display at the Museum of Historical Modeling in Voghiera, Italy depicts the Focke-Wulf Fw 190A-4 flown by Walter Nowotny. It is painted in the winter livery of Jagdgeschwader 54, which was known as "Grünherz" because its unit insignia was the "Green Heart" of Thuringia, a state in the heart of Germany. *Threecharlie photo licensed under Creative Commons*

scored his 200th kill. October began with Nowotny downing 32 Soviet aircraft in 10 days, and on October 14, he became the first of only five aces in history to reach a total of 250 victories. Five days later, he became the eighth German to have the Diamonds added to his Knight's Cross.

Despite his Diamonds and his national hero status, Nowotny continued to fly and fight with JG 54 through the blizzards of November. On November 15, however, as Nowotny scored his 255th Eastern Front victory, the Luftwaffe decided to bring him in from the cold. He was of more value at home as a living hero than on the Eastern Front where he might get killed. Nowotny would return to Germany, a celebrity, who would help the German propaganda mill to inspire the populace with confidence.

In February 1944, after a round of public appearances, Nowotny was assigned to command Schulegeschwader (literally, "school wing") 101, a training unit located at Pau in France. While Nowotny was in France, the first Messerschmitt Me 262 jet fighters were finally reaching the Luftwaffe, and were being worked through their initial teething troubles. Most new aircraft go through such a stage when they are first introduced, but the Me 262 represented such a leap into the stratosphere of unfamiliar technology that such problems were magnified. Despite their promise, the jets were plagued with difficulties. The Junkers Jumo engines were temperamental and fragile, and the Me 262s were vulnerable during take-offs and landings. Finally, it was decided that the best way to shape the Me 262s into an effective force was to get them into an operational unit commanded by an experienced fighter pilot and geschwader commander. The Luftwaffe's Inspekteur General der Jagdflieger (Inspector General of Fighters) Adolf Galland called Nowotny.

While a provisional Me 262 test unit already existed at Hesepe, Walter Nowotny was tasked with pulling together a jet fighter unit. On September 26, 1944, Nowotny formed his "Kommando Nowotny." The next day, it officially began operations at Achmer, near Osnabruck and not far from Hesepe, in the heart of the Ruhr industrial region. This is where the Eighth Air Force bombers were coming, and it was the place where interceptors were needed most. The idea was for Kommando Nowotny to become the prototype for the next generation of air defense.

On November 7, 1944, Adolf Galland came to Achmer to inspect the new air defense unit and its jet fighters. It was an inauspicious day. Because of numerous and varied mechanical problems, only two of the jets managed to get off. Nowotny himself was grounded with a plugged fuel line. Each of the two that flew would claim an Allied fighter, but it was not what Galland—or Nowotny—were looking for.

The following day, Galland observed six Me 262s—led by Nowotny—take off to intercept an Eighth Air Force bomber stream. Several USAAF bombers and fighters were reported shot down, and Nowotny reported that he was coming back with one of his two engines out. Galland watched him coming in on his final approach, but suddenly, the jet was bounced by a P-51D Mustang, which was later determined to have been piloted by R.W. Stevens of the 364th Fighter Group. Stevens broke off after his first pass and Nowotny reported that he was on fire. Nowotny's Me 262 hit the ground, bounced up, came down and disappeared in a fireball. Walter Nowotny was killed in action on November 8, 1944. His final score was 255 Eastern Front victories scored in Messerschmitt Bf 109s and Focke Wulf Fw 190As, plus three Boeing B-17s claimed while flying his Messerschmitt Me 262.

# RUDORFFER: THIRTEEN ON ONE MISSION

**THE LUFTWAFFE'S SEVENTH HIGHEST-SCORING EXPERTE OF WORLD WAR II**, Erich Rudorffer was also a master of multiple kills and he achieved the record of 13 victories—in 17 minutes—on a single mission. The fighter pilot folklore also tells of the day in 1940, when Rudorffer took pity on a Royal Air Force Hurricane pilot and saved his life.

Erich Rudorffer was born in Zwickau in Saxony on November 1, 1917. He joined the Luftwaffe at the relatively mature age of 23 and was assigned to JG 2 early in 1940. He participated in the Battle of France and scored his first victory against the Armée de l'Air on May 14, 1940. By the time that France surrendered in June, Rudorffer's score stood at nine.

The incident involving the Hurricane came in August, when Rudorffer shot up the British aircraft, but rather than delivering the coup de grace and forcing the pilot to bail out in the bitterly cold, uncertain waters of the English Channel, he flew with him until the damaged Hurricane crossed the English coastline. Two weeks later, a Royal Air Force pilot returned the favor when Rudorffer's Bf 109 was damaged over the channel.

Rudorffer received his Knight's Cross on May 1, 1941, having scored 19 victories, and he remained in Europe until November 1942, when JG 2 was relocated to North Africa. Here, Rudorffer was promoted to command the geschwader's II Gruppe. It was while JG 2 was located in Tunisia that Rudorffer began to achieve his mastery of multiple-kill dogfights.

Early in 1943, he scored 26 victories against the Royal Air Force over Tunisia, with 15 of them in the space of 52 minutes on two missions. On February 9, he downed eight in 32 minutes, and on February 15, he claimed seven in just 20 minutes.

In June, after spending three months in France flying patrols over the English Channel, Rudorffer received the assignment to the Eastern Front that was inevitable for high-scoring Luftwaffe pilots in 1943. He was given the task of organizing IV Gruppe for JG 54, the geschwader known as "Grünherz" because of its green, heart-shaped insignia. He was in Konigsberg in East Prussia working on this project when word came through on the last day of July that Heinrich Jung, the commander of II Gruppe, was missing in action. Erich Rudorffer was named as his replacement.

The master of the multiples was now in action against the VVS. On August 24, now flying the potent Focke-Wulf Fw 190, he would claim five Soviet aircraft before lunch, and another three in the afternoon. Rudorffer was setting impossible records on an almost weekly basis. On October 11, for example, he is recorded to have scored seven kills in the course of seven minutes. On November 6, he entered his name on page one of the record books when he downed 13 enemies in 17 minutes. This put him on the same page with Emil "Bully" Lang, who scored 18 victories in one day on the Eastern Front, and Hans Joachim Marseille, with 17 victories in one day against the Royal Air Force in North Africa.

By April 1944, when he received the Oak Leaves for his Knight's Cross, Rudorffer's score was up to 113. Still the multiple victories came. On October 28, he aborted a landing in order to chase a Soviet attack bomber force. He claimed nine of the heavily armored Ilyushin Il 2s, disrupted their attack, landed for lunch and claimed two more in the afternoon.

In January 1945, with Germany's ultimate fate sealed, Rudorffer was awarded the Swords for his 210th victory, and reassigned to JG 7 to be brought up to speed on the Me 262 jet fighter. He would go on to score 12 victories in the remarkable aircraft, tying him for fourth place among World War II jet aces. His total score was probably 219, plus two probables, but many sources list him with 222.

After the war, Erich Rudorffer would go on to serve with the civilian aviation agency of the German Federal Republic.

★
A line of Messerschmitt Bf 109G-6 aircraft.
The "DN" prefix in the markings suggests that
they were assigned to Jagdgeschwader 101, an
operational training unit formed in December 1942
and based at Pau in the south of France. They saw
limited action, defending Luftwaffe airfields in the
area from USAAF Eighth Air Force attacks.
*Author's Collection*

★
Heinz Bär inspects the largely intact fuselage of the American B-17F bomber *Miss Ouachita* (42-3040) which he shot down at Lingen near the Dutch border on February 22, 1944. Piloted by Lieutenant Spencer Osterberg, this Flying Fortress was one of several aircraft of the 91st Bomb Group targeting Luftwaffe airfields at Gutersloh and Achmer as part of Eighth Air Force "Big Week" operations. Though wounded, Osterberg managed a belly landing and most of the crew survived to be captured. *Wikimedia Commons*

# BÄR: THE TOP ME 262 JET ACE

**THE MAN DESTINED TO BE THE HIGHEST-SCORING ME 262 JET ACE IN WORLD WAR II,** Oskar-Heinrich (also seen as Oskar-Heinz) Bär, was born on March 25, 1913 in Sommerfeld, near Leipzig. "Pritzl," as he was called, grew up anxious to fly and made his first flights in a glider at an early age. He joined the Luftwaffe in 1937 and had been assigned as a Bf 109 pilot to JG 51 by the time World War II began September 1939. He scored his first victory on September 25 over Weissenberg, Germany. It was an American made Curtiss Hawk Model 75 fighter belonging to the French Armée de l'Air.

In 1940, Bär's geschwader shifted to the Western Front where, beginning in May, he would fly Messerschmitt Bf 109Es in both the Battle of France and the Battle of Britain. In the latter, he was the Luftwaffe's top scoring non-officer, with a total of 17 victories. It would be a year and another ten victories before Bär was commissioned as an officer, but on July 2, 1941, his commission as a leutnant was accompanied by a Knight's Cross.

Almost immediately, Bär became commander of IV Gruppe of JG 51, which was reassigned to the Eastern Front on July 27, 1941 a bit over a month after Germany invaded the Soviet Union. Bär's unit was re-equipped with Bf 109Fs and attached to JG 53, which was known as "Pik As" ("Ace of Spades") because of its insignia. On August 14, Bär scored his 56th victory and was subsequently awarded the Oak Leaves for his Knight's Cross. The Swords, and a promotion to captain, would come on February 16, 1942 after Bär's 90th victory. On May 1, Bär was transferred to the Mediterranean Theater, where he was made commander of I Gruppe of JG 77, based in Sicily. Over the course of the next year, Bär flew Bf 109Fs and Bf 109Gs on missions over North Africa and throughout the Mediterranean region, adding 45 victories to his total. However, as the story goes, the stress of combat and the blow of watching the Axis defeated in Africa and Sicily, pushed Bär into a nervous breakdown. Relieved of his command and demoted, Bär was sent back to Germany.

By the spring of 1944, the strategic bombing campaign being waged by the USAAF Eighth Air Force was in full swing, with raids hitting Germany's industrial heartland almost daily. Defense of the Reich now became a principal concern for the Luftwaffe, and pilots were needed to fly intercept missions. Bär was called back to duty to fly Fw 190As with JG 1. He proved that, once again, he had the "right stuff" and on April 22, 1944, he scored his 200th victory, one of 21 USAAF heavy bombers that he would shoot down over Germany.

In June, Bär was promoted again, and given a geschwader, JG 3, to command. On January 1, 1945, Bär led JG 3 in Operation Bodenplatte (Base Plate), the massive Luftwaffe attack on the Western Front that was launched in conjunction with the German Ardennes offensive that resulted in the Battle of the Bulge. It was over Eindhoven in the Netherlands during this operation that Bär scored his last victories in a piston-engine aircraft—a pair of Royal Air Force Hawker Tempests.

★
Hauptmann Heinz "Pritzl" Bär (right) is seen here circa July 1942, possibly at the Jagdgeschwader 77 base at Comiso, Italy. The Messerschmitt Bf 109F-4 on the left has a wreath of oak leaves surrounding the numeral "40," representing 40 aerial victories though Bär had exceeded 100 by this time. *McGoinz photo licensed under Creative Commons*

In January, after the collapse of the Ardennes offensive, Bär was reassigned to Reich defense duties, this time with jet fighters. He became commander of a training geschwader at Lechfeld, designated EJG 2 (Ergaenzungs Jagdgeschwader 2), which was created for the purpose of training pilots to fly the Messerschmitt Me 262 jet. He was taught to fly the new aircraft by Fritz Wendel, the Messerschmitt chief test pilot. In February, while he was flight testing the Me 262, Bär set a speed record of 645 mph and an altitude record of over 48,000 feet.

One gruppe of EJG 2 became operational, and Bär flew his first combat mission in the Me 262 on March 2. He scored his first victory—a USAAF P 51D Mustang—over Ingolstadt on March 13, and quickly increased his score to 13. On April 23, 1945, Bär transferred to Adolf Galland's Jagdverband 44 at Munich, the first operational all-jet geschwader. With this unit, Bär scored his last three victories—three P-47 Thunderbolts. His 220th kill—his 16th in a jet— came on April 28. When General Galland was injured on April 26, Bär became JV 44's last commander, serving until the unit surrendered to American troops on May 3.

Bär was the highest-scoring Me 262 ace of World War II, but Kurt Welter was the highest-scoring jet ace. He was a night fighter (nachtjager) pilot with 60 total victories (50 at night). He scored 29 of his 60 in various jet aircraft, including the Arado Ar-234B 2n (a converted bomber), the Me 262A 1a (such as Bär flew) and the two-seat Me 262B 1a, which was developed specifically to be a night fighter. Welter flew with his own "Kommando Welter" and with Nachtjagdgeschwader 11.

After the war, Pritzl Bär, like Adolf Galland, became an aerospace consultant and, eventually, a private pilot. On April 22, 1957, Bär was performing aerobatics in his light plane to mark the thirteenth anniversary of his 200th aerial victory, when he crashed to his death. The number 13 had always been considered his lucky number. Throughout World War II, he always flew an aircraft marked with "Lucky 13."

★
The Messerschmitt Me 262A jet fighter flown by Heinz Bär when he was with the elite Jagdverband 44 in 1945. Herbert *Ringlstetter illustration licensed under Creative Commons*

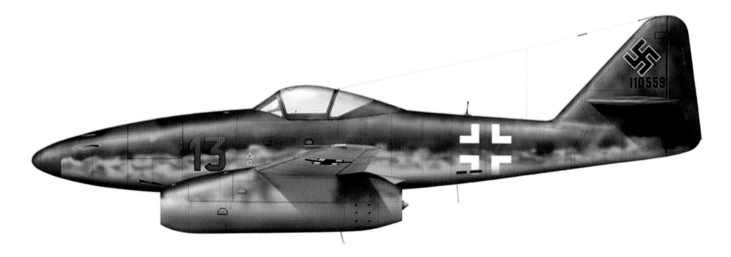

# STEINHOFF: THE MAN WITHOUT A FACE

**JOHANNES "MACKY" STEINHOFF** scored 176 victories during World War II, including six in jets, but he was also highly regarded as a tactician and as a leader. He is best remembered, however, for having overcome the disability of his face being destroyed by fire, to rise to the pinnacle of leadership in the postwar Bundesluftwaffe.

Steinhoff was born on September 15, 1913 in Bottendorf, and he joined the German navy, the Kriegsmarine, in 1934. Two years later, however, he transferred to the Luftwaffe. When World War II began in September 1939, Steinhoff was assigned to JG 26. He scored his first two aerial victories—a pair of Vickers Wellington bombers—on December 18, during the Battle of the German Bight, a daylight offensive against German ports. This offensive was so costly to the Royal Air Force Bomber Command in terms of the number of bombers lost that Bomber Command would switch to flying nighttime raids almost exclusively through the end of the war.

In February 1940, Steinhoff was transferred to JG 52, the jagdgeschwader with which he would serve through the Battle of Britain in August-September. JG 52 was moved to the Eastern Front in June 1941 in advance of the invasion of the Soviet Union on June 22. By August 30, when he was awarded his Knight's Cross, Steinhoff had raised his total score to 35. He was promoted to command II Gruppe of JG 52 in February 1942, and on September 2, the Oak Leaves were attached to his Knight's Cross. By this time, his score stood at 101.

On October 28, 1942, Steinhoff, now with 150 victories, was assigned to the staff of JG 77 in North Africa. In 1943, after the withdrawal of Luftwaffe forces to Italy, Steinhoff was promoted to command JG 77. On July 28, 1944, after having been relocated to France, Steinhoff received the Swords to his Knight's Cross to mark his 167th victory. In December, he was assigned to JG 7, which was starting to receive its first Me 262 jet fighters.

By the end of 1944, Steinhoff had become part of a political intrigue that was directed at trying to force Hermann Göring to use the Luftwaffe more effectively. Isolated behind his desk, Göring was ignoring the tactical recommendations made by flying officers and was running the Luftwaffe in a way that was costing lives unnecessarily. In January 1945, Steinhoff was one of the leading Luftwaffe commanders who demanded that Göring resign. The Luftwaffe chief screamed and threatened, but in the end, it was a virtual stalemate. Göring would not modify his flawed policies, but neither would he carry out his threat to execute those who had "conspired" against him.

General Adolf Galland lost his job as Inspekteur General, but he did get the opportunity to set up the Luftwaffe's all-jet "jagdgeschwader of experts," Jagdverband 44. Johannes Steinhoff was one of the first pilots asked to join, and he scored the first of his six aerial victories in the Messerschmitt Me 262 in February.

On April 18, 1945, Steinhoff was one of six jet pilots taking off to meet USAAF bombers when he hit a crater on the runway and collapsed the aircraft's landing gear. The Messerschmitt bounced down the runway at takeoff speed until the highly volatile jet fuel exploded in a fireball. This, in turn, ignited the air-to-air rockets, turning a fireball into an exploding inferno. Somehow, Steinhoff struggled free of the cockpit and ran from the aircraft.

Steinhoff had suffered severe disfiguring burns on every part of his body that was not covered. His face was effectively burned off. He survived, but years of skin grafts would never come close to repairing the damage.

Nevertheless, Steinhoff's indomitable spirit shown through, and he rebuilt his life in postwar Germany. He joined the government of the new Federal Republic of Germany (West Germany) in 1952, and was part of the organization that created a structure for the German Federal Armed Forces which would eventually be integrated into NATO. The new Bundesluftwaffe was officially created on November 12, 1955, and its first commanding officer, or Inspekteur General, was Josef Kammhuber, who had commanded Luftwaffe night fighter (nachtjager) units during World War II. He took office in June 1956, having been chosen over Adolf Galland, the only other serious candidate.

Among the officer corps of the Bundesluftwaffe were former Luftwaffe aces such as Gerhard Barkhorn, Günther Rall, Erich Hartmann—and Johannes Steinhoff. The new force was afflicted with many problems. Because of restrictions imposed on Germany by the Allies in 1945, Germany had not had an air force, nor even a means of training civilian pilots. Indeed, former Luftwaffe pilots were specifically forbidden to fly. Aviation in Germany had suffered from

the ten year break and had to re-associate itself with international standards. Only a handful of German pilots had experience in jet fighters, but not since 1945. In 1955, a group of select pilots—including Steinhoff—began training on new jets in Britain and in the United States, and operations also started in January 1957 at Landsberg and Furstenfeldbruck.

Steinhoff's career grew with the new Bundesluftwaffe, and in its relationship with NATO. In January 1965, now a general, he was named chief of staff and deputy commander of allied air forces Central Europe. In 1966, he was named as the commander of the force he helped create—or recreate—with the title, Inspekteur der Luftwaffe der Bundeswehr. He took over a force that was plagued by a series of crashes of the Bundesluftwaffe's newest fighter, the American-made Lockheed F-104 Starfighter. The deaths of many pilots had created a serious morale problem within the force, but also a serious scandal in the German government. Steinhoff is remembered for accepting the challenge of dealing with the crisis and reshaping procedures to correct the underlying problems.

In September 1970, he became the chairman of the military committee of NATO, a post that he held until 1974. In 1978, General Steinhoff wrote the manifesto that would help shape NATO strategy regarding tactical nuclear weapons through the end of the Cold War: "I am in favor of retaining nuclear weapons as potential tools, but not permitting them to become battlefield weapons. I am not opposed to the strategic employment of these weapons; however, I am firmly opposed to their tactical use on our soil."

Johannes Steinhoff lived to see the Cold War end and the Berlin Wall come down, but he died in February 1994.

# MARSEILLE: THE BEST FIGHTER PILOT EVER?

**HANS JOACHIM MARSEILLE'S** brilliant and deadly career as a fighter pilot was cut short in an accident that occurred on September 30, 1942, but in the months leading up to that date, he had become almost mythical—in the classical sense of the word. His ability to see the enemy and size up a situation before anyone else were remarkable. He was surrounded by accomplished pilots, many of them high-scoring aces, yet his marksmanship and his flying skills were beyond their comprehension. He was a man with an uncanny ability to score with impossible shots.

Watching him was like watching a magician. What he did was done in plain sight, but it was often impossible to tell just how he did it. He took virtually impossible, high-angle deflection shots and scored with short, split-second bursts of fire. Back on the ground after a mission where he had destroyed four or more enemy aircraft, ground crews were constantly amazed by how little ammunition Marseille had used.

Marseille's accomplishments became legendary throughout the Luftwaffe—and even with his foe, Britain's Royal Air Force (and its constituent Commonwealth air forces). The only aces in history that outscored him were the Luftwaffe aces who fought on the Eastern Front, where the VVS was consistently less well trained and equipped. Marseille scored all of his victories against the Royal Air Force, and he also scored more victories against the Royal Air Force than any other Luftwaffe pilot. Of his 158 victories, 154 were against fighters, rather than slower bombers or transports.

During the last year of his career, Marseille not only scored in almost all of his combat actions, but he scored multiple victories in most of them. He scored multiple victories in every combat action in which he fought during 1942. He scored 17 victories in one day against the Royal Air Force as part of a four-day period in which he claimed 32 British aircraft, including several Spitfires. In the last month of his life, Marseille flew in nine combat actions—one with a jammed cannon—and scored 56 victories. Just his daily average for that month exceeded the score required to become an ace in most other air forces.

At the time that he was killed, only a half dozen aces—all of them Luftwaffe pilots on the Eastern Front—were ahead of him. Erich Hartmann, the number one ace of all time, had not yet scored his first. Nor had any of the great American aces. Throughout the remainder of the war, no ace on any front—other than Luftwaffe pilots flying on the Eastern Front—would exceed his record. Had he lived, he would probably have been the leading ace of World War II.

★

Haptmann Hans Joachim Marseille, known as the "Stern von Afrika" ("Star of Africa"), in a September 1942 press photo. Twenty-two years old and the youngest hauptmann (captain) in the Luftwaffe, he was killed in action on the last day of that month. *Public Domain image from the Bundesarchiv, colorized by Ruffneck'88 and licensed under Creative Commons*

Hans Joachim Marseille was born on December 13, 1919 in the Charlottenburg district of Berlin, the son of Siegfried Marseille, who had been a pilot in World War I. The family was descended from French Huguenots who had emigrated to Germany in the seventeenth century seeking religious freedom, hence the origin of his French-sounding surname.

Marseille would join the infantry in October 1938, but he transferred to the Luftwaffe a month later. In November 1939, he was assigned to fighter pilot school in Vienna, and soon earned a reputation for his aerobatic skill. Marseille received his first operational assignment as a Bf 109 pilot with I Jagdgruppe of Lehrgeschwader 2 at Leeuwarden in the German-occupied Netherlands on August 10, 1940 during the Battle of Britain. He scored his first aerial victory over the English Channel on August 24, and his second in September. In the early days, his marksmanship left him disappointed, however. By December, he had scored seven victories and had been awarded the Iron Cross, but he was himself shot down four times. He knew he could do better.

Later in 1940, Marseille was transferred to JG 52, but he soon got into trouble. Because his flying skills came naturally, and because he seemed to have little regard for military regimentation, he quickly developed a reputation as an undisciplined daredevil. He dressed casually and always seemed to be grinning. His relaxed demeanor helped underscore his reputation for being undisciplined. Even in the air, where he was especially skilled, he lacked self-discipline.

Johannes Steinhoff kicked Marseille out of JG 52 and sent him to JG 27 in February 1941. Steinhoff recalled that he ejected him from JG 52 because of his "often irresponsible understanding of duty." However, Steinhoff added that Marseille had "irresistible charm."

JG 27 was assigned to the campaign in the Balkans on April 6, but Marseille flew primarily ground attack missions and scored no aerial victories. Meanwhile in North Africa, Germany's combat role was growing and more and more units were being assigned to support Field Marshal Erwin Rommel's Deutsche Afrika Korps . Parts of JG 27 were involved in an earlier deployment, but on April 21, after less than two weeks in the Balkans, Marseille's I Gruppe of JG 27 regrouped in Munich and went south to join the North African deployment. They would arrive at Gazala in Libya minus Marseille, who suffered engine trouble, crash-landed his Messerschmitt Bf 109E, and had to hitchhike. The brash young pilot had no qualms about asking to borrow General Hellmann's car and driver. The general, who respected Marseille's initiative, audacity and commitment to duty, agreed.

Despite his troubles, Marseille shot down a Royal Air Force Hawker Hurricane on April 23. It was his first victory in North Africa, but he took 30 hits in his own cockpit, forcing him into a crash landing—his second in three days. It was pointed out to him that he had lost more Luftwaffe aircraft in North Africa than he had shot down.

The typical mission for I Gruppe of JG 27 in North Africa was escorting Luftwaffe attack bombers—mainly Ju 87 Stuka dive bombers—that were flying in support of Deutsche Afrika Korps mechanized and armored ground forces. The Royal Air Force, on the other hand, would send out formations of fighters—usually at least a dozen or more Hawker Hurricanes—to shoot down the attack bombers. These would often be supported by more fighters whose job it was to fight JG 27's Bf 109Es that were there to protect the dive bombers. These actions were usually conducted in concert with ground operations, but often there were fighter sweeps known as frei jagd (free hunting), in which fighters from the opposing sides would hunt one another and attack one another's landing fields. On a typical day, there were a lot of aircraft in the sky.

On June 14, the British launched a major offensive in which Marseille was shot down twice in three days without scoring. Eduard "Edu" Neumann, commander of I Gruppe, recognized Marseille's potential, but he also realized—and he told Marseille—that the young pilot had best learn self-discipline before he ran the Luftwaffe out of aircraft and killed himself in the process. It was Edu Neumann's recognizing his potential and knowing how to compel him to channel that potential, that turned Marseille from being a pretty good fighter pilot into being an extraordinary one. On June 17, Marseille downed a pair of Hurricanes over Halfaya Pass. His score now stood at a relatively modest 18.

Things would change for Hans-Joachim Marseille in September 1941. Maybe it was his pondering the admonitions of Edu Neumann. Maybe it was pondering his own mortality when he got lost flying over a sandstorm. Maybe it was when JG 27 traded in its Bf 109Es for Bf 109Fs. Maybe it was just the practice. Somehow, in September, something just clicked.

On the morning of September 24, Marseille would shoot down four British aircraft, three of them from within a defensive circle that guarantees that any attacker will come under the guns of at least one defender. To shoot down one—much less three—under such circumstances is a major accomplishment. Marseille did it by channeling his aggressiveness and molding it with skill. He attacked fast, maneuvered with gut-wrenching tight turns and aggressive shooting— getting in close to his quarry so that he could not miss. Hans-Joachim Marseille had found himself as a fighter pilot.

Marseille went on to down 12 Royal Air Force aircraft in 14 days, and on November 3, he was awarded the Ehrenpokal, a gold trophy authorized by Luftwaffe chief Hermann Göring. As the story goes, Göring had now asked JG 27 to keep him up to date regularly on Marseille's accomplishments. Marseille spent most of November in Germany making the transition to the new Bf 109F-4, but on his return, he scored four kills in three missions between December 6 and December 10.

As the month wore on, JG 27 found itself in the difficult position of having to cover the Afrika Korps as it retreated from a British offensive. The Luftwaffe could not be beaten in the air, but on the ground, it was a different story—that is, until January 21, when Rommel launched a massive counteroffensive.

★ These two photos
show Hans Joachim
Marseille inspecting
a Hawker Hurricane
Mk. IIB of RAF No. 213
Squadron that he shot
down in North Africa
in September 1942.
*Wikimedia Commons*

As if to prove that his 17 victories on September 1 were not simply an anomaly, Marseille scored five on September 2 and seven on September 3. The legend of the Star of Africa had reached mythic proportions. Yet the story would continue, with four victories on September 5, four victories on September 6, three victories on September 7, two victories on September 11, seven victories on September 15, and seven more on September 26.

During September, Marseille was visited by Adolf Galland, and was invited to dine with Field Marshal Rommel. The Field Marshal, who was something of a folk hero himself, had been invited to make an appearance with Hitler and Göring at a big rally at the Sportspalast in Berlin on September 30. He asked Marseille to accompany him, but the Star of Africa declined. Marseille wanted to have a Christmas leave so that he could marry Hanneliese, and he was afraid that if he left again in September—after his July-August leave—his request for time off in December would be declined. Rommel was amused and delighted by the man who would rather spend Christmas with his girlfriend than be on the dais with Hitler at a rally.

On September 30, Marseille and other elements from JG 27 took off on a routine patrol. For the first time, Marseille was flying the new Bf 109G into combat. The new aircraft had just arrived and soon JG 27 would make the full transition. The patrol did not make contact with the enemy and was returning home, when Marseille reported an engine fire. With his schwarm five minutes from German lines, he had smoke in the cockpit.

Gasping and choking, Marseille nursed the Bf 109G back to friendly territory. Once there, Marseille announced that he had to get out. He rolled the aircraft over, popped the canopy and, as his comrades watched, he leaped into the slipstream. They watched him bounce slightly and then plummet away from the stricken Messerschmitt. They circled, waiting for his parachute to open. As they waited, it was obvious that something was wrong.

The Star of Africa fell to his death four miles south of Sidi el Aman at 11:26 on the morning of September 30, 1942.

The first on the scene was a doctor attached to a Deutsche Afrika Korps panzer regiment, but members of the JG 27 staff arrived soon after. It was soon determined that he had struck his hip on the rudder of the Bf 109G. The fall had crushed his skull. The evidence indicated that the shock of the initial blow must have incapacitated the young pilot, as the parachute ripcord was untouched.

Hans-Joachim Marseille's father, General Siegfried Marseille, was killed on the Eastern Front in 1943.

A monument was erected by Italian engineers on the site where Hans-Joachim Marseille fell, and he was interred with full military honors at Derna. His body was later moved to a memorial at Tobruk. A pyramid in his honor was dedicated in October 1989 at the German military cemetery at El Alamein in Egypt.

The dramatic film by Alfred Weidenmann, *Der Stern von Afrika*, was released in Germany in 1957. Starring Joachim Hansen (as Marseille) and Marianne Koch, it was popular at the box office.

# THE BRITISH COMMONWEALTH

**B**RITAIN'S ROYAL AIR Force became an instrument of national survival in World War II. It is the only air force that is officially credited with saving its nation from defeat in World War II. Technically, the Royal Air Force was the oldest independent air force among any of the major combatants, having been formed in 1917 from old Royal Flying Corps. The air forces of Germany and the Soviet Union were not formed until well after World War I, and the air forces of Japan and the United States remained subsidiaries of their armies and navies through World War II. Within the Royal Air Force were Bomber Command, Coastal Command and Fighter Command. The latter would be home to the aces of the British Commonwealth.

In World War I and World War II, the Royal Air Force was also the only air force that was the official "parent" air force to the air forces of several other nations. These included the Royal Canadian Air Force (RCAF), the South African Air Force (SAAF), the Royal Australian Air Force (RAAF) and the Royal New Zealand Air Force (RNZAF), whose aces are discussed in this section along with those of the Royal Air Force itself.

During both World War I and World War II, because of the sovereignty exercised by Britain over the nations of the British Commonwealth of Nations (formerly the British Empire), the air forces of these nations contributed pilots, aircrews and aircraft to support Royal Air Force operations—even though during the first two years of World War II, Britain was the only major Commonwealth nation whose actual territory was located within the war zone.

Operationally, during the 1939–1941 period, all of the Commonwealth air forces and pilots that were in combat, fought within the Royal Air Force command structure in Western Europe and the Mediterranean, with a large number of SAAF units in the Mediterranean and North Africa. After the war with Japan began at the end of 1941, many RAAF and RNZAF units and pilots returned to the Southwest Pacific Theater.

Britain is indeed indebted to its Commonwealth for supplying some of the top Royal Air Force aces. In World War I, only two of the top seven were English, and in World War II, the ratio was three in seven.

When the war began, the Royal Air Force was—after the air forces of Germany and Poland—the third to be mobilized. On September 1, 1939, the German Wehrmacht (armed forces) launched a full scale attack on Poland. At this point, Britain and France issued ultimatums because their mutual assistance treaties with Poland called for them to finally take action to halt Hitler's aggression. On September 3, Britain and France declared that a state of war had existed for two days.

For the Royal Air Force, the first combat came in November when a New Zealander flying with the Royal Air Force, E.J. "Kobber" Kain, shot down a pair of Dornier Do 17 bombers. He would claim three Messerschmitt Bf 109s during March 1940 to become the Royal Air Force's first ace of the war, but he was killed in an accident shortly thereafter.

Suddenly, on April 9, 1940, German troops quickly occupied Denmark and Norway. On May 10, the Germans began a great offensive to the west that duplicated their advance on Belgium and France in 1914 at the beginning of World War I.

★ (Previous)
The two most important British fighter aircraft of World War II, and those flown by the majority of Royal Air Force aces, were the Supermarine Spitfire and the Hawker Hurricane. Seen here are a restored Spitfire Mk. II (top) and a restored Hurricane Mk. I (bottom), photographed at the Royal International Air Tattoo at RAF Fairford in 2010. They entered service in 1938 and 1937 respectively and served throughout the war on battlefronts worldwide. More than 20,000 of the former were built, and there were nearly 15,000 of the latter. *Ronnie Macdonald photo licensed under Creative Commons*

In the air, combat was the most intense that had yet been seen in war, rivaling anything during World War I, especially in terms of the speed and armament of the aircraft. Of the air forces engaged, the Luftwaffe outscored the Royal Air Force, but the British managed to outscore the French Armée de l'Air.

After Kain, his mate from No. 73 Squadron was the only ace prior to May 10, but within nine days, two men in No. 85 Squadron—Geoffrey "Sammy" Allard and a South African, Albert Lewis—were aces twice over.

By May 28, Luxembourg, Belgium and the Netherlands had surrendered and German forces were pouring into France. On June 14, Germany had seized control of Paris, having accomplished in five weeks what it had been unable to do in four years of protracted fighting in World War I. France finally surrendered on June 22, leaving Britain to face the onslaught of Germany's blitzkrieg alone. Only 20 miles of English Channel separated Germany's crack troops from an army that had abandoned all of its equipment in France when it barely managed to escape from the Germans at Dunkirk on the French coast at the end of May.

While Hitler's forces prepared for a cross channel invasion of Britain, the English people rallied around Prime Minister Winston Churchill, who had taken office on May 10 telling them he had "nothing to offer but blood, toil, tears and sweat." He defied Hitler by informing him that his troops would meet relentless opposition on the beaches, on the streets and in every village. However, Luftwaffe commander Field Marshall Hermann Göring insisted that his bombers could easily subdue Britain, making the planned sea invasion a simple walk over.

Churchill braced the British people for the worst. On June 18, he told them: "The Battle of France is over. I expect that the Battle of Britain is about to begin.

Upon this battle depends the survival of Christian civilization. Upon it depends our British life, and the long continuity of our institutions and our Empire. The whole fury and might of the enemy must very soon be turned on us. Hitler knows that he will have to break us in this island or lose the war. Let us therefore brace ourselves to our duties, and so bear ourselves that, if the British Empire and its Commonwealth last for a thousand years, men will still say, 'This was their finest hour.'"

In August 1940, the Luftwaffe began a brutal, unremitting bombing assault on Britain's ports, factories and cities. The only thing that stood in the way of an easy victory was the courageous, but vastly outnumbered, pilots of the Royal Air Force, specifically of Fighter Command, who met the Germans like gnats attacking crows. Despite the fact that the British had fewer than 1,000 fighters to face a Luftwaffe onslaught four times as large, the Royal Air Force was able to destroy 12 bombers for each one of their own losses. Churchill called it the Royal Air Force's "finest hour."

Of the Royal Air Force Fighter Command pilots who met and turned back a vastly superior German Luftwaffe, Churchill said "Never, in the field of human conflict, have so many, owed so much, to so few."

Among the early heroes of the Battle of Britain were men like Sammy Allard and Albert Lewis, as well as Alan Christopher Deere of No. 54 Squadron and Robert Stanford Tuck of No. 92 Squadron. James Henry "Ginger" Lacey of No. 501 Squadron became a national hero on August 15, when he shot down the Heinkel He 111 that had bombed Buckingham Palace.

Many of "the few" were also shot down, but most of the time they managed to bail out, and since they were over friendly territory, they were back in action within days, if not hours. Frequently, because the Royal Air Force pilots were shot down multiple times. By August, Al Deere had been downed seven times—and each time he lived to tell the tale and to fly and fight again.

Although the Battle of Britain would technically drag on until the end of the year, the real turning point occurred on September 17 when Hitler made the decision to postpone the sea assault indefinitely. The highest-scoring Royal Air Force ace of the August-December Battle of Britain period was Eric Lock of No. 41 Squadron. He got his first two kills on August 15, the same day that Ginger Lacey downed the bomber that had bombed Buckingham Palace. By October 20, his score stood at 19.5 and he downed a pair of Messerschmitt Bf 109s, the same day that he was shot down and badly wounded. He would return to combat in June 1941 with No. 611 Squadron and would end the war with 26 victories, making him the 13th highest-scoring Royal Air Force ace and the seventh highest-scoring English ace of World War II.

At the end of the pivotal year of 1940, the two Royal Air Force aces with the highest cumulative scores were Sammy Allard and Ginger Lacey, tied with 23, compared to the 21.5 that Eric Lock had at the time. Allard and Lacey would end the war with 25 and 28, respectively.

The Battle of Britain was the first major battle in history to be decided solely by airpower, and it brought Hitler's remarkable string of successes to a halt. The Royal Air Force's turnback of Germany's Luftwaffe would later prove to be the point at which the tide of the war began to slowly turn in favor of the Allies.

The Battle of Britain was a major setback in Germany's effort toward world domination, but it had not stopped Hitler's armies. Britain remained alone and isolated while the rest of the countries in continental Europe either allied themselves with Germany, became occupied territories or waited in anticipation of a German attack.

The top scoring ace in the Royal Air Force was the South African, Marmaduke Thomas St. John Pattle, who may have scored at least 51 victories. He was followed by Englishman James Edgar "Johnny" Johnson with 38. George Frederick Beurling was the highest-scoring Canadian ace, scoring most of his 31.5 victories with the Royal Air Force before being reassigned to the RCAF.

In the pantheon of Commonwealth aces, there were several in the range of 28 to 29 victories. These were the Englishmen J.R.D. Braham, F.R. Carey, Neville Frederick Duke, Ginger Lacey and Robert Stanford Tuck, as well as the highest-scoring Australian, Clive Robertson Caldwell. The highest-scoring New Zealander was Colin Falkland Gray, who had a score of 27.5 when he was killed in May 1940. The fact that he died before the Battle of Britain leaves room to speculate what he might have contributed if he had lived.

★
A Hawker Hurricane Mk. I of No. 18 Squadron landing at Castle Camps, RAF Debden's satellite airfield, in July 1940. It is here flown by Pilot Officer Albert Gerald Lewis, a South African fighter pilot who scored five victories in a single day during the Battle of Britain. This aircraft was lost in action in August 1940, but Lewis went on to become an ace with 18 aerial victories. *UK Government photo in the public domain*

# DEERE: A HERO OF THE BATTLE OF BRITAIN

★
Wing Commander Alan Christopher "Al" Deere became an ace during the Battle of Britain while flying with No. 54 Squadron of the RAF. He is seen here in July 1944 in a photograph taken at the Air Ministry Studios in London.
*UK Government photo in the public domain*

**ONE OF THE BEST REMEMBERED** of "the few" is Alan Christopher Deere, who scored 22 confirmed victories, plus 10 probables and 18 damaged—most of them during the Battle of Britain. He was born in Auckland, New Zealand on December 12, 1917, but later moved to Britain. Deere joined the Royal Air Force in October 1937 and was assigned as a fighter pilot to No. 54 Squadron in September 1938. World War II began a year later, but the unit would see no action until May 1940.

Alan Deere scored his first aerial victory on May 23 while flying air cover for a rescue mission in northern France. In a precursor to the sorts of rescue missions that were common with helicopters a quarter century later in Vietnam, an attempt was being made to rescue a pilot downed behind enemy lines by using a trainer with short take-off and landing capabilities. Deere and another pilot were flying above in Spitfires to provide air cover.

A flight of German Bf 109s arrived on the scene just as the trainer was taking off. Deere bounced one of the Messerschmitts as it made a low-level pass and blew it away. Deere managed to damage more Bf 109s, as the other Spitfire shot down a pair. The rescue flight managed to get off and to reach the British coast without further incident.

Also on May 23, and very near to where Alan Deere was working, one of the largest rescue operations in history was underway. The evacuation of the 300,000-man British Expeditionary Force from defeated France could have turned into disaster for Britain had the Germans used mechanized forces instead of the Luftwaffe to attack the troops waiting on the beach at Dunkirk. Overhead, Royal Air Force Squadrons flew top cover for the operation, battling the Luftwaffe for control of the Dunkirk skies. During this operation, code-named Dynamo, Al Deere hit his stride, claiming three Bf 109s and three Bf 110s between May 23 and May 29 to become an ace.

Early in June, King George VI himself came to Hornchurch to award Distinguished Flying Crosses to several Royal Air Force aces, including Al Deere and Robert Stanford Tuck. It had been a huge morale triumph for Britain, but the Dunkirk operation was just a muted introduction to what the Royal Air Force would face in the coming months during the Battle of Britain.

For Deere, the weeks were filled with constant combat, day in and day out, as the Luftwaffe threw their numerical superiority at the embattled "few." During the Battle of Britain Deere reduced the size of the Luftwaffe by seven fighters and a bomber, for which he would have a Bar added to his Distinguished Flying Cross, the equivalent of a second Distinguished Flying Cross.

In January 1941, the Royal Air Force put Deere's expertise to work in the Fighter Command operations room as a controller. Eager to get back into the air, Deere finally was reassigned to an operational unit. He was posted to No. 602 Squadron in Scotland on May 7 as a flight commander, and he became squadron commander on August 1. In the meanwhile, three days

after he joined the unit, he was sent out to investigate a Messerschmitt Bf 110 that had penetrated Scottish air space. The aircraft crashed before Deere's flight could intercept it. Assumed at the time to have been a routine reconnaissance flight, the aircraft was actually piloted by Germany's Deputy Führer Rudolf Hess, who was on a clandestine mission to make contact with pro-German factions within Britain.

On the day that he took command of No. 602 Squadron, Deere downed a Bf 109. It was his first victory since September 1940. The days of intense combat were over for Alan Deere. In January 1942, shortly after the United States entered World War II, he was sent across the Atlantic to brief American pilots on operational issues. Between May and August 1942, he would command No. 403 Squadron, but this was his last operational tour, except for brief temporary duty with No. 611 Squadron in February 1943. During this month he saw action again and shot down a Focke-Wulf Fw 190. In March, he was assigned as wing leader of the legendary Biggin Hill Wing.

Alan Deere ended the war with 22 confirmed victories, 10 probables and 18 enemy aircraft damaged. His autobiography of his wartime experiences, Nine Lives, was published in 1959. In addition to his British Distinguished Flying Cross with Bar, Deere earned the American Distinguished Flying Cross, the French Croix de Guerre and a British Distinguished Service Order. When the war in Europe ended in May 1945, he was awarded an Order of the British Empire. Unlike many wartime aces, he remained in the Royal Air Force until 1977, retiring as Air Commodore Alan Deere.

★ [Above]
King George VI congratulates Flight Lieutenant Al Deere while decorating him with the Distinguished Flying Cross at Hornchurch in Essex. To the King's left is Air Chief Marshal Sir Hugh Dowding, commander-in-chief of RAF Fighter Command. *UK Government photo in the public domain*

★ [Below]
Wing Commander Alan Deere with Squadron Leader Denis Crowley-Milling at the time of the Battle of Britain in 1940. Crowley-Milling shot down four enemy aircraft during World War II but never achieved ace status. *UK Government photo in the public domain*

# PATTLE: THE TOP ACE
# IN THE ROYAL AIR FORCE

**THE ROYAL AIR FORCE'S** leading ace of World War II was the South African pilot, Marmaduke Thomas St. John Pattle, best known by his nickname, "Pat." His final score is usually listed as "at least 40," because the actual tally is unknown, and may exceed 51. He is probably unique among World War II aces to have scored his first ten victories in a biplane.

Pat Pattle was born in South Africa to English parents and joined the Royal Air Force in 1936. Posted in Egypt in 1938, Pattle was among the pilots of No. 80 Squadron who did battle with the Italians in Libya and Ethiopia during the early months of World War II. Unlike many of the other early Royal Air Force aces, Pattle would earn his victories in the Mediterranean region rather than in the skies over Britain and France.

No. 80 Squadron was not exactly equipped for modern combat, as they were flying the aging Gloster Gladiator biplanes at a time when "the few" in Britain were flying Hurricanes and Spitfires. Nevertheless, Pat Pattle managed to score his first four victories in rather short order. He was shot down himself in August, 1940 but was soon back in action.

Italy had invaded Albania in 1939, five months before World War II began, and in November 1940, Benito Mussolini's armies used their foothold in the diminutive former kingdom as a springboard for an invasion of Greece. Mussolini's plan had been to score a fast victory and to incorporate Greece into his idea of a "New Roman Empire" in the Mediterranean region. When this invasion occurred, Pattle's unit was among those air and ground forces being sent by Britain to Greece to help in a counterattack. The Italian invasion force became bogged down, and the Royal Air Force managed to exact a terrific toll on the Regia Aeronautica. By the end of the year, Pattle was an ace twice over and had been awarded the Distinguished Flying Cross.

It was not until February that No. 80 Squadron finally received its first Hawker Hurricanes. On February 28, finally flying the Hurricane, Pattle downed a pair each of Fiat BR-20 bombers and CR.42 fighters in a single day. His innate skill as a fighter pilot was clearly manifesting itself. Five days later, he added three G.50 fighters to his score during one sortie.

In March 1941, Pat Pattle was promoted to squadron leader and placed in command of No. 33 Squadron, which had just been sent to Greece from North Africa, where it had seen action against the Italians in Egypt and Libya. Pattle had brought his score to 25.66 by the time that he first tangled with the Luftwaffe.

By April, the stalemated and embarrassed Mussolini was compelled to ask Hitler for help. On April 6, Germany attacked Greece within the greater context of their spring 1941 drive into the Balkans. As air cover for the invasion, the Luftwaffe sent in the fighters of JG 52. Pat Pattle and No. 33 Squadron met them on the first day, and Pattle shot down two Messerschmitt Bf 109Es.

It was here that the story of the Royal Air Force's highest-scoring ace fades from documented fact to the stuff of legend and folklore. This is because all of the records of No. 33 Squadron from this day forward were lost. Based on anecdotal evidence and the accounts of men who were there, Pattle had an extraordinary run of successes, matching his Hurricane against the Messerschmitts of JG 52. Evidence generally confirms that he scored five kills on April 14 alone, and six on April 19 to bring his score to no less than 38.

The successes that Pattle had against the Luftwaffe are even more remarkable in light of the overall tactical situation. The Greek Army, which had held the Italians at bay, were no match for the battle-hardened Germans. The Greeks—and the British ground troops that had come to their aid—were never able to put up more than token resistance. The Luftwaffe, meanwhile, took a terrible toll on retreating troops. The Royal Air Force units did the best they could, but they were outnumbered ten to one. On April 19, when Pattle scored his six-in-one-day, the Germans had Athens surrounded and were closing in for the kill.

The following morning, Pattle awoke sick with fever. In a normal situation, a flight surgeon should have grounded him, but this was a desperate day in a desperate campaign. A Luftwaffe bomber attack was incoming. He had to go up.

The ailing squadron leader led the lads of No. 33 Squadron against the attack. He was observed as having killed two Messerschmitt Bf 110 Zerstorers, and he had scored a probable against a Bf 109, when another Hurricane pilot got in trouble. As he went to the aid of this pilot, Pattle was jumped by a cluster of Bf 110s who tore his Hurricane to shreds. Pat Pattle spiraled down into Eleusis Bay.

Three days later, the Greek government capitulated and the British troops scrambled to escape. As they did, any hope of nailing down an exact final score for the Royal Air Force's top-scoring ace was lost. The evidence combines to suggest a minimum of 51, with "at least 40" that are considered certain.

★ (Above) Squadron Leader Marmaduke Thomas St John "Pat" Pattle (left), commander of No. 33 Squadron RAF, with the Squadron Adjutant, Flight Lieutenant George Rumsey, standing by a Hawker Hurricane at Larissa, Thessaly, Greece in March 1941. *UK Government photo in the public domain*

★ (Below) The Hawker Hurricane Mk. I was a mainstay of Royal Air Force fighter squadrons in the early days of World War II. The Hurricane was flown by Pat Pattle and the men of No. 33 Squadron. *Author's Collection*

# JOHNSON: THE TOP-SCORING ENGLISHMAN

**JAMES EDGAR "JOHNNY" JOHNSON** is remembered as not only the highest-scoring Englishman in the Royal Air Force, but also as having survived the war with his aircraft being hit only once—by a single shell—in all his aerial combat career. Furthermore, he made it a practice to engage only the toughest of foes—high-performance air superiority fighters—rather than lumbering bombers and attack aircraft.

Johnson had joined the Royal Air Force Reserve prior to the war, and his unit, No. 616 Squadron, was one of those called up in August 1939 when war seemed inevitable. However, he was hospitalized through much of the Battle of Britain and did not score his fifth victory to achieve ace status until early in 1942.

His leadership skills led Johnson to a series of promotions and he became commander of No. 610 Squadron in time to lead it as part of the air cover for the ill-fated Dieppe raid on northern France in August 1942. During this fight, he scored two assists.

Typically, men in higher command are more insulated from combat than pilots of lesser rank, but Johnny Johnson's success as fighter pilot really began to take off early in 1943, when he was promoted to head the Kenley Wing. Composed primarily of RCAF units, the Kenley Wing was equipped with the relatively new Spitfire Mk. IX.

Wing Commander
Johnnie Johnson
with his pet Labrador
dog, Sally, at
Bazenville Landing
Field in Normandy
on July 31, 1944.
At this time, he
commanded No. 127
Wing, comprised
of three Canadian
Spitfire squadrons,
and had scored 35
of his eventual 38
aerial victories.
*UK Government*

First introduced in July 1942, this aircraft was essentially a Spitfire Mk. V upgraded with the powerful new Model 60 series Merlin engine that was turbo-supercharged for high altitude interception duty. It was developed as an interim fighter to replace the earlier marks until the Spitfire Mk. VIII—with strengthened fuselage as well as a more powerful engine—was available. The Spitfire Mk. IX equipped many Fighter Command units based in Britain through the winter of 1942–1943, and was produced in much larger numbers than originally anticipated. When it finally entered squadron service in June 1943, the Spitfire Mk. VIII was used primarily overseas.

Between April and September, Wing Commander Johnson claimed 18 victories, all of them save one against the top German air superiority fighters such as the Focke Wolf Fw 190 and later model Messerschmitt Bf 109s. The one exception was a Bf 110, Johnson's only multi-engine victory.

Johnson was a careful and meticulous fighter pilot. As he said later, "In a dogfight when the odds are heavily on your side, there is a great temptation to lower your guard, to get in close, and hammer your enemy until he falls. Too many pilots concentrate on one target and forget to keep a sharp lookout for friend or foe; too many airplanes converge, in a dangerous funnel-like movement, on the single quarry and the risk of mid air collision is high."

By the autumn of 1943, Johnson's score stood at 25, enough to put him in the upper echelon of Allied aces, and he was reassigned to a staff job with No. 83 Group of the 2nd Tactical Air Force. By late spring 1944, however, he managed to get himself back into a flying command, this time with another Canadian unit, No. 144 Wing. He scored three kills on the eve of the June 6 Normandy Invasion, and another 10 over Europe during the Allied sweep across northern France.

In early 1945, Johnson was promoted to group captain, and given his last assignment of the war, as commander of No. 125 Wing. By that time, it was equipping with the Spitfire Mk. XIV, which was powered by the supercharged Model 61 Rolls Royce Griffon engine with its distinctive, five-bladed Rotol propeller.

Johnny Johnson's final score officially stood at 38, making him the Royal Air Force's second highest-scoring ace. After World War II, he would have a long career in the Royal Air Force, retiring as Air Vice Marshal James Edgar Johnson, but still "Johnny" to those with whom he had shared comradeship when they were "the few."

★ (Left)
Johnnie Johnson smiles from the cockpit of his Spitfire. Though he missed the Battle of Britain because of an injury, he participated in all the major subsequent campaigns from Normandy to Operation Market Garden, from the Battle of the Bulge to the offensive into Germany. Among other decorations, he received the Distinguished Service Order with two Bars and a Distinguished Flying Cross with one. *UK Government photo in the public domain*

★ (Lower)
A restored Spitfire FR.XIV in markings which replicate those of the Spitfire flown by Johnnie Johnson. *Alan Wilson photo licensed under Creative Commons*

★
Adolph Gysbert "Sailor" Malan was a South African fighter pilot and ace who flew with the Royal Air Force throughout the war. He commanded RAF No. 74 Squadron in 1940 and 1941, and later No. 19 Wing, No. 20 Wing and No. 145 (Free French) Wing. At the time of this official portrait, he led No. 20 Wing. *UK Government photo in the public domain*

# MALAN: THE SAILOR WAS AN AIRMAN

**THE ROYAL AIR FORCE'S NUMBER THREE ACE**, like its number one, was a South African. Born in 1910, Adolph Gysbert Malan left home to join the British Merchant Marine and spent his formative years on the high seas. In 1935, having arrived in Britain, he joined the Royal Air Force, where his previous career earned him the enduring nickname, "Sailor." During World War II, it was easily a more popular name than "Adolph."

Whatever his aptitude for sea life, Sailor Malan's skill as a pilot was considerable, and by the time that the war began, he was already commanding a flight within No. 74 Squadron at Hornchurch. He first saw action in late May 1940, leading his Spitfire-equipped squadron into battle over the Dunkirk evacuation beaches during Operation Dynamo. For his part in the operation, he earned a Distinguished Flying Cross. In less than a week, his score stood at three victories, two shared kills and a pair of probable.

He would earn a Bar to his Distinguished Flying Cross on the night of June 19, when he downed a pair of Heinkel He 111 bombers over southern England. This was only a prelude to what would come two months later when Hermann Göring launched the air offensive that became the Battle of Britain. By that time, Sailor Malan had been promoted to command No. 74 Squadron. In the life or death battle for the future of Britain, Malan would find himself and his No. 74 Squadron very much in the thick of the fight. By mid-August, his score stood at 10.

During a rest and recuperation leave, Malan wrote his famous Ten Rules for Air Fighting, which would fast become required reading for a generation of combat pilots.

In September 1940, No. 74 Squadron moved from Hornchurch to Biggin Hill, where it was assigned high altitude interceptor duties, and Malan resumed his command. At the beginning of 1941, he was placed in charge of the entire Biggin Hill Wing, with the newly created rank of "wing commander." By this time, his own score stood at 14 solo kills, plus four shared victories.

During the summer of 1941, he had an exceptional run of victories, raising his official score to 27 destroyed (though some sources give him as many as 34), plus seven shared and five unconfirmed or probable. Withdrawn from action and sent to the United States on a liaison mission that also included fellow ace Robert Stanford Tuck, he would not see combat again.

When Sailor Malan returned from America, he rose steadily through the ranks, eventually becoming Group Captain Malan. In 1944, he was placed in command of the Royal Air Force Advanced Gunnery School at Catfoss.

Malan would remain in the Royal Air Force until 1946, when he retired to return home to South Africa. After having become a successful businessman, he became an energetic voice in opposition to apartheid. He would remain active until he became debilitated by Parkinson's Disease. He died in 1963, at the relatively young age of 53.

★ (Above)
The Supermarine Spitfire Mk.XII, an example of which is seen here banking away from the camera, was the first Spitfire powered by a Rolls-Royce Griffon engine. The Mk.XII began entering service October 1942. *Author's Collection*

★ (Opposite, top)
Group Captain Sailor Malan (second from left), Commanding Officer of No. 145 (Free French) Wing discusses the operational situation over the Normandy invasion beaches on the morning of June 6, 1944 with some of his pilots at Merston, Sussex. On the left is Free French pilot, Lieutenant Raoul Duval; second from the right is Wing Commander William Crawford-Compton; and third right is Commandant C. Martell, Commanding Officer of No. 341 (Free French) Squadron RAF. Crawford-Compton, a New Zealander, was an ace with 21.5 aerial victories. *UK Government photo in the public domain*

★

Squadron Leader
Robert Stanford "Bob"
Tuck, commander of
No. 257 Squadron,
in the cockpit of his
Hawker Hurricane at
Martelsham Heath in
November 1940. His
aircraft carries the
"kill marks" of the first
23 of his eventual
30 aerial victories.
*UK Government photo
in the public domain*

# TUCK:
## THE CAGED EAGLE

**ROBERT ROLAND STANFORD "BOB" TUCK** is listed in various sources as having either 29 or 30 aerial victories, placing him in a near tie with William "Cherry" Vale, often credited with 30 victories, as the second highest-scoring Englishman in the Royal Air Force.

Bob Tuck was born on July 1, 1916 at Catford in Greater London and, like "Sailor" Malan, he left school in his teens to join the British Merchant Marine. Also like Malan, Tuck left his life at sea in 1935 to join the Royal Air Force for a life in the clouds. He was mustered in at Uxbridge and took his pilot training at Grantham in an Avro Tutor biplane in October. When he graduated in 1936, he was assigned to No. 65 Squadron at Hornchurch. He would spend the next two years perfecting his skills with the Gloster Gladiator biplane. In January 1938, he was involved in a midair collision with two other aircraft, in which another pilot was killed and Tuck was injured. His biographers have credited the incident as a turning point in his career that curbed an impulsive streak and helped mold him as a combat pilot.

At the end of 1938, Tuck was among those pilots that were picked to transition into the new Supermarine Spitfire at Duxford.

When the war began in September, there was an urgency within the Royal Air Force to form new Spitfire squadrons, and in May 1940, Tuck was transferred to become deputy squadron leader for No. 92 Squadron, based first at Croydon and later at Hornchurch along with No. 54 Squadron, No. 65 Squadron and No. 74 Squadron. These squadrons were tasked to fly air cover for Operation Dynamo, the evacuation of the British Expeditionary Force from Dunkirk on May 23.

During the course of the morning, Tuck's formation was bounced by Messerschmitt Bf 109Es. As the formation broke, Tuck chose one enemy fighter and promptly shot it down. After a quick refueling stop at Hornchurch, the Spitfires were back over Dunkirk. This time, it was No. 92 Squadron's turn to do the bouncing, and the target was a flight of Messerschmitt Bf 110C Zerstorers. Tuck claimed one and pursued a second into a low altitude gun duel in which the Zerstorer was forced into a crash landing. As the story goes, Tuck circled the downed flyer and waved. The German shot at him with a pistol, and with uncanny accuracy, almost hit the circling Englishman. Enraged, Tuck finished off the "unsporting" German with his machine guns.

Robert Stanford Tuck had scored three victories on his first day in action and No. 92 Squadron had claimed 20 against a loss of only five. One of these, however, was the squadron commander. Tuck, second in command—and top scorer in the squadron—got a battlefield promotion to squadron leader.

On May 24, Tuck led No. 92 Squadron back into action over Dunkirk. This time, they spotted a formation of about 20 Dornier Do 17 bombers. Tuck picked one off from the edge of the group

and then plunged in for a second kill. In less than two days, Robert Sanford Tuck had gone from being a pilot with no combat experience to an ace and squadron leader.

On June 28, 1940, King George VI himself came down to Hornchurch to award decorations to the Royal Air Force heroes—including such men as Robert Tuck and Alan Deere—of Operation Dynamo. For Tuck, it was to be the Distinguished Flying Cross for his "initiative" and "personal example."

The beginning days of the Battle of Britain found No. 92 Squadron assigned to the Royal Air Force Fighter Command's 11th Group in southeast England where it was heavily engaged in stemming the tide of German bombers that were sweeping across the English Channel daily. During two days in mid-August, Tuck shot down three Ju 88 bombers, and on August 18 he took off in the midst of a raid on the Royal Air Force base at Northolt. He gave chase, shooting down one Ju 88, and getting shot down himself by another.

A week later, Tuck was shot down again. On August 25, he was over the Channel, leading his last patrol as commander of No. 92 Squadron, when he attacked a Dornier Do 215 bomber that was trying to sink a British ship. The Dornier's gunner managed to shoot up his engine, forcing him into a long, powerless glide that fortunately brought him across the English shoreline.

On September 11, 1940, Bob Tuck became squadron leader at No. 257 Squadron, a Hawker Hurricane Mk. I unit based at Martlesham. While he did not like the Hurricane at first, Tuck eventually took to it, finding it to be a "good gun platform" for the work of killing bombers, which was, after all, the primary business of the Royal Air Force in the autumn of 1940.

★
Squadron Leader Bob Tuck (center) with pilots of No. 257 Squadron RAF under the nose of Tuck's Hawker Hurricane at Martlesham Heath. They are displaying souvenirs of their action against Italian aircraft on November 11, 1940. *UK Government photo in the public domain*

★

The "Burma" on the side of Bob Tuck's Hurricane is a reference to No. 257 Squadron as the "Burma Gift Squadron." It was paid for by the Burmese people and adopted the slogan "Thay Myay Gyee Shin Shwe Hti," meaning "Death or Glory." Tuck and his aircraft are seen here at Coltishall in Norfolk. *UK Government photo in the public domain*

Tuck had gotten the reassignment because Fighter Command had decided that No. 257 Squadron was a "problem" unit that was incapable of combat. He introduced a series of drills and mock dogfights in an effort to sharpen the skills of the pilots, and within a few days, he was able to report his new squadron ready to face the enemy. This was music to the ears of the powers that be at Fighter Command Headquarters, because the Battle of Britain was taking its toll. Every plane and every pilot were necessary to defeat the Luftwaffe onslaught.

On the afternoon of September 15, Bob Tuck led No. 257 Squadron, along with No. 17 Squadron and No. 73 Squadron, to intercept a huge formation of German bombers—plus escorting fighters—who were flying against London. Word of the impending attack came too late for the interceptors to get an altitude advantage on the attackers before they reached London, so they were forced to climb into the strike force from below. Nevertheless, the interceptors managed to disrupt the attack, and Tuck scored one confirmed kill of a Bf 110 and claimed a Bf 109 as damaged.

By now, Robert Stanford Tuck had become the kind of fearless, yet effective, young fighter pilot that the British media loved. He was often written up in the London newspapers. In October, when he shrugged off the honor of an added Bar to his Distinguished Flying Cross by saying simply that he had been "bloody lucky," the public loved it. On January 28, 1941, he was awarded his Distinguished Service Order for his work in turning the "problem" No. 257 Squadron into a well-oiled fighting machine.

Early in 1941, No. 257 Squadron began converting to the Hurricane Mk. IIC, with its 20mm cannons in place of .303 caliber machine guns. Tuck was a firm proponent of this extra firepower, which proved useful in March, when No. 257 Squadron was tasked with intercepting German night bombers.

By June, No. 257 Squadron was flying missions over the English Channel and the northern edges of the continent, repaying the aggressive Germans with a bit of aggressiveness of their own. On June 21, Tuck was on a solo flight over the Channel when he was jumped by three Bf 109s. He quickly claimed one of them and outmaneuvered a second enemy pilot at a wave-top level before finally nailing him as well. He got into a shoot-out with the third that left both aircraft badly damaged. Finally, both opponents turned away. Tuck attempted to nurse his Hurricane home, but the aircraft gave out and Tuck was forced to abandon it over the water. Badly injured in both shoot-out and bail-out, he would eventually be picked up, but he spent nearly a month recovering.

When Bob Tuck returned to duty, it was as a wing commander at the Duxford Wing, where he now had three squadrons to oversee.

One was a Spitfire unit, No. 12 Squadron, flying the Spitfire Mk. V, and it was with this unit that Tuck himself chose to fly. The other units were No. 56 Squadron, equipped with the new Hawker Typhoon Mk. IA, and No. 601 Squadron with its American-made P 39 Airacobras. This mix of aircraft was a problem operationally, because each type had a different performance level and it was hard for them to operate together. Again, as it had been with No. 257 Squadron earlier in the summer, Tuck was tasked with flying missions over the continent.

In October 1941, Tuck was one of several leading Royal Air Force pilots sent to the United States on a liaison mission that predated the American entry into the war by two months. By December, when the United States actively entered World War II, Tuck was back in Britain, where he was given command of the five squadrons of the Biggin Hill Wing. Unlike the Duxford Wing, the Biggin Hill Wing had a unified family of aircraft, with four of the squadrons being equipped with Spitfires. These were No. 72 Squadron, No. 91 Squadron, No. 124 Squadron and No. 401 (RCAF) Squadron. The odd squadron was No. 264 Squadron, which was a night fighter squadron flying the somewhat elderly Boulton Paul Defiant Mk. II, a two-man fighter with a rear-firing turret as defensive armament.

Tuck's last mission came on January 28, 1942. It was a fighter sweep over northern France, in which the Biggin Hill Spitfires were assigned to destroy targets of opportunity. The 29-victory ace attacked a train that was parked on the outskirts of Boulogne, but when he emerged from the steam cloud that erupted from the exploding locomotive, he was hit by antiaircraft artillery fire. He managed to crash land his Spitfire, but he was soon surrounded by German soldiers.

The news spread quickly that Robert Stanford Tuck was in custody. Within hours, he was summoned by the commander of Luftwaffe JG 26, Adolf Galland. Also an ace, Galland would later command all Luftwaffe fighter operations, and would end the war with 111 victories. In a bizarre situation that is illustrative of the camaraderie that existed between aces—even while they were at war—Galland invited Tuck to dine with him, and they spent the evening talking about other Luftwaffe and Royal Air Force aces as though they were all part of the same fraternity.

On the morning of January 29, however, Tuck awoke as just another prisoner of war. Eventually, he found himself in Stalag Luft III, a prisoner of war camp at Sagan, near Berlin. For more than three years, the man who had been the toast of the London media would endure the gradually-worsening conditions of captivity in the German stalag archipelago.

Bob Tuck and his fellow pilots made numerous unsuccessful escape attempts. For years, they were working on a major tunnel project that would inspire numerous postwar movies, including The Great Escape, which was based on the March 24, 1944 breakout from Stalag Luft III that used the tunnel. A total of 76 men sneaked 400 feet through the tunnel to freedom, but the results were not so good. Only three men were able to elude capture. Of the others, 23 were recaptured and thrown back into imprisonment. The rest were shot and killed. But Robert Stanford Tuck was not among any of these groups. A few weeks before "the great escape," he and several other POWs were transferred to another stalag.

Nearly a year later, Tuck and many other prisoners were moved again, but by now a pall of chaos had descended over the Reich and the Germans were not nearly as well organized as they had once been. Tuck and another man managed to elude roll call one morning after an overnight stop during the prisoner move, and they got away. Making their way through the snow and sleet for several weeks, they finally linked up with the vanguard of an advancing Soviet column on February 22, 1945. The Soviets sent them to the rear, and eventually they were put aboard a British ship at the Russian Black Sea port of Odessa on March 26.

Robert Stanford Tuck enjoyed a homecoming before the war had actually ended, but by the time that he had fully recuperated, there would be no more combat flying for him. He would go on to fly jet fighters—albeit never in combat—and he would play a role in the postwar evolution of the Royal Air Force, remaining in the service until May 1949. As a civilian, Tuck moved to Kent, where he would spend his life as a farmer, until his death on May 5, 1987.

★
The No. 257 Squadron Hurricane Mk. I belonging to Squadron Leader Robert Stanford Tuck refueling at Coltishall in early January 1941. *UK Government photo in the public domain*

# BADER: THE LEGLESS ACE WHO COULDN'T BE CAUGHT

**ONE OF THE MOST INDOMITABLE ACES** to serve with the Royal Air Force during World War II, Douglas Robert Steuart Bader was one of the top aces in the Royal Air Force during the difficult days of the Battle of Britain and its aftermath, and he scored 23 victories despite the fact that he had no legs.

He joined the Royal Air Force in 1928 at the age of 18 and showed immediate promise as a pilot. Assigned to No. 23 Squadron, he demonstrated so much skill that he became part of the squadron's aerobatic team. In 1931, No. 23 Squadron converted from Gloster Gamecocks to Bristol Bulldogs, an aircraft that was much better suited to aerobatics. The aircraft's appellation might well have been an allegory for the aggressive Bader, whose skill led him to be a bit reckless. In December 1931, his luck ran out. In a crash, he lost the lower part of his left leg, and his right leg was cut off above the knee.

Despite his debilitating injuries, Bader got himself a set of crude artificial legs, and soon had learned to walk without a cane. He also learned to drive and, at last, to fly again. When the

Royal Air Force refused to assign him to flying duty, he quit the service in 1933 and went to work selling fuel at an airport. It was work that he detested, but at least it kept him near the aircraft.

By 1939, things had changed. With the winds of war blowing, the Royal Air Force needed pilots badly, and, when Bader applied, he was promised a flying job if he would reenlist. In February 1940, he was assigned as a Spitfire pilot with No. 19 Squadron at Duxford, but before long he was promoted to flight leader and transferred to No. 222 Squadron at Hornchurch. It was with No. 222 Squadron that Bader would get a taste of combat over France at the end of May 1940, during Operation Dynamo, the evacuation of the British Expeditionary Force from Dunkirk.

The following month, he was named to command No. 242 (RCAF) Squadron, a Hawker Hurricane unit which was being formed at Coltishall as the first Canadian fighter squadron in the Royal Air Force. Leading No. 242 Squadron into combat during the Battle of Britain in August and September, Bader decided to employ the tactic of a massed formation—such as Baron Manfred von Richthofen had used during World War I with his so-called "Flying Circus"— rather than small cells of fighters. With Bader, however, the favored nickname was "beehive." Unlike the Red Baron, Bader took his hives to the ceiling, so that when attacking bombers, they could dive to build up a speed advantage.

Bader liked speed, on the ground as well as in the air. According to one story, during the time that he was becoming a hero of the Battle of Britain, he had a warrant out for his arrest for unpaid speeding tickets.

When Bader was given command of the Tangmere Wing in 1941, the "Bader Beehives" were often composed of up to 200 Spitfires. He had started with 60, but when his flight claimed 152 German bombers in a month, Fighter Command gave him all he wanted. The call sign of the

★
Group Captain Douglas Robert Steuart Bader (center), acting commander of No. 242 (Canadian) Squadron of the RAF. With him outside the officers' mess at Duxford, Cambridgeshire in September 1940 are Pilot Officer W.L. McKnight and Acting Flight Lieutenant G.E. Ball. *UK Government photo in the public domain*

Tangmere Wing was "Green Line," a reference to an English urban bus line, so another nickname was "Bader's Bus Company." Bader is also credited with the development of the "finger four" formation in which the two leaders of a four-ship formation fly abreast, with their respective wingmen also flying abreast.

By August 1941, Douglas Bader was hitting his stride as a fighter pilot and as a commander. He had raised his score to 22, and he had been awarded both the Distinguished Flying Cross and the Distinguished Service Order. Then the war ended abruptly for him. During a dogfight over northern France, his Spitfire was involved in a midair collision with a Bf 109. In the process of bailing out of the mortally crippled aircraft, his right artificial leg became entangled and was ripped from his body. He survived the parachute landing, and was captured.

As was the case when Robert Stanford Tuck was shot down and captured in France five months later, Bader was quickly recognized as a celebrated catch and was invited to dine with Adolf Galland, the commander of Luftwaffe JG 26, at his officers' mess in Abbeville. The Germans also retrieved Bader's prosthesis from the wreck of his Spitfire and returned it to him. It was smashed beyond being useful, and his other was damaged, so Galland graciously made a request through the International Red Cross. The British were offered safe passage for an aircraft to drop replacement artificial legs. They dropped the legs, but bombed Galland's base.

Bader was fitted and sent to a German prison hospital, where he returned the favor by escaping, using the classic trick of tying bed sheets together. A fugitive in France, Douglas Bader was eventually recaptured and thrown into a succession of stalags from which he would escape again, only to be recaptured a second time. He escaped a third time and was recaptured again. After this, the Germans put him in Colditz, the infamous eighteenth century castle prison that was located on a mountaintop with sheer cliffs all around.

When the war ended, Douglas Robert Steuart Bader was welcomed home as a returning hero. He was awarded Bars to both his Distinguished Flying Cross and the Distinguished Service Order, the equivalent of a second of each. In 1976, he became Sir Douglas Bader, having received a knighthood for his service to the United Kingdom. In later years, he met Adolf Galland again, under more congenial circumstances, and they became good friends.

Bader died in 1982, at the age of 72. Today, the Douglas Bader Sports Centre at St. Edwards in Oxford, his former school, is a living tribute to the legless air ace whom the Germans could not keep from escaping.

★
In August 1955, having overcome the limitations of his own orthopedic disability, Douglas (later Sir Douglas) Bader paid a courtesy call to Sophies Minde Ortopedi (Queen Sophie's Memorial Orthopedic Hospital) in Trondheimsveien, Norway. Paul Brickhill's biography of Bader, *Reach for the Sky*, was published in 1954, becoming the biggest-selling hardback in postwar Britain, and Bader had become an inspirational speaker. *National Archives of Norway*

# BEURLING: THE HIGHEST-SCORING CANADIAN ACE

George Frederick "Buzz" Beurling, Canada's highest-scoring ace, on a publicity tour visit to Vancouver in March 1943. *Department of National Defence*

**MANY PILOTS FROM CANADA** distinguished themselves during World War II, flying for both the Royal Air Force and Canada's own RCAF. George Frederick "Buzz" Beurling would fly for both, scoring 29.5 victories with the Royal Air Force and two with the RCAF for a total of 31.5, making him one of the top half dozen aces scoring victories with the Royal Air Force.

Beurling was born in 1921 at Verdun in Quebec, and took an early interest in aviation, devouring books about World War I aces and watching airplanes at the local airport. He took his first ride at age nine and had made his first solo flight by age 17. He then quit school to work as a bush pilot, flying mail and supplies to mining camps in the far north of Canada.

At one point, Beurling won an aerobatic contest in Edmonton, Alberta, flying against a number of RCAF pilots. In commenting about his victory, he made some pointed remarks about the quality of RCAF flight training and pilots that would not be forgotten. In 1939, he applied to join the RCAF and was refused. They claimed that it was his deficiency in "academics," but Beurling knew the real reason.

World War II had begun and Beurling was itching to get into the action. He had been rejected by the RCAF, but when the Soviet Union invaded Finland at the end of November 1939, he decided that he would join the Finnish Air Force. However, the Finnish embassy asked for his parents' permission because he was just 18. They said no.

Undaunted, Beurling signed on as a hand on a ship bound for Glasgow, and upon arrival headed for the first Royal Air Force recruiting office that he could find. They were ready to sign him on, based on his knowledge of aviation, but they needed his birth certificate, which he didn't have. In a scene that could have been from a movie, Beurling walked out, signed on to another ship and made a round trip across the Atlantic—during which his ship was hit by a torpedo from a German U-Boat—to retrieve his birth certificate.

Once in the Royal Air Force, Beurling progressed quickly, and he had soon earned the nickname "Buzz" for his low-level—often unauthorized and unsanctioned—aerobatics. During his early months with the Royal Air Force, Beurling crossed paths with—and was trained by—James Henry "Ginger" Lacey, who would soon be one of the leading aces in the Royal Air Force, and who was the man who shot down the bomber that bombed Buckingham Palace. Lacey was impressed by Beurling's flying skills, and so were the RCAF squadron commanders who offered him an RCAF commission. Beurling refused, deciding that he'd rather remain an enlisted pilot in the Royal Air Force than an officer in the RCAF. It was his turn to snub the RCAF.

Beurling scored his first victory in March 1942 while flying a Spitfire Mk. V with No. 41 Squadron on a sweep over northern France. He was flying last place in a four-ship formation, when five German fighter pilots attacked, especially keen to pick off the man at the end of the queue. Beurling pulled up and let the Focke-Wulf Fw 190s overshoot him. He then got one in his sights and picked him off. Two days later, again over France, Beurling saw a flight of Fw 190s and broke formation to attack them. He shot down the lead aircraft but was sanctioned for breaking formation for a second time.

Displeased with the leadership at No. 41 Squadron, Beurling volunteered for duty with No. 249 Squadron, which was based on the British island garrison at Malta in the Mediterranean. Malta was being referred to as an unsinkable British "aircraft carrier" in the Mediterranean and the Germans and Italians wanted it out of commission. This was because the British used it as a base from which to attack the Mediterranean supply lines used by the Germans and Italians to resupply their forces in North Africa. For General Erwin Rommel's Deutsche Afrika Korps, these supplies were the key to victory. The Luftwaffe and the Regia Aeronautica were tasked with eliminating Malta as an interference to Axis operations in the Mediterranean and North Africa, and No. 249 Squadron was about all that stood in their way. It was not pleasant duty, but for George Beurling it offered a welcome change.

Along with 16 new Spitfire Mk. Vs and 15 other pilots, Beurling was soon on the way aboard HMS Eagle. Because the Germans controlled the air over the continent, one of the only ways that the Royal Air Force could get aircraft to Malta was to send them aboard Royal Navy aircraft carriers. The only problems, beyond the danger of being torpedoed by the Germans, were that the Spitfire Mk. V was never designed for carrier operations, nor had the Royal Air Force pilots been properly trained for this kind of take-off.

Beurling managed to get off HMS Eagle and fly the last 600 miles to Takali Field on Malta, when he was ordered to take off immediately to intercept a strike force of German bombers headed for the island. He would soon learn that flying an intercept mission was something to look forward to. Despite the danger, anything was better than being on alert for a mission at Takali, which meant sitting in an oven-like cockpit under the blistering Mediterranean sun—and waiting.

On July 6, 1942, George Beurling and seven other Spitfire pilots intercepted three Regia Aeronautica bombers en route to Malta, escorted by an estimated 30 Macchi C.200 fighters. Beurling led the assault, diving straight through the Macchi formations and pulling up to fire on a big Cant Z.1007 bomber. Beurling's first pass damaged a bomber, and he quickly shot down two of the Macchis. These were his first victories since coming to Malta.

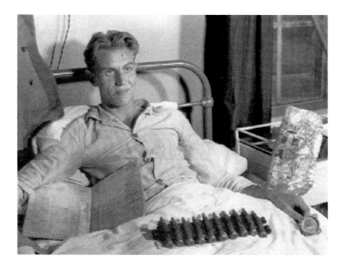

★
George Beurling in a hospital in 1943 after escaping from a transport aircraft that was taking the already injured fighter pilot to Britain. He jumped out just as the plane crashed near Gibraltar and then swam 160 yards with a heavy cast on his foot. Only three people survived the crash. *Department of National Defence*

# WOODWARD: CANADA'S NUMBER TWO ACE

**THE SECOND HIGHEST-SCORING CANADIAN ACE** of World War II was a study in contrasts and similarities with George "Buzz" Beurling. They both had what it took to be excellent combat pilots and they were both pragmatic men who put their missions ahead of red tape. However, while one alienated himself from the Royal Air Force establishment, the other made the system work for him. Vernon Crompton "Woody" Woodward commanded squadrons in North Africa and scored, by various accountings, between 20 and 21.8 victories. Woodward flew with the Royal Air Force's number three ace from the First World War, and he flew as wingman to the Royal Air Force's greatest ace of the Second World War on his last successful mission.

Woodward was born on Vancouver Island, north of Victoria, British Columbia, on December 22, 1916, and grew up in the woods of the Pacific Northwest, learning to be an extraordinary marksman. He also took an interest in aviation, and in 1938 enlisted in the Royal Air Force because, unlike the RCAF, they were actively expanding and they wanted pilots—especially bomber pilots.

Woodward went through his initial flight training in Perth, Scotland and because of his aptitude for aerobatic flying, he was steered toward fighters rather than bombers. From Perth, the Royal Air Force sent him south to No. 6 Flying Training School at Little Rissington, north of Oxford, for intermediate and advanced training in Hawker Audaxes and Furies. He earned his wings in December 1938 and took advanced training at Warmwell in Dorset.

In June 1939, with the war just three months away, Woodward was assigned to No. 33 Squadron, part of Egypt Group, based at Ismailia in Egypt and flying the aging Gloster Gladiators. Their commander at Egypt Group was none other than a fellow Canadian, Air Commodore Raymond Collishaw, the third highest-scoring ace in the Royal Air Force during World War I.

For Britons at home, the Axis threat was obviously Germany, but in North Africa it was Italy. To the west of Egypt lay Libya, an Italian colony since 1911, and to the south lay Italian Somaliland and recently conquered Italian Ethiopia. When World War II began in September 1939, Italy remained neutral, but Egypt Group went on alert.

On June 10, 1940 when Germany invaded France, Italy declared war on Britain and France, and the Italian forces in Libya went on the offensive. No. 33 Squadron was in action immediately, and on June 14, while on patrol near the Libyan border, Woodward and another Gladiator pilot attacked a Caproni Ca.310 bomber and Woodward got a "probable" on a Fiat CR.32 fighter.

He scored his first confirmed victories over a pair of CR.32s on June 20. In a battle four days later, No. 33 Squadron Gladiators downed four out of five Fiats, with Woodward claiming one of the four, and a "probable" on the fifth. He would become an ace the following day with one confirmed and a shared kill.

In October, No. 33 Squadron started to convert from Gladiators to Hawker Hurricanes, a quantum leap in fighter aircraft technology. From elderly biplanes, they had switched to the aircraft that had outscored the Supermarine Spitfire in the recent Battle of Britain. Woodward flew his first Hurricane mission on October 11, 1940.

Through the autumn, the Italian forces had managed to push deep into Egypt, while the British withdrew to regroup. In December, the British forces launched Operation Compass, a major counteroffensive aimed at pushing the Italians in Libya. As the attack went over the top, No. 33 Squadron was overhead flying air cover. On December 9, Woodward's flight attacked a large number of CR.42s. He shot down a pair and damaged a third. Within three days, Operation Compass was deemed a success, with 38,000 prisoners and vast quantities of equipment and materiel captured as well.

On December 19, Woodward shot down two more CR.42s, bringing his score for the month to five, plus two damaged Savoia SM.79 bombers. By February 1941 the British Commonwealth forces had occupied a large slice of Libya, including the city of Benghazi.

In October 1940, while his legions were on the offensive in Egypt, Benito Mussolini launched his ill-fated invasion of Greece. With British Commonwealth—mainly Australia and New Zealand—reinforcements, the Greeks stopped the Italians and held them in a stalemate, until Mussolini finally asked Adolf Hitler for help.

In February 1941, No. 33 Squadron was sent to Greece, and in March it was placed under the command of the legendary fighter ace Marmaduke St. John "Pat" Pattle. At this time, the Royal Air Force was still facing only the Italian Regia Aeronautica, as the Germans had not yet intervened. Nevertheless, the Italians were outnumbering the British two-to-one in most engagements. For some pilots, such as Woodward, this just meant more targets. On April 6,

★
Flying Officer Vernon Crompton "Woody" Woodward was Canada's second highest-scoring ace. He is seen here strapping on his parachute beside his Hawker Hurricane Mk. I, at Fuka, Egypt in the summer of 1941. He was then a member of "B" Flight of No. 33 Squadron of the RAF. He had already downed a half-dozen enemy aircraft, but he would add 19 more victories to his tally before he left the Middle East Theater in September 1941. *UK Government photo in the public domain*

he shot down three Cant Z.1007 bombers in one day, despite withering defensive fire from the gunners aboard the bombers. One of an original five had been shot down after a raid, and Woodward scrambled to intercept the survivors.

When he landed, Woodward found out that Germany had just invaded Greece, and now No. 33 was facing the Luftwaffe. Instead of being outnumbered two-to-one, the Royal Air Force was now outnumbered ten-to-one. They had just 80 fighters to counter a force that numbered 800. Woodward first faced the Luftwaffe on April 13, but he managed to down one of three Messerschmitt Bf 109s that attacked while he was on a solo patrol. The following day, he and his wingman intercepted and downed three Ju 87 Stukas while they were dive-bombing an Anglo-Greek position.

Five days later, Woodward was part of a three-ship patrol with Pat Pattle when they were jumped by nine Messerschmitt Bf 109s. Pattle and Woodward managed to get behind them, with Pattle claiming two and Woodward a single. This was the day that Pattle scored his six-in-one-day. Meanwhile, however, the third Hurricane had been hit. Time was running out for the Royal Air Force—and for Pat Pattle.

The following day, April 20, the Germans launched their huge air offensive against Athens. Pattle ordered everybody aloft, and he flew himself, despite a debilitating fever. Woodward managed to claim a Bf 110 that day, possibly one of those that shot down Pat Pattle. Woodward also claimed two Bf 110s and a Ju 88 damaged.

Within days, the Commonwealth troops evacuated mainland Greece for the island of Crete. On May 20, with a powerful Luftwaffe flying air cover, the Germans invaded Crete. In the face of overwhelming enemy numbers, it was obvious that the only Commonwealth troops that would live to fight again were those who managed to escape to the south side of the island to be picked up by the Royal Navy. Woodward took charge of the Royal Air Force contingent and started across the island. Moving by night, they crossed through German lines several times before finally being picked up by the Australian destroyer HMAS Nizam. From there, they were evacuated to Egypt.

Back where he had started the war, Woody Woodward picked up the Distinguished Flying Cross that he had been awarded while he was fighting for his life in Greece. The remnants of No. 33 Squadron joined No. 30 Squadron and went back into action in the desert, where the enemy now included Field Marshal Erwin Rommel's Deutsche Afrika Korps as well as the Italian armies. Woodward managed to down an Italian Fiat G.50 on almost his first outing with No. 30 Squadron, but he was coming near the end of his tour.

Woodward's final score marked a technological turning point. On July 12, 1941 he was directed to intercept a Junkers Ju 88, not by a pilot or spotter who actually had seen it, but by a radar operator miles away in the Mediterranean aboard the HMS Formidable. Vectored by radar, as modern interceptors are, Woodward got a visual on the Ju 88 and sent it flaming into the desert sand.

Woodward's score now stood officially at 21.8, although it might be higher—No. 33 Squadron's records were lost in the evacuation from Greece. In September 1941 he was reassigned to the Rhodesian Air Training Group at Salisbury, Southern Rhodesia (now Harare, Zimbabwe). Through June 1942 he flew as an instructor, training new pilots to fly and fight under the combat conditions that he had experienced so vividly during the first year of the war in the Mediterranean Theater.

Late in 1942, Woodward returned to an operational command as head of No. 213 Squadron, based at Martuba near Alexandria, Egypt. By this time, the war had moved far to the west and the nature of the missions being flown from Egypt had changed considerably. Instead of flying life and death duels in skies dark with the enemy, the No. 213 Squadron Hurricanes flew escort duty on missions where the Germans and Italians were never seen.

In August 1943, Woodward had a Bar attached to his Distinguished Flying Cross, and was reassigned to the headquarters for Air Defense, Eastern Mediterranean, and then to the Royal Air Force Staff College at Haifa in Palestine. His final squadron command was the Middle East Communications Squadron, which was actually an executive transport unit tasked with ferrying visiting dignitaries, both military and civilian, throughout the region. After the war, Woodward remained in the Royal Air Force, and in 1946, he was assigned the staff at the Central Fighter Establishment, back in Britain.

Woodward would have a variety of assignments in the postwar years, including several tours commanding flying squadrons. Between 1948 and 1950, he commanded No. 19 Squadron, which was equipped with de Havilland Hornets, a long-range attack bomber with twin piston engines that was a successor to the great de Havilland Mosquito of the war years. In 1955, he was assigned to command No. 122 Wing, a fighter unit based at Jever in West Germany that was equipped with Hawker Hunter jet fighters, which represented leading edge technology for the time.

In the interim, Woodward was assigned to a project with Fighter Command that was tasked with developing a network of underground and hardened shelters for aircraft and communications facilities throughout Britain for use in time of nuclear war. He also served a tour with the Royal Air Force Flying College at Manby. Woodward's last command was No. 39 Squadron at Luqa on the island of Malta. Equipped with English Electric Canberras configured for high-altitude photographic reconnaissance missions, No. 39 Squadron conducted such missions around the periphery of Soviet satellite nations in southeastern Europe. In the event of a nuclear war, No. 39 Squadron would have had the dubious distinction of flying post-strike reconnaissance missions over targets of nuclear strikes in the southern Soviet Union.

Woody Woodward retired from the Royal Air Force in 1963, and operated an air charter company until 1967, when he retired to his native British Columbia.

★
Some of the pilots of No. 33 Squadron standing with a Hawker Hurricane Mk. I at their airfield in at Larissa, Greece in March 1941. From left to right, They are P. R.W. Wickham, D. T. Moir, Vernon Crompton "Woody" Woodward, J. M. "Pop" Littler, E. H. "Dixie" Dean, F. Holman, E. F. "Timber" Woods, C. A. C. Chetham, A. M. Young, Pat Pattle, H. J. Starrett, George Rumsey, A. R. Butcher, W. Winsland, and R. Dunscombe. Woodward was Canada's second highest-scoring ace in World War II. *UK Government photo in the public domain*

# CALDWELL: THE TOP-SCORING AUSTRALIAN ACE

**WHEN BRITAIN WAS PULLED INTO WORLD WAR II IN 1939,** many Commonwealth pilots joined the Royal Air Force to fight the Germans, many not thinking that the war would soon spread closer to home. Clive Robertson "Killer" Caldwell was one of these pilots. He was an ace in the European Theater, but when his native Australia became a battleground, he came home to defend Australia and to become an ace in the Pacific Theater as well. The 28.5 victory marks painted on his aircraft at the end of the war included the insignias of Germany, Italy and Japan—all three Axis powers.

Caldwell was born at Lewisham in suburban Sydney on July 28, 1911. He had a civilian pilot's license when the war began in 1939, so he enlisted in the RAAF. He became an officer, but when he saw that he was going to be assigned as an instructor rather than as a combat pilot, he resigned and reenlisted as an enlisted aircrew trainee. The RAAF got the idea. His commission was reinstated in January 1941, and he was sent to the Middle East where he was assigned to the Royal Air Force's No. 250 Squadron, flying Curtiss Tomahawks in Syria and Cyprus.

As the Deutsche Afrika Korps replaced or supplemented the Italian forces in North Africa, the British were forced to rush reinforcements to blunt the Axis drive toward the Suez Canal. No. 250 Squadron was part of this reinforcement effort.

By the middle of 1941, when Caldwell had scored no victories for three dozen outings, he had begun to wonder whether he had the "right stuff" to be a fighter pilot. As he pondered the "how to" of being a successful pilot one day, he was watching his own aircraft's shadow flitting across the desert. He opened fire and watched the hits relative to the position of the moving shadow of the Curtiss Tomahawk. Gradually, he began to understand the physics of deflection shooting relative to speed and position.

During the last four days of June, he added 3.5 kills to his roster, including 2.5 on the last day of the month over the Mediterranean off Tobruk—two Ju 87 Stukas and a shared Bf 110. He became an ace on August 16, claiming a Regia Aeronautica G.50 over the Mediterranean.

Two weeks later, Caldwell was on patrol over Sidi Barrani, when he was jumped by a pair of JG 27 Messerschmitt Bf 109Es. One was piloted by Werner Schroer, an ace with 114 kills against people just like Caldwell. Bullets and cannon shells riddled the Tomahawk's fuselage and cockpit, hitting Caldwell in the back, shoulder, and leg. The aircraft was also badly damaged. Nevertheless, Caldwell managed to return fire, downing Schroer's wingman, as the great ace himself slipped away.

Out of action for a month, Caldwell proved that he still had that "right stuff" when he returned to the fray in September. On September 27, he downed a Bf 109 over Buq Buq, and he claimed another the following day in a fight over Bardia. On November 23 he shot down two

★
Clive Caldwell,
wearing his standard
issue felt hat and
sitting on his No. 452
Squadron Supermarine
Spitfire Mk VIII at
an airfield on the
island of Morotai in
the Dutch East Indies
in 1944. *Australian
War Memorial via
Wikimedia Commons*

Bf 109s in a single day, including one piloted by Wolfgang Lippert, the Knight's Cross holder who commanded II Gruppe of JG 27.

The best day of Caldwell's career as a fighter pilot came on December 5, when he plunged into a massed formation of Ju 87 dive bombers over El Adem during the British Operation Crusader offensive. Caldwell attacked from the rear, claiming two of the Stukas. He then went after the leader and downed two more after that, for a total of five. This brought his score to 14, plus two shared kills. The El Adem action also led to the nickname "Killer Caldwell" being assigned, much to the discomfort of the honoree, who did not feel it to be accurate.

After another pair of Bf 109 kills, Caldwell was awarded a Distinguished Flying Cross—with Bar—on December 26. In January 1942 he was promoted to squadron leader and assigned to lead No. 112 "Shark" Squadron. Caldwell soon experienced the difficulties of command, as many of the "Sharks" proved to be inexperienced and vulnerable. In a battle with JG 27 Messerschmitt Bf 109s on February 21, Caldwell would claim one of the enemy, but No. 112 Squadron would lose three of its own. On March 13 two Sharks went down, but the following day Caldwell claimed a pair of Regia Aeronautica Macchi C.202s over Tobruk—one of them a shared kill.

Caldwell's last victory in North Africa—another Messerschmitt Bf 109—came on April 23 during the great battle for the French Foreign Legionnaire fortress at Bir Hakeim.

★
Flight Lieutenant Clive Caldwell as a member of No. 250 Squadron of the RAF at Cyrenaica, Libya in December 1941 during the North African Campaign. On December 5, flying a Curtiss Tomahawk, he downed five Ju 87 Stuka dive bombers in a single mission. *Australian War Memorial via Wikimedia Commons*

Things were turning ugly down under, and his presence was required at home. The Japanese were on the offensive, and the northern cities of Australia were under attack. The Philippines, Hong Kong and Singapore had fallen like dominos and it was feared that Australia itself might be invaded. The RAAF wanted its best pilots at home.

Before he left North Africa, however, the Royal Air Force awarded Caldwell a Distinguished Service Order. Because of the Polish pilots in No. 112 Squadron that he'd commanded and nurtured, the Polish government awarded him the Walecznych Cross (Cross of Valor).

Back in Australia, Caldwell was given command of RAAF No. 1 Fighter Wing, which was based at Darwin, in Northern Territory. He would get his first victories against the Imperial Japanese Navy Air Force on March 2, 1943 off Point Charles, when he claimed one of Japan's dreaded Mitsubishi A6M Zero fighters, as well as a Nakajima B6N bomber. On May 2, he would claim another pair of Zeros in a dogfight less than 60 miles from Darwin.

During June, Caldwell downed another pair of Zeros and a Mitsubishi G4M bomber. His final victory of the war came on August 20, when he claimed a Mitsubishi Ki-46 reconnaissance aircraft of 202 Sentai near Cape Fourcroy.

In April 1944, after an extended leave, Caldwell commanded RAAF No. 80 Wing, with aircraft based at both Darwin and Morotai. By this time, Japanese aircraft were no longer a threat to Australia. Indeed, they had been virtually eliminated from the skies of the Southwest Pacific, and RAAF operations centered around ground attack missions against isolated Japanese troop concentrations. These units were no longer capable of offensive operations, and many people in the RAAF—Caldwell included—felt that attacking them was a waste of time.

By 1944, there was a seething dissatisfaction with how the RAAF had been relegated by the American-dominated command structure to mere nuisance work. The RAAF pilots, who had proved themselves in the darkest days of the war, wanted to be used in the offensive against Japan in the Philippines and farther north—where the "action" was.

This displeasure finally reached its boiling point with the Morotai Mutiny in April 1945. Eight front line RAAF officers, including Caldwell, resigned in protest over the RAAF's allowing itself to become a second-class air force in the final battles for the defeat of Japan. In a major government crisis, much of the RAAF's top leadership, including Air Commodore A.H. Cobby—himself a World War I ace—were compelled to resign.

The action was anticlimactic. In April, the war was expected to last for another two years, with the final invasion of Japan's main island of Honshu not even scheduled until March 1946. However, Japan announced its surrender on August 15, 1945.

By this time, Clive Caldwell had been named to the headquarters staff of the RAAF 1st Tactical Air Force at Melbourne. He left the RAAF in 1946 and pursued a successful business career until his death in August 1994.

# **GRAY:** NEW ZEALAND'S TOP ACE

**WHILE CLIVE CALDWELL**, Australia's leading ace, went home to finish his wartime career fighting the Japanese, the top-scoring New Zealander would serve his entire wartime career with the Royal Air Force in Europe, ending World War II with 27.5 victories. Colin Falkland Gray and his twin brother Ken were born in Christchurch on the South Island on November 9, 1914. Having moved to Britain, Clive became a fighter pilot in the Royal Air Force in 1939, a year after Ken became a bomber pilot. When World War II began in September 1939, Ken Gray was one of the pilots who flew the first tenuous raids against the Reich. Two months later, he was awarded a Distinguished Flying Cross. Colin Gray, meanwhile, was posted to No. 54 Squadron in November 1939 and saw very little action through the winter.

In May 1940, everything changed. Ken Gray was killed in an accident and Colin Gray faced his first combat. On May 26, during a bomber escort mission, Colin Gray's flight was bounced by German fighters. Gray managed to shoot down a Bf 109 before his Spitfire was hit. He managed to recover from a steep dive and nurse the damaged Spitfire back to Britain. Mrs. Gray would not lose two sons in one month.

Gray's second victory, another Messerschmitt Bf 109, came on July 13 over Calais. During the Battle of Britain he saw a great deal of combat, and by the first week of September, he had raised his score to 14 kills and 14 probables. By then Colin, like Ken, had pinned a Distinguished Flying Cross on his shirt. In January 1941, after a short assignment with No. 43 Squadron, Gray became a flight commander with No. 54 Squadron, replacing fellow New Zealander Alan Deere, who was one of the highest-scoring Battle of Britain aces.

In June, Gray was transferred to No. 1 Squadron as a flight commander and in August was given command of No. 616 Squadron. By September 20, when he received a Bar on his Distinguished Flying Cross, he had raised his score to 17 victories.

Colin Gray spent most of 1942 behind a desk, but late in the year, he was reassigned to North Africa as commander of No. 81 Squadron, the first squadron in the theater to be equipped with the new Spitfire Mk. IX. Gray quickly added five kills and four probables to his victory tally, and by the time the campaign ended in May 1943, he had added a Distinguished Service Order to his Distinguished Flying Cross.

With Operation Husky—the invasion of Sicily—in the planning stages, Gray was promoted to command the Malta-based No. 322 Wing. During June, as Allied forces were getting into position for the coming fight for Sicily, Gray led patrols over the Axis-held island. During this period, he claimed a Bf 109 and a Macchi C.202. On July 10, while flying air cover for the invasion forces, he downed a Bf 109. No. 322 Wing relocated to Lentini on Sicily after it was occupied by Allied troops and continued to fly patrols from there. On July 25, Gray was leading such a patrol when they encountered a large number of German Ju 52 transports landing reinforcements at Cap Milazzo. In the ensuing fight, five German fighter escorts went down, along with 21 Ju 52s, two of which were destroyed by Colin Gray.

After the successful conquest of Sicily, Gray was reassigned to Britain to help train newer pilots. In July 1944, when the Germans began to launch their V-1 cruise missiles at Britain, the Royal Air Force turned to Colin Gray to help coordinate intercept operations.

When World War II ended, Colin Gray remained with the Royal Air Force until March 1961. After his retirement he returned to New Zealand, where he lived until his death at Waikanae in 1995.

# WADE: THE YANK IN THE ROYAL AIR FORCE

**THE 1941 HENRY KING FILM** *A Yank In The RAF*, starring Tyrone Power and Betty Grable, wasn't about Lance Wade but he would have made a better subject. With his dark eyes, Texas drawl and black mustache, Wade had the same leading man charisma as Power, but he was the real thing, the American who felt strongly about defeating the "Jerries"—or at least strongly about feeling the rush of combat from the cockpit of a Spitfire.

Lance Wade was indeed the real thing. He would score 25 victories (some sources list 23) with the Royal Air Force, putting him in the top ten among American aces, and among the top dozen Royal Air Force aces. He was born in Broaddus, Texas in 1915, and when World War II began he decided that he wanted to be part of the action. He traveled to Canada to join the Royal Air Force in December 1940.

He was assigned to No. 33 Squadron—Pat Pattle's old unit—in Egypt in September, where he was flying the Hurricane Mk. I against the Italian Regia Aeronautica. He scored his first victories, a pair of Fiat CR.42s, on November 18 and scored the magic fifth on November 24. By September 13, Wade had scored 13 victories flying a Hurricane Mk. II since April, and he had been awarded the Distinguished Flying Cross.

With the United States now in World War II, Wade could have chosen to transfer to the USAAF, but he remained in the Royal Air Force. He did, however, spend some time in the States during late 1942 on a liaison mission for the RAF. When he returned to combat in early 1943, Wade became a flight leader with the Royal Air Force's Desert Air Force No. 145 Squadron, but was soon promoted to squadron leader.

Now flying a Spitfire Mk. V, Wade scored eight victories in the Tunisia campaign to raise his score to 21 by April 1943, and had a Bar attached to his Distinguished Flying Cross. At the end of April, No. 145 Squadron converted to Spitfire Mk. IXs and relocated to a base in Italy. By autumn they had upgraded to Spitfire Mk. IXs, and Wade scored his first kills in the new machine, a pair of Focke-Wulf 190s, on October 2. By now he was the highest-scoring ace in the Desert Air Force, slightly ahead of his nearest rival, Neville Duke, also of No. 145 Squadron.

The last claim in Wade's logbook was three damaged Fw 190s, penciled in on November 3. After that, Wade was awarded a Distinguished Service Order, promoted to wing commander and kicked upstairs to a desk job on the staff of the Royal Air Force Desert Air Force headquarters. On January 12, 1944, he was killed in a flying accident at Foggia, Italy.

Neville Duke ended the war as the leading ace of the Desert Air Force, and the third highest-scoring Allied ace in the Mediterranean, with 26.83 victories. Lance Wade was fourth in the Mediterranean, behind Pat Pattle, George Beurling and Duke. Wade was also the highest-scoring American ace ever to serve exclusively with a non-American air force.

Neville Duke went on to a distinguished career as one of Britain's most important test pilots. In 1953, at the Royal Air Force base at Tangmere, he flew the prototype of the Hawker Hunter jet fighter to a speed record of 727 mph.

★
Lance Cleo "Wildcat" Wade was born in Broaddus, Texas and traveled to Canada in December 1940 to join the Royal Air Force. He flew with No. 33 Squadron and was an ace before the United States entered the war. He is seen here in the cockpit of his Supermarine Spitfire HF Mk.VIII at Triolo Airfield, south of San Severo, Italy on November 12, 1943. At the time, he commanded No. 145 Squadron. *UK Government photo in the public domain*

CHAPTER

05

JAPAN

T HE INVOLVEMENT OF THE JAPANESE EMPIRE IN WORLD WAR II was a direct
outgrowth of its prewar foreign policy that called for the Empire's political and
economic domination of the Far East through a political and economic initiative
called the "Greater East Asia Co-Prosperity Sphere." Having defeated China in
1895 in the First Sino-Japanese War and Russia in 1905 in the Russo-Japanese
War, Japanese set about building its empire. Formosa (Taiwan) and Korea were
incorporated in 1895 and 1910, respectively. Emperor Hirohito, who came to
power in 1926, presided over a dramatic expansion of the Japanese Empire. In 1931, Japan
incorporated Manchuria into the Empire, renaming it Manchukuo and setting up a puppet
emperor. In 1937 Hirohito's forces moved on China itself in the Second Sino-Japanese War.
Shanghai, Beijing (then known as Peiping) and Nanjing (then Nanking) were battered into
submission and occupied.

Within its military establishment, Japan, like the United States, had no single independent
air force. Its military air assets were distributed between its army and navy. Both the Imperial
Japanese Navy Air Force (IJNAF) and the Imperial Japanese Army Air Force (IJAAF) were
closely linked to their parent services, between which a bitter rivalry had always existed.

Many of the principal IJNAF aces would get their start in China. Among them was Tetsuzo
Iwamoto, who was the leading ace in the Second Sino-Japanese War and one of the top two in

the Pacific Theater of World War II. He began his career as a fighter pilot in early 1938 when he was assigned to the 12th Kokutai (12th Air Group). On February 25, he became the first Imperial Japanese Navy Air Force pilot to score five victories in a single day, and on April 29, he scored four in one day over Hankow. When Iwamoto returned to Japan in September 1938, he had flown 82 missions and had scored 14 victories.

Another IJNAF ace in the Sino-Japanese War was Kuniyoshi Tanaka. He scored 12 victories in China, flying with the 13th Kokutai. He and Iwamoto would be the only top China aces to add additional victories during World War II. As it would be in World War II, most of the aerial victories scored during the Sino-Japanese War were scored by IJNAF pilots.

However, the army pilots of the IJAAF would experience much more air combat in a few short months in an all-but-forgotten border war with the Soviets in 1938–1939 than the IJNAF did throughout the entire Sino-Japanese War.

This war, sometimes called the Second Russo-Japanese War, began with a Japanese incursion from Manchukuo into Soviet-controlled Mongolia, and involved the major battles of Lake Khasan in 1938 and at Khalkin Gol (the "Nomonhan Incident") in 1939. During the final phase of this war, while their brothers on the ground were being routed by the Soviets, the IJAAF pilots achieved air superiority over the vast, dusty dry steppes of central Asia. This little-remembered side show in Mongolia accounted for some of the fiercest aerial combat among all the minor conflicts that simmered on the eve of World War II, although few of the veterans of Mongolia were around to use their experience.

Japan took a major step toward World War II on September 27, 1940, when they signed the Tripartite Pact, or Triple Alliance, with Italy and Germany to form the Berlin-Tokyo-Rome Axis. Japan occupied former French Indochina as a spoil of war. The Japanese were beginning to expand their empire into Southeast Asia under the guise of the Greater East Asia Co Prosperity Sphere, by which Japan assumed a claim to occupy Indochina, Malaya, the Philippines and the Netherlands East Indies (now Indonesia). President Franklin Roosevelt, increasingly concerned about Japanese aggression, ended exports to the Empire and began to consider further sanctions. Japan viewed these actions as a major impediment to their plans to dominate the Far East and decided to take action.

On Sunday morning, December 7, 1941, IJNAF bombers launched from Japanese aircraft carriers struck at American military installations in Hawaii, particularly the naval base at Pearl Harbor. The attack was a complete surprise and an immense success for the attackers. The following day, President Roosevelt, calling December 7 "a day of infamy," asked Congress for a declaration of war. On December 11, Germany and Italy declared war against the United States and Japan declared war on Britain.

In the months following the attack on Pearl Harbor, the military successes achieved by the Japanese were reminiscent of the German blitzkrieg of 1939 and 1940. Within a month of Pearl Harbor, they had captured Wake Island, Guam and Hong Kong, and were marching toward the allegedly impregnable British fortress at Singapore. After landing in the Philippines, they seized control of Manila within a month.

During World War II, the IJAAF would see most of its action on the Asiatic mainland, while the IJNAF saw nearly all of its combat in the Pacific Theater and Southwest Pacific Theater. IJAAF aces were often eclipsed in prominence by their more well-known comrades in the islands. However, IJAAF aces would earn most of their victories over Burma and in China.

★
Kuniyoshi Tanaka of the Imperial Japanese Navy Air Force scored victories over China in the Sino-Japanese War and in the Pacific during World War II. *Kokutai Gallery*

The highest-scoring IJAAF ace was Master Sergeant Satoru Anabuki, who claimed 53 victories in his memoirs, but whose score was probably fewer. The second highest-scoring IJAAF ace was Isamu Sasaki who, like Anabuki, flew with the 50th Sentai in Burma. He scored 32 victories in Southeast Asia before being rotated back to the homeland. Flying air defense interception missions, Sasaki succeeded in shooting down six B-29s to bring his score to 38.

The victory scores for Japanese aces are somewhat ambiguous because of lost records, and because victories were officially attributed to groups rather than individuals, therefore meaning that individual scores were kept informally.

Thanks to their being assigned to the Pacific Theater, where air combat was more intense than over the Asiatic mainland, the pilots of the IJNAF included Japan's top seven aces. The top two were probably Hiroyoshi Nishizawa and Tetsuzo Iwamoto, who are discussed below.

Other top-scoring IJNAF aces included Shoichi Sugita, who is generally credited with 70; Hinomichi Shinohara with 58; Takeo Okumura with at least 54; Saburo Sakai, who had at least 28, but claimed 64; and Junichi Sasai with 27. The leading fighter unit in Japanese history was the Tainan Kokutai (Tainan Air Group), which was named for its original base at Tainan on the island of Taiwan (then known as Formosa). The Tainan Kokutai achieved its notoriety during early to mid-1942—when the IJNAF ruled the skies over the Southwest Pacific—while based at Lae on the island of New Guinea. The Tainan Kokutai brought some of the best fighter pilots in the Imperial Japanese Navy Air Force together in what was probably the most elite Japanese fighter group to exist during the war. Especially notable about the Tainan Kokutai in 1942 was the fact that four of Japan's top aces—Nishizawa, Sakai, Sasai, and Okumura—were all assigned to it at the same time.

★
Isamu Sasaki was the number two ace of the Imperial Japanese Army Air Force. *Kokutai Gallery*

★
Pilots of the legendary Tainan Kokutai of the Imperial Japanese Navy assemble at their base at Lae on New Guinea during the peak of their prowess in June 1942. This air group included more aces than any other Japanese unit. The first two in the middle row are Toshio Ota (34 victories) and Saburo Sakai (64 victories). Hiroyoshi Nishizawa, seen at upper left, was Japan's top ace ever, with at least 87 victories, though he may have scored more than 100. *Wikimedia Commons*

# ANABUKI:
## TOP IJAAF ACE

**BORN IN 1921,** Satoru Anabuki joined the Imperial Japanese Army Air Force late in 1941 and was assigned to the 50th Sentai (Fighter Group) flying a Nakajima Ki-27. Anabuki first saw action in the Philippines during the Japanese invasion in December 1941, where he claimed three American aircraft.

In 1942, the 50th Sentai was reassigned to action in Burma and reequipped with the fast and maneuverable Nakajima Ki-43 Hayabusa (peregrine falcon). Known by the Allied code name "Oscar," the Ki-43 was produced in larger numbers than any other Imperial Japanese Army Air Force fighter, and it was very effective until improved Allied aircraft reached the field in 1943.

It was in Burma, between June 1942 and October 1943, that Satoru Anabuki shot down 13 American and 28 Royal Air Force aircraft. On January 26, 1943, he became possibly the first Japanese pilot in Southeast Asia to bring down a Consolidated B-24 Liberator strategic bomber. On October 8, 1943, Anabuki had his best day ever, shooting down three B-24s and a pair of P-38 fighters in a single action near Rangoon. Having exhausted his ammunition shooting down these five, Anabuki rammed the tail of a third B-24 and then crash-landed his Hayabusa. In the Japanese armed forces, decorations for heroism were almost never given to individuals and especially not to living individuals. The theory was that heroism was a team effort and that individual heroism—when it occurred—was defined by a person sacrificing his life. Nevertheless, Satoru Anabuki's actions on October 8, 1943 were so outstanding that he was decorated.

He is also credited with developing an air combat tactic known as "The Anabuki Run," which was widely used throughout the Imperial Japanese Army Air Force. In this move, a pilot who is attacked from behind, pulls up, rolls his fighter into an inverted position, then dives vertically, opening fire at 300 feet.

In 1945, Anabuki returned to Japan to fly air defense missions, piloting the new Nakajima Ki-100 fighter. This fighter, one of the best high-altitude interceptors flown during the war, was the last production aircraft put into service by the IJAAF, but only a handful saw action. Anabuki's last victory came during an air defense mission in June 1945 when he shot down a Boeing B-29 Superfortress, a far more formidable foe than the B-24 Liberator of two years before.

Satoru Anabuki's final score was probably around 39, but he claimed 53 in his 1985 memoirs.

★
Satoru (Satoshi) Anabuki was the highest-scoring ace in the Imperial Japanese Army Air Force. *Kokutai Gallery*

# NISHIZAWA AND IWAMOTO:
## THE TWO AT THE TOP

**OF THE LEADING PAIR IN THE PANTHEON OF JAPANESE ACES**, Hiroyoshi Nishizawa and Tetsuzo Iwamoto, the latter was already an ace twice over before the war even started. He had scored his initial victories against the Chinese in the Sino-Japanese War, and he would go on to be the top-scoring Imperial Japanese Navy Air Force ace to serve aboard an Imperial Japanese Navy aircraft carrier. He was also the only one of the top Pacific Theater aces who flew on the opening day of World War II in the Pacific—December 7, 1941.

Tetsuzo Iwamoto's career as a fighter pilot began in early 1938 when he was assigned to the 12th Kokutai to fly Mitsubishi A5M fighters against the Soviet-built Polikarpov I-16s of the Kuomintang Chinese Air Force during the assault on Hankow. On February 25, he became the first Imperial Japanese Navy Air Force pilot to score five victories in a single day, and on April 29, he scored four in one day over Hankow. When Tetsuzo Iwamoto returned to Japan in September 1938, he had flown 82 missions and scored 14 victories.

During the coming years, Iwamoto became part of Japan's ambitious plan to create aircraft carrier battle groups for offensive operations in the Pacific. In 1941, having made the transition from the clumsy Mitsubishi A5M to the exceptional A6M, Tetsuzo Iwamoto was assigned to the Fifth Carrier Division, specifically to the Zuikaku Kokutai aboard the carrier Zuikaku, whose sister ship Shokaku was also part of the Fifth Carrier Division. The Zuikaku was commissioned on September 25, 1941 and underwent a shakedown cruise in the Kobe and Kure area, moving out to Oita and Saeki.

On November 26, Zuikaku was added to Vice Admiral Nagumo Chuichi's First Air Fleet, which departed from Hittokapu Bay in the Kurile Islands to be part of the four-carrier task force destined for the attack on Pearl Harbor, Hawaii. On December 7, the fighters of the Zuikaku Kokutai and Shokaku Kokutai escorted the bombers against the Pearl Harbor Naval Base and other targets, engaging the Americans who rose to intercept them.

After the Pearl Harbor raid, the Japanese task force withdrew quickly, returning to Japan on December 23. Zuikaku sailed for the island fortress of Truk on January 8, 1942 and moved south to provide air support for Japanese operations against Rabaul and Lae on January 21. During the first week of February, the Zuikaku was part of a strike force operating against American shipping in the Marshall Islands, after which it returned to the Yokosuka Naval Base in Japan by way of Truk.

After a layover in Japan through early March, it sailed for air attack operations in the Indian Ocean with First Air Fleet, Carrier Division 5. On April 5 and April 9, Zuikaku launched air strikes against the cities of Colombo and Trincomalee in the British colony of Ceylon (now Sri Lanka). In the latter attack, Tetsuzo Iwamoto added four Royal Air Force aircraft to his

日本 西澤広義

撃墜王 厳本善治

★ [Above]
Hiroyoshi Nishizawa of the Imperial Japanese Navy Air Force was probably Japan's top ace of all time. Having scored as many as 102 aerial victories, he died when the transport aircraft in which he was a passenger was shot down. *Kokutai Gallery*

★ [Below]
Tetsuzo Iwamoto of the Imperial Japanese Navy Air Force scored at least 80 aerial victories, but some sources credit him with more than 100. He and Hiroyoshi Nishizawa were almost certainly Japan's top two aces. *Kokutai Gallery*

score. On April 19, the Zuikaku began operations in the Coral Sea which would culminate in its involvement in the Battle of the Coral Sea on May 7 and 8, 1942. This battle was a milestone in the history of aircraft carrier operations in that it was the first battle in naval history conducted by air. The ships of the opposing combatants were not visible to one another. For his part, Tetsuzo Iwamoto claimed two American aircraft. Though losses were heavy and it was not a victory for either side, it was a moral victory for the US Navy because it was the first major operation since the beginning of the war in which Japan did not win decisively.

Her sister carrier Shokaku was badly damaged in the Battle of the Coral Sea, but the Zuikaku managed to slip away into a rainstorm. The Zuikaku Kokutai, however, took severe losses in terms of both pilots and aircraft, and the ship was forced to sail for Japan to take on replacements. As such, the Zuikaku missed the Battle of Midway, which was a major defeat for the Imperial Japanese Navy, a rout that cost the Japanese four of its carriers—Akagi, Hiryu, Kaga and Soryu—along with nearly 300 aircraft and many of its best pilots. The losses represented more than a third of Japan's carrier strength. On July 14, 1942, Zuikaku would receive a new assignment as part of the Striking Force, of the Third Fleet's Carrier Division 1, but she would be in drydock until August 12 and unable to get into action.

It was in early August 1942 that the US Marines had landed on the island of Guadalcanal in the Solomon Islands, so the Third Fleet's Carrier Division 1 and the Zuikaku were ordered south to take part in operations in the eastern Solomons. The force would remain in combat in the Solomons area essentially continuously for the next two months, taking part in Guadalcanal operations and the Battle of Santa Cruz on October 26, where she was bombed, but undamaged. On October 30, Zuikaku returned to Truk and then back to Yokosuka by way of the naval base at Kure.

For Tetsuzo Iwamoto, the Solomon Islands action would mark an end to his career as a carrier pilot, but he returned to the same area as part of the land-based Imperial Japanese Navy Air Force 281st Kokutai. In November 1943, he was transferred to the 204th Kokutai, based ashore at Rabaul, New Britain.

During his first month with the 204th Kokutai, Tetsuzo Iwamoto is credited with 15 victories and five probables, including three Curtiss SB2C bombers and a pair each of Lockheed P-38 and Bell P-39 fighters. On December 10, he claimed a pair of Vought F4U Corsairs and four bombers.

In February 1944, having painted another 25 kill marks on his Zero, Tetsuzo Iwamoto was reassigned to the 253rd Kokutai to fly air defense for the big Imperial Japanese Navy base at Truk. On March 6, he destroyed five Consolidated B-24 Liberator strategic bombers in one of the most dramatic attacks in the history of aerial combat. With one swift blow, Iwamoto dropped a phosphorous bomb on one Liberator, igniting its bombs in a fireball that consumed the other four aircraft.

After reassignment to Japan, where he was finally promoted to lieutenant, Tetsuzo Iwamoto was assigned briefly to the 252nd Kokutai in the Philippines in October 1944. Coincidentally, the Zuikaku was sunk on October 25, 1944, during the Battle off Cape Engano. She was the last surviving carrier of those that took part in the attack on Pearl Harbor.

By this time, Japan's home islands were starting to come under attack, and a man of Tetsuzo Iwamoto's skill was considered to be an important asset in the air defense of his homeland. He was assigned to the 203rd Kokutai, an air defense interceptor unit. By this time, attacks against Japan's major cities were an almost nightly occurrence. With the 203rd Kokutai, Tetsuzo Iwamoto scored 23 victories between February and April 1945, including seven American fighters on February 16 alone.

On April 6, 1945, when the Imperial Japanese Navy super-battleship Yamato was sent against the US Navy forces off Okinawa, the 203rd Kokutai was assigned to provide air cover. The 64,000-ton Yamato and her sister ship Musashi carried 18-inch guns and were the largest battleships ever built. The big ship was, ironically, sunk by US Navy air power before ever firing a shot at another capital ship, but during the air attack, Tetsuzo Iwamoto succeeded in shooting down three F4U Corsairs and three F6F Hellcats. Tetsuzo Iwamoto would not live to see the end of World War II, but his final combined score of 94 in China and the Pacific is generally accepted as having made him Japan's highest-scoring ace overall.

Not counting his 14 in China, however, Iwamoto's score of 80 during World War II is second to the 87 that were scored by Hiroyoshi Nishizawa, the top-scoring Japanese ace of World War II.

Nishizawa was a sullen loner. He was an unassuming man who was ill at ease on the ground. Almost sickly in appearance, Hiroyoshi Nishizawa was a man who one hardly noticed in a group, but when he got into the air he suddenly became—as Saburo Sakai remembers—"The Devil." For him flying was less second nature than first nature. He flew with the best units in the Imperial Japanese Navy Air Force during the intense early days of the war and he achieved the best record of any pilot of any nation in the Pacific Theater of World War II.

This pilot who was called "The Devil" even by his comrades, was born on January 27, 1927, the son of a sake brewer in rural Nagano Prefecture. He left school in his mid-teens to work in a textile factory, but in 1936, he decided on a whim to volunteer to become an aviation trainee with the Imperial Japanese Navy Air Force. He earned his wings in 1939 and served with several air groups in Japan over the ensuing two years, winding up in 1941 at the Chitose Air Base with the Chitose Kokutai (Chitose Air Group). During these years, he never tasted the action that all the young men of his generation craved. He was never assigned to units that were then in combat in China, nor did he participate in the attack on Pearl Harbor in December 1941, or the subsequent offensive operations in Southeast Asia.

While the high profile activities of the Imperial Japanese Navy Air Force were the carrier actions against Pearl Harbor and later at the battles of Midway and the Coral Sea, most of the Imperial Japanese Navy Air Force fighter groups were actually based on land in such areas as the Solomon Islands, New Guinea and the Philippines. In January 1942, the Chitose Kokutai was assigned to the newly captured air base at Rabaul on New Britain. Now a petty officer, first class, Hiroyoshi Nishizawa claimed his first aerial victory on February 3 in an A5M, although the Royal

Australian Air Force Catalina that he thought he shot down had actually survived.

The unit would soon make the transition from the Mitsubishi A5M to the Mitsubishi A6M Zero. By March, the Zeros of the Chitose Kokutai were incorporated into the larger 4th Kokutai headed for New Guinea. Here, where the air war in the Southwest Pacific would soon be the most intense, Nishizawa was able to prove himself in several air battles, as 4th Kokutai Zeros tangled with USAAF and RAAF fighters.

Strategically, the Japanese high command had decided to capture the island of New Guinea as a steppingstone to neutralizing Australia, and this set the stage for the vicious fighting that would result in many significant combat actions over the next two years.

In early March 1942 the Japanese captured Lae on the northern coast of the island, and established a major—albeit crude—air base. A further reorganization of the Imperial Japanese Navy Air Force resulted in the fighter units of the 4th Kokutai being incorporated into the Tainan Kokutai.

During April and May, the Tainan Kokutai flew numerous missions—mainly against the big Allied base at Port Moresby on the opposite side of New Guinea—escorting bombers and conducting fighter sweeps aimed at drawing Allied fighters into dogfights. In the latter, the A6M Zeros of the Tainan Kokutai often achieved decisive victories over superior numbers of Allied P-39 Airacobras and P-40 Warhawks. Nishizawa was an ace twice over by the summer of 1942, claiming five P-39s between June 1 and July 4 alone.

Meanwhile, on May 17, in an account that is vividly described by Sakai in his 1957 book *Samurai*, he, Nishizawa and Ota brazenly flew a series of aerobatic maneuvers—including six tight close formation loops—over the Allied field at Port Moresby. The Allied gunners, apparently stunned by this audacious display, didn't fire a shot at the trio.

The spring and summer of 1942 were the best of times for the pilots of the Imperial Japanese Navy Air Force and its Tainan Kokutai. They flew a superior aircraft, they had better training, and they had the Allied air forces thoroughly outclassed in every regard. Japan was still on the offensive, and the eventual Allied superiority in numbers, equipment and training had not yet begun to manifest itself.

Only the formidable Boeing B-17 Flying Fortresses, with their bristling defensive armament proved to be an obstacle. By August, however, Nishizawa and Sakai developed the tactic of attacking them head-on, and after that, even the Fortresses were just huge sitting ducks for the Zeros of the Tainan Kokutai.

It was in early August 1942, when the US Marines landed on the island of Guadalcanal in the Solomon Islands, that the Tainan Kokutai was relocated to Rabaul, New Britain. Initially, the level of air superiority that the Tainan Kokutai and the Imperial Japanese Navy Air Force had enjoyed in New Guinea would continue, but soon it would begin to fade, never to be seen again.

On August 7, in the Tainan Kokutai's first battle with US Navy carrier-based fighters after arriving back at Rabaul, Hiroyoshi Nishizawa shot down six Grumman F4F Wildcats, primarily of VF-5, based on the USS *Saratoga*. The score for the Tainan Kokutai for the day would include at least nine F4Fs and a Douglas SBD Dauntless dive bomber.

The air battle raged over Guadalcanal through September and October, with Nishizawa and the Tainan Kokutai being forced to battle larger and larger numbers of US Navy and US Marine Corps aircraft. In November, the Tainan Kokutai was redesignated as the 251st Kokutai and strengthened for a struggle that would continue until February, when Japanese troops were finally withdrawn from Guadalcanal. It was a major psychological blow to the Japanese, who had, a year earlier, been virtually invincible.

After the evacuation of Guadalcanal, Nishizawa was out of action until May 7, 1943, when the 251st Kokutai was sent back to Rabaul. It was on June 7 that Hiroyoshi Nishizawa shot down his first Vought F4U Corsair on a fighter sweep over Guadalcanal. In October, after a brief assignment to the 253rd Kokutai, Nishizawa was promoted to warrant officer and rotated back to Japan. He would remain in the home islands, essentially out of action, for a year. By this time, he is reported to have achieved a total of 85 aerial victories.

While in Japan, Hiroyoshi Nishizawa spent time training recruits at Atsugi Air Base—a task which he disliked, because there was no longer time to give them the level of training that he had received—and patrolling the Kurile Islands north of Japan waiting for American air attacks from Alaska. These patrols were endlessly boring because the attacks, which Japanese intelligence was sure were imminent, never came.

When American forces invaded the Japanese-occupied American Commonwealth of the Philippines in October 1944, Nishizawa was sent back into the fray at last. He was assigned to the 201st Kokutai, which was sent to the island of Cebu to help defend Japanese occupation forces being pounded by American bombers.

By now, the shortage of good pilots in the IJNAF, combined with ever-growing American strength, led the Imperial Japanese Navy to resort to the desperate option of sending inexperienced pilots on suicide missions. Under the kamikaze (divine wind) doctrine, it was believed that the suicide pilots were religiously inspired heroes of the highest order. Experienced pilots were assigned to escort the novices on their one-way missions.

On October 25, Nishizawa was chosen to provide a fighter escort for what was to be the first kamikaze attack against American ships. The attack succeeded in sinking the carrier USS *St. Lo*, and Nishizawa shot down two Grumman F6F Hellcats in his first and last air duel with the US Navy's premier fleet air defense fighter.

Later that day, Nishizawa reportedly had a premonition of his own death and requested to fly a kamikaze mission himself. His request was denied because his skill as a fighter pilot was still needed by the Imperial Japanese Navy Air Force.

The following day, October 26, 1944, Hiroyoshi Nishizawa and several other 201st Kokutai fighter pilots were to be ferried north to Clark Field on the island of Luzon to pick up several A6M Zeros, which they were to fly back to Cebu. Having imagined his own death, Japan's leading ace was flying as a passenger in a transport and not at the controls of a fighter.

There are different versions of what happened that morning. Nishizawa may have been piloting the aircraft or just a passenger. The aircraft may have been a twin-engine Nakajima Ki-49 bomber or (according to Saburo Sakai) an unarmed DC-3 airliner. In either case, the aircraft was attacked by a pair of Hellcats and shot down. There were no survivors.

Hiroyoshi Nishizawa was posthumously promoted to lieutenant (junior grade). The final score of Japan's top-scoring ace in World War II was 87 victories, with 85 of them between February 1942 and October 1943. As noted above, this placed him second in Japanese history to Tetsuzo Iwamoto, who scored a generally accepted 80 during World War II, plus 14 in China for a total of 94. However, each man is mentioned in various sources as having claimed more than 200.

# SAKAI: THE MAN WHO LIVED TO TELL THE TALE

**SABURO SAKAI WAS JAPAN'S THIRD (SOME SOURCES WOULD SAY FOURTH) HIGHEST-SCORING ACE IN WORLD WAR II**, but he is best remembered for being the only major Japanese ace to live to tell about his experiences during the war.

He was born on August 26, 1916 in Saga, on Kyushu, the southernmost main island of Japan. Ironically, for a man who was at home in the sky, he enlisted in the Imperial Japanese Navy, envisioning a life at sea. He was mustered in at Sasebo Naval Base in May 1933 as a seaman recruit, and in 1935 was assigned as a gunner's mate aboard the battleship Haruna. Two years later, as a petty officer, third class, he applied for and was accepted into the naval flight training program at Tsuchiura. As noted above, Imperial Japanese Navy Air Force flight training was the most demanding in the world at this time. The numbers of students who would pass the course were relatively few, but their quality was extremely high.

Saburo Sakai became a naval aviator in July 1937 and was assigned to various units within Japan before being sent into action in the Sino-Japanese War in May 1938. Based at Kiukiang in China, Sakai flew the clumsy Mitsubishi A5M open-cockpit fighter, escorting bombers against targets such as Hankow. It was on one such mission that he scored his first victory, against a Soviet-built Polikarpov I-16 of the Kuomintang Chinese Air Force.

Sakai would spend the next year in Japan, leisurely training to fly the new Mitsubishi A6M Zero fighter. There was still no particular urgency to Japanese pilot training. In May 1941, Sakai returned to Hankow for more missions against the Kuomintang. After having scored his first two victories in an A6M, Sakai was transferred to the Tainan Kokutai which was being formed at Tainan on the island of Formosa. It was here that IJNAF units began to prepare for the invasion of the American Commonwealth of the Philippines.

On December 7, 1941 (December 8 across the International Dateline in Taiwan and the Philippines), the IJNAF attacked the United States Naval Base at Pearl Harbor Hawaii, with simultaneous raids being launched from Taiwan against the Philippines. The Tainan Kokutai and accompanying bombers struck at Clark Field, the big American air base on Luzon, and Saburo Sakai scored his first victory against the Americans, a USAAF P-40 Warhawk.

Three days later, he shot down a B-17 piloted by Captain Colin P. Kelly, who had, according to American media reports, just sunk the battleship Haruna, coincidently, the same ship on which Sakai had served as a seaman. In fact, the Haruna was not in the area and Kelly had missed, not sunk, the heavy cruiser Ashigara, off Aparri, Luzon. Nevertheless, Kelly was posthumously awarded the first Medal of Honor of World War II, and he would become a patriotic rallying point for Americans.

★
Saburo Sakai was one of the top half-dozen aces of the Imperial Japanese Navy Air Force. His best-selling memoir *Samurai* was published in 1957. *Kokutai Gallery*

After the Imperial Japanese Navy Air Force had destroyed the USAAF units in the Philippines, the Tainan Kokutai was sent into the Netherlands East Indies to support the Japanese offensive in this area. Here, Sakai enjoyed a remarkable series of victories flying his A6M Zero against American and Dutch aircraft, mainly Brewster Buffalos and Curtiss P-36s and P-40s.

In April 1942, the Tainan Kokutai was sent to a crude airfield, recently captured at Lae, New Guinea. Strategically, the Japanese high command had decided to capture the island of New Guinea as a steppingstone to neutralizing Australia, and this set the stage for vicious fighting that would result in many significant combat actions over the next two years.

As discussed above, it was at Lae that some of the best fighter pilots in the Imperial Japanese Navy Air Force were brought together in the Tainan Kokutai, transforming it into Japan's ultimate fighter unit.

During April and May, the Tainan Kokutai flew numerous missions—mainly against the big Allied base at Port Moresby on the opposite side of New Guinea—escorting bombers and conducting fighter sweeps aimed at drawing Allied fighters into dogfights. In the latter, the A6M Zeros of the Tainan Kokutai often achieved decisive victories over superior numbers of Allied P-39 Airacobras and P-40 Warhawks, as well as against B-25 Mitchell and B-26 Marauder medium bombers that ventured to attack Lae and other Japanese positions on New Guinea. Both Hiroyoshi Nishizawa and Saburo Sakai were aces twice over by the summer of 1942.

In early August 1942, when the US Marines landed on Guadalcanal, the reinforcements sent by the Japanese included the Tainan Kokutai, which was based at Rabaul, New Britain. On August 7, when the Tainan Kokutai was assigned to escort a bomber force headed for Guadalcanal, the force was attacked over the target by a large number of Grumman F4F Wildcats. They proved to be among the most skilled opposition that the Tainan Kokutai had encountered, but Nishizawa destroyed six and Sakai shot down a Wildcat and a Douglas SBD Dauntless, his 59th and 60th victories.

Sakai then engaged eight Grumman TBF Avenger torpedo bombers, which he had never seen before, and which he mistook for Grumman Wildcats, because of the general similarity that might be expected of two single-engine types from the same manufacturer. A principal difference, which he had not counted on, was that the Avengers had a rear-facing gunner that could fire at an attacker coming in from behind.

Sakai shot down two TBFs, but the rear gunners in the remaining six badly damaged his Zero, and the battering that he took knocked him unconscious. He regained consciousness before the aircraft hit the water, and managed to recover it, although he was blinded in one eye and his vision in the other was seriously impaired. He had suffered severe head wounds and the left side of his body was paralyzed, but somehow he managed to keep the Zero in the air, navigate for more than 500 miles and land at Rabaul.

Having suffered wounds that should have killed him, Saburo Sakai was sent back to Japan, where a series of operations saved one of his eyes and repaired much of the remaining damage to his body. In April 1943, when he was finally released from the hospital, he begged to be allowed to fly again, and was assigned as an instructor at Omura Air Base.

Had the IJNAF not become desperately short of combat-experienced pilots, Saburo Sakai would probably never have seen combat again. A year after being released from the hospital, the partially-blind ace was transferred to the Yokosuka Kokutai at the huge naval base at Yokosuka. This kokutai was sent to Iwo Jima in June 1944 to fend off the American invasion that was expected imminently, but which would not materialize until February 1945. Ironically, an invasion in June 1944 would have caught the Japanese totally unprepared. But by February, they had turned the volcanic island into a virtually impregnable fortress that would cost the Americans over 6,000 men.

It was on June 24 that Sakai had his initial opportunity to duel with the Grumman F6F Hellcat, the US Navy fighter that was the first such aircraft to have a clear superiority over the Zero. A force of 40 Zeros engaged a large number of Hellcats. Sakai shot down one of the F6Fs, but barely eluded being shot down by others in what was his first aerial combat in nearly two years. In a further action, he shot down another Hellcat, but the Iwo Jima defenders were badly mauled by the US Navy. They were withdrawn to Yokosuka to prepare for the defense of Japan.

Beginning in September 1944, Sakai, now promoted to ensign, test flew a number of advanced fighter aircraft, including both the Kyushu J7W Shinden and the Mitsubishi J2M Raiden. In June 1945, he would test-fly the successor to the great Zero, the Mitsubishi A7M Reppu. However, he was never to fly these aircraft, all designed to match or better the Hellcat, in combat. His last combat mission came on the night of August 13, 1945, less that 48 hours before the announcement of Japan's unconditional surrender. He was part of a 10-ship formation of Yokosuka Kokutai Zeros that downed what they thought was a Boeing B-29 Superfortress, but was actually a Convair B-32 Dominator.

Saburo Sakai's final score—excluding the shared kill of the B-32—is seen listed variously as 62 or 64, although it may have been much higher. After the war, Sakai worked as a day laborer for nearly a decade before scraping together the money to start a small printing company. The 1956 publication of his autobiography *Samurai* (co-authored with Martin Caidin and Fred Saito) brought him worldwide notoriety and provided a valuable account of the Japanese side of the air war in the Pacific.

The choice of the word "samurai" was a good one. Nothing exemplifies the attitude of Japan's World War II fighter pilots better than the code of the samurai, the classical Japanese warrior. This code is known as bushido, dates back to the twelfth century, and exemplifies in the samurai, the same kind of dedication to duty and honor as the code of chivalry that has defined European knighthood since the Middle Ages.

# THE SOVIET UNION

**W**HEN RANKING THE AIR FORCES OF WORLD WAR II, that of the Soviet Union must be, without dispute, listed as "most improved." From the moment the Germans invaded in June 1941 to the moment of Germany's final surrender in May 1945, the Soviet Air Force (Voenno Vozdushnie Sily or VVS) went from being a cadre of ineffective pilots in vulnerable, obsolete aircraft to a well-oiled and formidable force. Within VVS, the principal tactical organization for fighter operations was the Fighter Regiment (Istrebitel'naya Aviatsiya Protivovozdushnoi or IAP). Throughout the Soviet armed forces, organizations that distinguished themselves valiantly in combat received a designation as a "Guards" (Gvardiya) unit. As the war went on, many IAPs were honored (and renumbered) with a "Guards IAP" designation.

Part of the reason for the lack of preparedness on the part of the VVS in 1941 lay at the feet of the enigmatic, capricious and contradictory man who was the Soviet Union's absolute leader.

Josef Vissarionovich Djugashvili, who took the name "Stalin," meaning "man of steel," had a greed for absolute power that led him to undertake a series of purges that resulted in the execution or imprisonment of tens of thousands of the best and the brightest individuals in Soviet society and government—and in the armed forces.

In aviation, Stalin was a proponent of dramatic stunts rather than building a first-rate indigenous aviation industry. The 1930s in the Soviet Union are remembered for long, dramatic, record-setting flights and large, pretentious aircraft. This, he felt, was good publicity for the Communist economic experiment that he was compelling his people to endure. However, the level of quality seen in the front line aircraft of Germany, Britain and the United States in the late 1930s was never matched, or even approached, in most prewar Soviet aircraft.

Even before World War II, the ideological rivalry between Fascism and Communism—and between two obsessive nationalists, Adolf Hitler and Josef Stalin—erupted into warfare on and over the dusty, yellow hills of Spain. Stalin felt obligated to intervene in 1936 when Hitler sent covert forces to assist the Fascists in the Spanish Civil War. The VVS found itself fighting the Luftwaffe's Condor Legion in what was to be a dress rehearsal of the air combat that would take place on the Eastern Front during World War II. The Soviets, in their primitive, open-cockpit Polikarpov I-15s and I-16s, were no match for the German Condor Legion pilots in their Bf 109s, and Stalin was forced to withdraw the VVS in 1938.

This was not before several of the Polikarpov pilots achieved ace status flying against the Fascists and their Condor Legion comrades. Anatoli Serov—better known as "Carlos Castejon"—the top-scoring Soviet ace, scored 16, including the first night fighter kill of the conflict. Pavel Rychagov—who flew under the name "Pablo Palencar"—had 15 victories. The highest-scoring VVS ace to add to victories in Spain with further kills in World War II was Vladimir Bobrov, who scored 13 victories against the Germans in the Spanish Civil War before increasing his count to 43 in the later conflict.

In the little-known border conflict between the Soviet Union and Japan that took place in Mongolia during the summers of 1938 and 1939, the Imperial Japanese Army Air Force

thoroughly outfought the VVS. Nevertheless, several Soviet pilots managed to achieve ace status. The highest-scoring among them was Grigori Kravchenko, who scored 15 kills flying a Polikarpov I-16.

On August 24, 1939, Stalin stunned the world—especially his staunch socialist friends in the West who had supported him against the Fascists in Spain—by signing a nonaggression pact with the Hitler. This gave Stalin's rival the flexibility that he needed to initiate the mischief that rapidly became World War II. A week later, on September 1, the German army invaded Poland. Britain and France issued ultimatums because their mutual assistance treaties with Poland called for them to finally take action to halt Hitler's aggression. The Soviet Union quickly occupied half of Poland as its bonus for Stalin's pact with Hitler, but otherwise remained on the sidelines for nearly two years, while the German juggernaut consumed Europe.

Despite Stalin's innate brutality and paranoia—not to mention his hatred for Hitler—the Soviet Union was totally unprepared when Germany suddenly launched its invasion on June 22, 1941. For the Soviets, World War II was now the Great Patriotic War.

Known as Operation Barbarossa, the German attack advanced swiftly on all fronts. The VVS lost over 4,000 aircraft in the first week alone, many of them on the ground. In the early days of the German onslaught, the Soviet defenders were brutally hurled back into Mother Russia and the Luftwaffe swept through the VVS like it was swatting flies. Flying relatively primitive Mikoyan-Gurevich MiG-3s and the Polikarpov I-16s, the Soviet Union's air arm was ill-equipped to deal with the Luftwaffe's Messerschmitt Bf 109s. Nowhere were they able to challenge the Luftwaffe successfully.

It was to be the same story on the ground until December, when the severity of the Russian winter finally stalled the German invaders at the gates of Moscow. For the great Luftwaffe, the weather was so cold that engine oil congealed and the engines refused to turn over. The combination of the Russian winter and the armed resistance of the Russian military forced a retreat. However, in the spring of 1942, the Germans counterattacked, successfully regaining much—albeit not all—of what they had lost. The city of Stalingrad—named for the dictator himself—became the symbol of Soviet resistance. When the Soviets defeated the Germans and captured the entire German Sixth Army in January 1943, it was a psychological and military triumph that marked the turning point in the Great Patriotic War.

For the VVS, the initial losses in Barbarossa would cost it 74 percent of its combat strength, but most of its pilots survived because the aircraft were caught on the ground. At the same time, the VVS didn't lose very many first-rate, modern combat aircraft, because Stalin's iron-handed central economic planning hadn't produced very many.

The Soviet Army, aided by the respite afforded by the bitter Russian Winter, was able to rebuild itself in time for the 1942 Spring Offensive, and so too was the VVS. A number of factors contributed to the phoenix-like rebirth of the VVS. One was a pragmatic flexibility in developing tactics, and another was the ability of the VVS to replace losses. With virtually unlimited manpower and open space, the Soviet Union was able to quickly build new factories out of reach of the advancing Germans, and these turned out a new generation of warplanes— especially the fighter aircraft that were designed by the Lavochkin and Yakovlev design bureaus.

★
Boris Safonov, who flew with Soviet Naval Aviation, was the first Soviet ace of World War II. He had 25 victories at the time he was killed in action in March 1942. *Wikimedia Commons*

At the same time, American Lend Lease aircraft were starting to make their way to the Eastern Front via Alaska by the summer of 1942. Notable among the American-made Lend Lease aircraft was the Bell P-39 Airacobra, an aircraft that would ironically be more important to the VVS than to the USAAF.

Finally, the VVS was able to rebuild itself through an influx of thousands of brave and dedicated men—and women—who became its combat pilots. Many of these people were merely schoolchildren during the purges of the 1930s and felt an allegiance to their "Rodina" (Motherland) rather than to Stalin and his cronies. Indeed, many of the fighter pilots who became the top aces of the VVS were still in school when the Soviet Union was invaded in 1941.

There were at least 60—and possibly four times that number—Soviet aces during the Great Patriotic War, and at least 16 who matched or outscored America's top ace, Dick Bong, who had 40 victories. At the head of this list was Ivan Kozhedub, whose 62 kills made him the deadliest combat pilot of any nation who fought against the Axis in the global war that raged between 1939 and 1945.

The first Soviet pilot to achieve ace status through victories scored during the Great Patriotic War was probably Boris Safonov, a naval aviator whose unit was later incorporated into the VVS. He scored his first victory, a Heinkel He 111, on June 24, 1941. His unit converted from I-16s to Lend Lease Hawker Hurricanes and later American-made Curtiss P-40 Warhawks. On May 30, 1942, flying one of the latter, he scored two victories while flying top cover for a British convoy bound for Murmansk. This brought his score to 25, but it was the day his luck ran out. His engine was hit and he crashed into the Arctic Ocean. Safonov was the first fighter pilot to be awarded the Rodina's top decoration for bravery—the Hero of the Soviet Union—twice.

★
A bust of Alexander Pokryshkin, the second-place Soviet ace of World War II is adjacent to that of Kozhedub in the Museum of the Great Patriotic War in Moscow's Victory Park. *Bill Yenne Photo*

# KOZHEDUB: THE SOVIET UNION'S ACE OF ACES

**BORN IN 1920**, Ivan Nikitich Kozhedub was the leading Soviet ace of all time and one of only five men in history to earn the Hero of the Soviet Union three times. He was part of the second generation of Soviet fighter pilots to see action during the Great Patriotic War. Only 21 years old when Germany invaded the Soviet Union in June 1941, Kozhedub was unlike the pilots who were just a few years older than he, those who had firsthand experience with Stalin's dreadful purges of the Soviet armed forces during the 1930s, and who would experience the desperate battles of 1941–1942, when the Red Air Force was hopelessly outclassed by the German Luftwaffe.

Ivan Kozhedub had enlisted in 1940 and qualified for flight training in 1941, even as the German armies were sweeping eastward across the borders of the Soviet Union. Because of his natural abilities as a pilot, he was kept on as a flight instructor after his training. This was a source of great frustration and disappointment for him because of his eagerness to get into the field in a combat unit, but it meant that by the time he actually did get into the field, the tide of the Great Patriotic War had turned in favor of the Soviet Union.

Kozhedub watched nearly two long years of war go by before he finally got his wish for a combat unit assignment in March 1943. However, his first major combat action did not come until July. This coincided with the great battles in the Kursk salient, which turned out to be some of the largest armed clashes in human history.

Ivan Kozhedub scored his first aerial victory on July 6 when his squadron, led by a Major Soldatienko, spotted a group of 20 Junkers Ju 87 Stuka dive bombers attacking a Soviet ground position near Kursk. Kozhedub downed one of the Stukas that day and added another seven to his total through July 16. In August 1943 Ivan Kozhedub was promoted to squadron commander and, by the first week of November, his score stood at 26. He was awarded his first Hero of the Soviet Union decoration on February 4, 1944.

Early in 1944, Kozhedub was transferred to the elite 176th Guards IAP, a rapid-reaction unit that was designed specifically to be moved at any time to any place on the front where air superiority was especially critical.

One such place was the sky over the Dnieper front, and the 176th Guards IAP arrived to take charge of this aerial battlefield. It was here that Kozhedub was to down 11 German aircraft in the space of just ten days. In April 1944 he shot down three in one day, and his second Hero of the Soviet Union came on August 19, 1944, in the wake of his 34th victory.

By the beginning of 1945, the Soviet Army and Air Force were clearly on the offensive. Ivan Kozhedub was now the vice commander of the 176th Guards IAP, and still taking his toll on the Luftwaffe. In February 1945, having traded his Lavochkin La 5 for the lighter, more powerful and much improved Lavochkin La 7, Kozhedub was possibly the first Soviet pilot to fight and shoot down a Messerschmitt Me 262 jet fighter.

When the war ended, Ivan Kozhedub had completed 326 missions and was the top scoring Soviet ace. He was officially credited with 62 victories, although some sources suggest that his score may actually have been in excess of 70. The official total included 22 Focke-Wulf Fw 190s, 19 Messerschmitt Bf 109s, 18 Ju 87s and various bomber types, as well as the Messerschmitt Me 262. His third Hero of the Soviet Union was awarded on August 18, 1945.

After the war ended, Kozhedub remained in the Red Air Force and attended the Zhukovski Military Aviation Academy. Meanwhile, he also remained active as a fighter pilot, making the transition from the piston-powered Lavochkins, to the MiG-15 jet fighter, which was arguably the best fighter in the world in the late 1940s.

★
One of the actual Lavochkin La-7 fighters flown in combat by Ivan Kozhedub. It is preserved at the Central Air Force Museum at Monino, east of Moscow. *Bill Yenne Photo*

# POKRYSHKIN AND RECHKALOV:
## TOP RUNNERS-UP

★
Grigory Rechkalov, seen here after having received his second Hero of the Soviet Union medal, was the Soviet Union's third highest-scoring fighter pilot of the war. *Wikimedia Commons*

**THE SECOND AND THIRD HIGHEST-SCORING SOVIET ACES OF THE GREAT PATRIOTIC WAR** flew and fought together through much of the conflict. Depending on sources, Aleksandr Ivanovich Pokryshkin is officially credited with at least 56 aerial victories while Grigori Andreevich Rechkalov is credited with between 56 and 61 solo victories, plus between four and six shard victories.

During 1941 and early 1942, the two men flew with the VVS 55th Fighter IAP, which was redesignated as the 16th Guards IAP on March 7, 1942. By 1943, Pokryshkin was an escadrilli (squadron commander) with the 16th Guards IAP, and Rechkalov is often mentioned as having been his wingman on the Caucasus Front and during the Kuban battles in 1942 and 1943.

Aleksandr Ivanovich "Sasha" Pokryshkin is the man regarded as perhaps the premier Soviet air combat tactician of the Great Patriotic War. He was also the Soviet Union's second highest-scoring ace, and one of a small number of top Voenno-Vozdushnie Sily aces whose combat career began with a victory on June 23 when the war was just hours old and spanned the entire war.

Born in 1913, Sasha Pokryshkin joined the VVS in 1933 and survived the chaotic days of the Stalinist purges. He was on duty as a fighter pilot when the Germans launched Operation Barbarossa. The outclassed VVS defenders fought back bravely. Flying a MiG-3 with the 55th IAP, Senior Lieutenant Aleksandr Pokryshkin and his wingman engaged five Luftwaffe fighters over the Germans' Prut River bridgehead. Pokryshkin succeeded in shooting down a Bf 109, but he took a cannon shell in his right wing. He then went low and successfully managed to lose the Bf 109s that were chasing him.

This Bf 109 was not the only aircraft that Pokryshkin would claim during the war's first 48 hours. The 211th Attack Regiment (Bronirovanny Aviatsiya Protivovozdushnoi or BAP) assigned to the Odessa Military District had launched nine Sukhoi Su 2 ground attack planes to attack German forces crossing the Prut River. Only 75 of the still-classified Su-2s were in service and even most Soviet pilots knew that it existed.

When Pokryshkin observed the formation of unfamiliar aircraft, he assumed they were German and dove to the attack. He hit one of the aircraft but broke off from a second pass when he saw the red stars on the wings and spent several frantic moments trying to wave off his squadron-mates—without breaking radio silence—before they made the same mistake. It is believed that the crippled Su-2 managed a crash landing with no loss of life. The crisis of meeting the German invasion diverted attention away from this faux pas and Pokryshkin was never reprimanded for the incident. A month later he was, himself, shot down but he managed to escape and make his way back to Soviet-held territory.

During the bitter winter of 1941–1942, as the Soviet Union fought its desperate battle for survival, the VVS braved extremely brutal weather conditions. As for Pokryshkin, he earned the nickname "Mustafa," because of the frozen cheeks that he suffered while flying an open-cockpit I-16.

By 1942, a Bell P-39D had become Aleksandr Pokryshkin's signature aircraft. He would eventually graduate to the more powerful, Soviet-built Lavochkin La-7, but 48 of his 59 aerial victories were scored in the American Airacobra.

Pokryshkin was also coming to be regarded as an extraordinary tactician. In that role, he is often compared to the great World War I French ace René Fonck and Adolph "Sailor" Malan of the Royal Air Force—who were not only excellent combat pilots but developed air-to-air tactics that they could teach to others to make them effective in combat as well.

After helping to defeat the Germans on the Kuban Front in 1943, the 16th Guards IAP was operational on the First, Second and Fourth Ukrainian Fronts through 1944 and followed Soviet advances through Romania and Hungary toward the final victory in 1945.

In July 1944, Aleksandr Pokryshkin was promoted to colonel and placed in command of the 9th Guards IAP Division. The units that he commanded contained 30 pilots who were awarded the Hero of the Soviet Union, the nation's highest military decoration. As for Pokryshkin

★
Alexander Pokryshkin after he received his third Hero of the Soviet Union on August 24, 1943. In the background is an American-made Bell P-39 Airacobra fighter plane, the type in which he scored most of his aerial victories. *Wikimedia Commons*

himself, he was one of only three men to be awarded the Hero of the Soviet Union three times. The other two were fellow fighter ace Captain Ivan Kozhedub and Marshal Georgi Zhukov, the supreme commander of all Soviet armed forces in the Great Patriotic War.

Aleksandr Pokryshkin flew 550 missions, engaged in 139 air battles and ended the war with 59 victories, second only to Kozhedub with 62. Some sources say that his score was actually 73 because of victories scored over German territory during the fighting around Kuban in 1943. During this period, enemy aircraft not downed over Soviet territory were not counted. Possibly this is because it would suggest that the Soviet pilots were not defending Soviet territory. Pokryshkin would eventually graduate from the P-39 Airacobra to the more powerful, Soviet-built Lavochkin La-7, but most of his aerial victories were scored in American fighters.

Aleksandr Pokryshkin, a leading tactician in the history of the Red Air Force, and three times a Hero of the Soviet Union, died on November 13, 1985.

Close behind Pokryshkin, the third-place Soviet ace of the Great Patriotic War was his sometime wingman, the baby-faced Grigori Rechkalov. He was born on February 9, 1920 in the village of Khudyakovo near the city of Ekaterinburg, which was known as Sverdlovsk between 1922 and 1991. By the time that he joined the VVS in 1938, he had already learned to fly at the Sverdlovsk Aeroclub. He graduated from the Perm Military Air College in 1939, but he was grounded by the flight surgeon when he was discovered to be color blind. However, by 1941 this was no longer an issue and he was assigned to a fighter squadron, the 55th IAP, based in the Soviet Republic of Moldavia (now Moldova), which was equipped with Polikarpov I 153s and I 16s. He flew 13 missions on the first two days of the Great Patriotic War and killed his first Bf 109 on June 27. By July, when he was shot down for the first time, he was flying an I-16.

In March 1942, when the 55th IAP received its "Guards" redesignation as 16th Guards IAP, it was re-equipped with the newer Yak-1 fighters. Through 1942, Rechkalov's combat prowess had not yet begun to be demonstrated. He had scored three kills during the summer of 1941, but by the end of 1942 he was listed with just four victories, plus two shared. This would have given him five, enough to be classed an ace, however.

Through the winter, the regiment was re equipped with its Bell Airacobras, and by the spring of 1943, it was reassigned to the North Caucasus Front for operations over the Kuban River area. On the unit's first operational sortie with Airacobras, Rechkalov and Pokryshkin shared a Messerschmitt Bf 109 in a fight over Krymskaya. By April, Rechkalov had started to hit his stride as a fighter pilot. Between April 15 and April 21, he claimed three Bf 109s and a Junkers Ju 88.

On April 21, Rechkalov was part of a six-ship patrol led by Pokryshkin when they encountered four Ju 87 Stukas escorted by four Bf 109s. Pokryshkin immediately attacked the Stukas while ordering Rechkalov to engage the fighters. Pokryshkin would claim a pair of Stukas, and Rechkalov a pair of Bf 109s. Rechkalov was awarded his first Hero of the Soviet Union decoration on May 24, 1943.

During the summer of 1944, as the 16th Guards IAP was shifted to the 4th Ukrainian Front in the Crimea, Rechkalov saw action over the Sea of Azov as well as in the Kishinev campaign and completed his 415th mission in June. However, by the time that Rechkalov received his second Gold Star of the Hero of the Soviet Union on July 1, he was no longer on the best of terms with his commander. Pokryshkin had come to strongly disapprove of the brash, 21-year-old pilot's obsession with personal victories at the expense of unit cohesion.

When Aleksandr Pokryshkin was promoted to colonel and placed in command of the 9th Guards IAP Division, it was assumed that Rechkalov would be promoted to head the 16th Guards IAP. But, at Pokryshkin's urging, the corps commander brought in Boris Glinka from the 100th Guards IAP instead. However, when Glinka was badly wounded a few weeks later, Rechkalov, the deputy commander, became the de facto regimental commander.

By the autumn of 1944, the 16th Guards IAP was transferred to the 1st Ukrainian Front for operations in the Lvov area and then throughout Poland. The regiment was flying air cover when Soviet armies crossed the Oder River and plunged into Germany itself. By this time, they had transitioned from the Airacobras to Lavochkin La 7s, and it was in this type that Rechkalov scored his last victory over Berlin in April 1945. This is calculated to have been on his 450th mission.

Of his score, which is between 56 and 61 depending on sources, 44 kills were made in the Airacobra, making him the highest-scoring Airacobra ace of any air force.

In addition to being named Hero of the Soviet Union twice, Rechkalov was awarded the Order of Lenin, the Order of the Red Banner (four times), the Order of Alexandr Nievski and the Order of Patriotic War (First Class). After the war, Rechkalov remained with the VVS, retiring as a major general in 1959. He is also the author of two autobiographical books, *The Smoking Skies of War* and *In Moldavian Skies*.

# LITVYAK AND BUDANOVA:
## NOT ALL THE ACES WERE MEN

★ [Above]
Lidiya Vladimirovna Litvyak, known universally as "Lilya," was the highest-scoring woman air ace in history. They called her the "White Rose of Stalingrad," though it was actually a white lily painted on the side of her aircraft. *University of Texas via Author's Collection*

★ [Below]
Ekaterina Vasylievna Budanova, known as "Katya," was the second highest-scoring woman ace in history. Like Lilya Litvyak, she scored her first victory with the 437th Fighter Aviation Regiment, and eventually flew with the elite 73rd Guards Fighter Aviation Regiment. *Author's Collection*

**MOST OF THE AIR FORCES OF THE NATIONS ENGAGED IN WORLD WAR II HAD WOMEN IN THEIR RANKS.** The German Luftwaffe had its corps of helferinnen, who played a major role in numerous tasks, including staffing the fighter control centers that managed air defense operations. The British Royal Air Force used women in a similar role, and in the United States, the Women Air Service Pilots (WASP) logged tens of thousands of hours ferrying every type of combat aircraft in the USAAF inventory to and from every corner of the country.

However, only in the Soviet Union did women fly regular, routine missions in live-fire combat. Of all the major air forces that were engaged in the war, only the VVS had units comprised specifically of women.

In the armies of the Soviet Union, over 58,000 women endured the harsh conditions at the front, fighting and dying next to their brothers, fathers and sons.

Initially, as with other air forces, the Red Air Force maintained an all-male policy among its combat pilots. However, as the apparently invincible German juggernaut sliced through Soviet defenses like the proverbial hot knife through butter during the summer of 1941, the Red Air Force began to rethink its ban on women. By October 1941, authorization was forthcoming for three regiments of women pilots.

Credit for this policy change can be traced to a surge of volunteers from among the women who were members of the pre-war state-sponsored flying clubs—and to the vision of the great prewar aviatrix, Marina Raskova. As the story goes, she made a personal plea to Stalin himself to secure authorization for official all-female combat units.

In 1934, at the age of 21, Marina Raskova graduated from the Zhukovski Aviation Academy, the first Soviet woman to pass the navigation examination, and the following year she earned her pilot's license. In 1937–1938, in the span of less than a year, she made a mark for herself as a crewmember on three record-breaking flights. In October 1937, she and Valentina Grizodubova set a Soviet women's distance record of 867 miles flying a Yakovlev AIR 12. (The aircraft is better known as the UT 1. The AIR prefix stood for Communist Party official A. I. Rykov who was killed in one of Stalin's purges, and had evidence of his existence erased).

In July 1938, Raskova, Polina Osipienko and W. Lomako flew a Polikarpov MR 1 flying boat a distance of 1,345 miles, and in September she and V. Grizodubova and P. Osipienko made a non stop flight of 3,545 miles in a Tupolev DB-2 (aka Ant 37) twin engine bomber.

According to the legends that are told about her, the young Raskova was a very remarkable young woman. In addition to being an excellent pilot, she was a classical pianist, spoke both French and Italian and was a charismatic leader. Because of her accomplishments in aviation, she was appointed to the People's Defense Committee and moved in all the right circles at the apogee of Moscow society.

When Germany invaded the Soviet Union in June 1941, there was an obvious and immediate need for qualified pilots, and thousands—male and female—volunteered. However, the VVS initially rejected the notion of using women pilots in combat, despite their qualifications and the fact that many were part of the Soviet Grazhdanski Vozdushny Flot (GVF), the civil air fleet. Raskova proposed to Stalin himself that there should be all-woman units within the VVS that could be staffed by all the girls who were in the pre-war flying clubs. At first the answer was no, but that soon changed and the Stavka (Shtab Glavnogo/Verkhovnogo Komandovaniya, the Supreme High Command) okayed Raskova's plan.

The initial selection took place at the Zhukovski Aviation Academy, but training would be centered near the city of Engels on the Volga. The women were issued ill-fitting men's uniforms, and boots so big that they had to fill them with paper. The female pilots were organized into three aviation regiments, which were numbered in the "500" series, indicating that they were designated as reserves under the control of the Soviet State Committee for Defense, the GKO (Gosudarstveny Komitet Oborony). The units were the 586th IAP, the 587th BAP and the 588 NBAP (Night Bomber Regiment).

Commanded by Major Tamara Kazarinova, the 586th IAP first saw action on the Moscow front in the spring of 1942, flying Yak 1 fighters. On September 3, 1942, Lieutenant Valeria Ivanovna Khomyakova was the first woman pilot to down a German aircraft, a Junkers Ju 88 bomber. Before joining the VVS, she had been an engineer and a flight instructor.

Because of the losses that were being suffered in the Battle of Stalingrad, and the general lack of trained male replacements, many women fighter pilots were transferred from the 586th IAP to all-male IAPs. On the ground, and in the air, the women suffered the torment and ridicule of their male counterparts, who did not like the idea of the women invading their profession. Initially, they refused to fly with them. Reluctantly however, they soon incorporated the female pilots into their combat formations. Soviet fighters flew in cells of four, with two "shooters" at the number one and three slots. Initially the women were assigned to a three-man cell in the number four slot.

Gradually the women began to prove themselves, and as the all-female units got into action, they demonstrated that they were capable of the task at hand. Eventually the 587th BAP, flying Petlyakov Pe 2 twin engine bombers, became the 125th Guards BAP. The 588th NBAP became the 46th Guards NBAP—both with the coveted "Guards" designation.

The 46th Guards NBAP was the legendary women's night bomber regiment that came to be known to the Germans as the much-feared "Night Witches" because of their combat effectiveness flying Polikarpov Po 2 biplanes against German positions in the darkness of night. Among the Night Witches, there were over 20 pilots who were awarded the Hero of the Soviet Union decoration.

The Yak-1M, in which
the "M" stands for
"Moskit" or "Mosquito,"
was the most advanced
of the early generation
of Yakovlev fighters.
It was designed as a
steppingstone to the
Yak-3, the "ultimate"
development of the
Yak family. *Author's
Collection*

Luftwaffe fighter pilot Johannes Steinhoff of JG 52, an ace with 176 victories, would later write: "We simply couldn't grasp that the Soviet airmen that caused us the greatest trouble were women. These women feared nothing. They came night after night in their very slow biplanes, and for some periods they wouldn't give us any sleep at all."

Meanwhile, the pilots of 586th IAP flew an average of over 3,000 combat sorties between 1942 and 1945 in Yakovlev Yak 1s, Yak-3s and later YaK 7s. They are credited with at least 38 victories, and with playing an important role in the defeat of the German Sixth Army at Stalingrad.

Luftwaffe Major Bruno Meyer, who commanded a ground attack unit during the Battle of Kursk, called the 586th IAP "an elite unit. . . brave daredevils, well trained and excellent fliers with a sure flair for German weaknesses [who] attacked in a superior manner with short bursts of fire from all guns at short distances, directing their fire mainly at the lead aircraft of the German squadron or flight, eight of which were shot down in one week."

Of all the women fighter pilots who flew with the 586th IAP and other units within the Voenno-Vozdushnie Sily, perhaps none proved themselves more effectively than Lidiya Vladimirovna "Lilya" Litvyak and her friend and comrade, Ekaterina (Katarina) Vasilyevna "Katya" Budanova. With 12 and 11 victories respectively, they are confirmed as having been the highest-scoring female aces of all time.

While these scores are generally accepted as exact, some sources credit Litvyak with as many as 20 victories, and others suggest that Olga Yamshchikova may have had as many as 17 victories. Whatever the numbers, Lilya Litvyak was probably the highest-scoring woman ace. Given the diminishing level of intensity in aerial combat, she is likely to retain this distinction in perpetuity.

Litvyak's story, for all its glory, is not a happy tale. She grew up in the shadow of her father having been on the unlucky side of one of Stalin's mad purges, and she never lived to see the ultimate victory in which she played a small but important role.

Lidiya Vladimirovna was born in Moscow on August 18, 1921, amid the chaos and confusion of the consolidation of power that followed the Bolshevik Revolution of 1917. In the course of Stalin's purges, Lidiya's own father was discredited and put to death as an "an enemy of the people." This would have eventually hampered her own career, had she not gone to great lengths to keep it a secret.

She took an early interest in becoming a pilot and, despite her family difficulties, soloed at the age of 15 at the Chkalov AeroClub. In 1940, having graduated from high school, she became a flight instructor, first at the Kherson flight academy and later with the Osoaviakhim, the Society for the Support of Defense and Aviation.

Best remembered by her nickname "Lilya" which translates as "Lily," Lidiya Litvyak began her training as a military pilot at the Engels training center near Stalingrad on October 15, 1941. In January 1942, she was assigned to the 586th IAP, then based at Saratov, also near Stalingrad.

The women flew without rank insignia, identification or parachute, because it was assumed that women who survived being shot down behind enemy lines would suffer a cruel death. The women themselves decided that if they ever survived a crash behind German lines, they would have to shoot themselves.

By the summer of 1942, the initial inclination of the Red Air Force to not take the women's regiments seriously had dissipated as the women proved themselves in combat. Meanwhile, the tactical situation had deteriorated to the point where the Red Air Force wanted its best pilots—regardless of gender—flying the most essential missions. In September 1942, several of the best women fighter pilots—including Starshina (Senior Sergeants) Lilya Litvyak and Katya Budanova—were ordered to join the previously all-male 296th IAP, flying Lavochkin La 5s on the Stalingrad front.

Flying her second mission with the 296th IAP on September 13, Lilya Litvyak shot down a Messerschmitt Bf 109 and a Junkers Ju 88. Two weeks later, she added a third victory, shooting down another Ju 88. By the time that she was awarded the Order of the Red Banner on February 17, 1943, her unit had transitioned to the nimble Yakovlev Yak-1, and she had added another score to her tally, as well as a shared victory over a Focke-Wulf Fw 190, then considered to be the Luftwaffe's best operational fighter.

On March 1, Litvyak and Budanova, flying as half of a four-ship flight, intercepted a dozen Fw 190s on a ground support mission near Stalingrad. Two of the Focke-Wulfs were shot down, one of them claimed by the guns of Lilya Litvyak's Yak-1. The Germans broke off the fight, and the Russians promptly engaged and mauled a flight of Ju 88s. Lilya Litvyak claimed one of the four Ju 88s that were shot down and returned to base with an overall score of 6.5.

Promoted to Junior Lieutenant and now an ace, Lilya Litvyak was a rising star in the Red Air Force. Meanwhile, the fact that she was a female ace was not lost on the hero-hungry Soviet media, and soon her name became well-known. It also didn't hurt the image of the Soviet Union's new star that Litvyak was a very colorful character. She wore long silk scarves made of parachute cloth, carried bouquets of fresh-cut wildflowers in her cockpit and, although she was already blonde, bleached her hair white.

As a reference to her nickname, she painted a large white lily on the side of her Yak-1. The Germans, who mistook the lily for a rose—but knew through the rumor mill that this pilot was a woman—started calling her "The White Rose of Stalingrad."

She is recalled in anecdotal accounts as being a strikingly beautiful woman, although the handful of photographs that exist show her as somewhat plain. Nevertheless, she caught the attention of fellow fighter pilot Alexei Salomatin, an ace with a dozen victories of his own, and with whom she often flew in the wing position. The couple fell in love and were engaged to be married, a turn of events that was popular content for the Soviet media, which was keen for tales of patriotism to punctuate its reporting from the battlefronts of the Great Patriotic War.

By then, word had come through that Marina Raskova was dead. She was one of several women pilots who had volunteered to help ferry a group of Pe 2 bombers to the Stalingrad front. On the night of January 4, 1943, during a blinding blizzard, Raskova crashed into the cliffs overlooking the Volga River, north of Stalingrad.

On March 15, during a mission on which she downed a pair of Ju 88s, Lilya Litvyak was badly wounded but managed to bring her Yak-1 back to base. By the time she recovered from her wounds to return to action, her regiment was redesignated as the 73rd Guards IAP. The heroism

★
Lilya Litvyak, Katya Budanova and Mariya Kuznetsova are seen here studying paperwork on the tail of a Yak-1. They started out with the all-female 586th Fighter Aviation Regiment, but transferred to the 437th Fighter Aviation Regiment in September 1942. It was with the latter regiment that Lilya and Katya scored their early aerial victories. *Author's Collection*

that warranted the "Guards" designation included the continued bravery of Lilya Litvyak, who claimed her ninth solo victory on May 5.

To add to the evolving legend of The White Rose of Stalingrad, Lilya Litvyak—now promoted to Senior Lieutenant—was shot down behind enemy lines twice during the ensuing weeks. Both times she was unhurt, and both times she escaped to fly again—once by evading the Germans on foot, and another when rescued by a fellow pilot who landed behind enemy lines to save her.

On May 21, the storybook romance with Salomatin ended tragically when he was shot down and killed. But Lilya Litvyak continued to fly and fight, adding an observation balloon to her tally of victories on May 31.

By July 18, Katya Budanova and Lilya Litvyak were aces twice over, tied with 10 victories each. Then tragedy again visited Litvyak. Katya Budanova was attacked by a pair of Messerschmitt Bf 109s and shot down. She managed to take one of the Germans with her before she was killed. This final victory made Budanova the top-scoring Soviet female ace with 11 victories to Lilya's 10 (plus three shared victories).

On August 1, 1943, Lilya Litvyak was flying her 168th mission as part of a flight of eight Yak-1s escorting a flight of Il-2 Sturmovik bombers on a ground attack mission, when they were bounced by a large number of German fighters. As the story goes, eight Messerschmitt Bf 109s ganged up on the Yak-1 with the white lily on its side, as though determined to put the legend to an end, once and for all.

According to the final chapter of that legend, Litvyak took two of the Messerschmitts with her, to end her life and career with at least 12 victories.

The White Rose of Stalingrad fell near the village of Dmitriyevka. Like Katya Budanova a few days earlier, she apparently survived the crash only to die in her wildflower-bedecked cockpit, and was buried under the wing of her aircraft. She was two weeks short of turning 22.

In the coming months, the legend of The White Rose of Stalingrad faded, pushed from the headlines by other stories of defeat, victory and heroism in the global war. Amazingly, the location of her grave was forgotten when the wreckage of the Yak-1 was removed, and her body was not recovered for 46 years.

The fact that she was officially "missing" through all those years also precluded her being posthumously awarded the USSR's highest decoration, that of Hero of the Soviet Union, a distinction that she had certainly earned. This shortcoming was rectified on May 5, 1990—during the Soviet Union's final days—in a decree signed by Mikhail Gorbachev. Three years later, on October 1, 1993, President Boris Yeltsin officially designated Lidiya Vladimirovna "Lilya" Litvyak as a Hero of Russia.

Her full story is told in great detail in this author's internationally popular biography *The White Rose of Stalingrad: The Real-Life Adventure of Lidiya Vladimirovna Litvyak, the Highest Scoring Female Air Ace of All Time.*

**O**F ALL THE AXIS LEADERS OF WORLD WAR II, Benito Mussolini was the first to come to power. He was named prime minister of Italy in 1923 and ruled as a dictator from 1926 to 1943. In 1919, Mussolini and other World War I veterans founded a revolutionary, nationalistic group called the Fasci di Combattimento, named for the ancient Roman symbol of power, the fasces—an axe in a bundle of reeds. The group, which became a political party, were known as "fascists." This term would subsequently be applied to the nationalists in Spain, the National Socialists (Nazis) in Germany and the imperial nationalists in Japan. By 1922, the fascists had become so powerful that King Victor Emmanuel III asked Mussolini to form a coalition government. By 1926, the coalition had evolved into a single party, totalitarian dictatorship.

In terms of foreign policy, Mussolini imagined himself as a reconstituted Roman emperor, and set out to rebuild what he could of the Roman Empire. In northern Africa, he had inherited Italian Somaliland and Libya, and he conquered Ethiopia in 1936. In Europe, he annexed Albania in 1939. He aided the Spanish Nationalist leader, General Francisco Franco, in the Spanish Civil War and he allied himself with Adolf Hitler's Nazi Germany. On October 25, 1936 Hitler and Mussolini formally created the alliance called the Rome-Berlin Axis. Japan joined with Germany and Italy to form the Berlin-Tokyo-Rome Axis on September 27, 1940 when it signed the Tripartite Pact or Triple Alliance with the first two Axis powers.

In the course of re-creating his Roman Empire, Mussolini recreated his Roman legions by building up the Italian army, navy and air force. By 1939 the latter, known as the Regia Aeronautica, was built into a sizable, modern force.

The first place that Italian combat pilots would see action between the world wars was in the Spanish Civil War. Both Hitler and Mussolini sent air power to aid their friend Franco in defeating the Spanish Republic. Mussolini sent a selection of Regia Aeronautica pilots organized as the Aviazione Legionaria, and Hitler sent a selection of Luftwaffe pilots organized as the Condor Legion. They would fight alongside Nationalist Spanish pilots, against Republican Spanish and Soviet pilots from 1936 to 1939.

Italy would not enter World War II until June 1940, when Germany defeated France. The first Regia Aeronautica actions were against France's Armée de l'Air in the south of France, but the Regia Aeronautica would see extensive action against the Royal Air Force (and later the USAAF) in North Africa and the Mediterranean region from 1940 through early 1943.

In terms of air superiority fighters, the Regia Aeronautica began World War II with such types as the Fiat G.50 and the Macchi C.200 (MC.200), both durable, low-wing monoplanes having top speeds of about 300 mph. The best Italian fighter to see widespread service with the Regia Aeronautica during World War II was certainly the Macchi C.202, which was introduced into squadron service in 1941.

★
Giulio Reiner was a test pilot turned fighter pilot, who participated in testing the Macchi C.202. He commanded the 73a Squadriglia of the Regia Aeronautica, but switched sides to the Aeronautica Co-Belligerante (Co-Belligerent Air Force) in 1943. He ended the war with 10 individual victories and 57 shared victories. *Wikimedia Commons*

★
Teresio Vittorio Martinoli was Italy's third highest-scoring ace. When Italy surrendered to the Allies in 1943, he joined the Aeronautica Co-Belligerante (Co-Belligerent Air Force) and fought on the side of the Allies until he was killed in an accident in August 1944. *Wikimedia Commons*

The year 1943 was a turning point for Italy in World War II. By that time, Mussolini had lost the African portion of his empire, and on July 9, the Allies invaded Sicily. The war had come home to Italian soil. On July 25, King Victor Emmanuel III fired Mussolini and on September 3, the Allies invaded Italy proper. Italy surrendered unconditionally five days later and the Germans occupied the country, which would remain a battleground until the war ended in May 1945. Mussolini fled to the northern, German-occupied portion of Italy and formed a puppet government under the name, Republica Sociale Italiana. Mussolini himself lived under German protection until April 28, 1945, when he was captured by partisans as he and his mistress tried to escape to Switzerland. He was executed and hung by his heels.

Many diehard Fascist members of the Regia Aeronautica continued to fight on as part of the air force of the Republica Sociale Italiana, but the majority surrendered and some actually fought alongside the Allies in the new Co-Belligerent Air Force (Aeronautica C-Belligerante).

Italy produced over 120 aces during World War II, four of them with scores in excess of 20 (including shared victories). Like the French Armée de l'Air, the Regia Aeronautica gave full scores for shared victories. However, none of the Italians in World War II topped the score of Francesco Baracca, who was Italy's top-scoring ace in World War I with at least 34 victories.

The highest-scoring Italian ace of World War II was probably Adriano Visconti, who is credited with as many as 26 victories. This score was perhaps equaled by Franco Lucchini, who is generally believed to have scored five in the Spanish Civil War, plus as many as 21 in World War II for a maximum total of 26. All of Visconti's victories were scored in World War II. Other aces of note were Teresio Martinoli, who scored all of his 22 victories (plus 14 shared victories) in World War II, and Giulio Reiner, a test pilot who had helped evaluate the Macchi C.202 and later commanded 73 Stormo (Fighter Squadron). He scored 10 individual victories, as well as 57 shared victories and 8 probables.

★
This Macchi C.202 painted in the markings of the one flown in combat by Giulio Reiner is preserved at the Museo Storico dell'Aeronautica Militare (Historical Museum of the Italian Air Force) at Vigna di Valle, on Lake Bracciano in central Italy. *Photo by Zerosei licensed under Creative Commons*

# VISCONTI:
## NUMBER ONE

**ADRIANO VISCONTI** scored his first victory in North Africa while flying as a reconnaissance pilot in 1940, but he later qualified to fly fighters. He was active with 7 Gruppo (Group) of the Regia Aeronautica's 54 Stormo in combat over Malta in 1941 and 1942. During this period, he would claim a pair of Bristol Blenheim bombers and a pair of Hawker Hurricane fighters.

At the end of 1942, Visconti moved to 16 Gruppo and scored 14 victories against the Allies during the final campaign in Tunisia and the battles over Sicily in August 1943. During the latter campaign, Visconti was among the first to operate the new Macchi C.205 in combat. When Italy capitulated in September 1943, Visconti did not. He flew north to continue fighting the Allies under the banner of the Republica Sociale Italiana. Flying his C.205 for the new Fascist Italian government's 1 Gruppo, Visconti claimed seven victories, including a Lockheed P-38 and three Republic P-47 Thunderbolts.

As was the case with Benito Mussolini, Adriano Visconti met an ignominious end. After surviving dozens of difficult combat missions across the length of the Mediterranean, he was shot in the back by the Russian bodyguard of a Communist guerilla leader after he surrendered in April 1945.

★
Adriano Visconti, Italy's leading ace, was the recipient of four Medaglia d'argento al Valor Militare medals and a pair of Medaglia di Bronzo al Valor Militare decorations. *Author's Collection*

Count Francesco
Baracca, Italy's
leading ace of World
War I, still loomed
large in the folklore
as an inspiration for
Italian fighter pilots
of the next generation.
He died in 1918. His
insignia of a black
horse was cited by
Enzo Ferrari as the
inspiration for his
automotive logo.
*Public Domain*

# LUCCHINI: BARACCA DELLA SEGUNDA GUERRA MUNDIAL

**IN WORLD WAR II**, air ace folk hero Francesco Baracca was the man most emulated by Italian fighter pilots. For a pilot to be called "Baracca Della Segunda Guerra Mundial" ("The Baracca of World War II") was the highest honor that could have been bestowed, greater than any award or decoration. Franco Lucchini was the man.

Having scored five victories to become an ace in the Spanish Civil War, Lucchini scored 21 more in World War II while flying with the Regia Aeronautica's 10 Gruppo. Born in Rome on Christmas eve in 1917, he joined the Regia Aeronautica as a reserve officer and earned his wings at the Foggia training base in July 1936. He was initially posted to the 91 Squadriglia (Squadron) of 4 Stormo, and in July 1937 he volunteered with the Aviazione Legionaria for duty in the Spanish Civil War. At the time, Spain was the place to go for Europe's aspiring young knights of the skies. Over the course of a year, Lucchini flew 122 sorties in Spain, flying Fiat CR.32 biplanes with 19 Squadriglia of 23 Gruppo. In 1938, Lucchini was shot down twice. The second time, in July 1938, he would remain a prisoner of war for six months until he was able to escape.

Back in Italy, Lucchini returned to 10 Gruppo, where he was serving with 90 Squadriglia when war was declared against Great Britain and France in June 1940. At first, 90 Squadriglia was assigned to Libya and equipped with Fiat CR.42s. He had two shared victories during June 1940, a Gloster Gladiator and a Short Sunderland flying boat, and scored his first solo kill, a Royal Air Force Gladiator, on August 4. Through the end of the year, Lucchini would fly 94 missions and score three confirmed victories, four probables and 15 shared victories.

Early in 1941, 10 Gruppo rotated back to Italy for conversion to the new Macchi C.200 fighter. They were then assigned to Sicily to take part in the offensive against the British garrison on the Mediterranean island of Malta. Lucchini's first confirmed victories of the Malta campaign came on July 11 during a major Regia Aeronautica attack against the island. He shared two Hawker Hurricanes in aerial combat and participated in destroying or damaging five Vickers Wellingtons and three Bristol Blenheims on the ground.

Another major assault on Malta came on July 17, when three Regia Aeronautica groups launched 49 C.200s. The Royal Air Force claimed two C.200s destroyed, while 10 Gruppo claimed four Hurricanes. One of these would be a shared victory for Lucchini. On August 19, it was the turn of the Royal Air Force to go on the offensive, with a dozen Hurricanes intercepting a dozen C.200s over Sicily. Lucchini would claim a probable shared victory.

Late in 1941, 10 Gruppo re equipped with the C.202 and after a training period was re-assigned to Sicily in April 1942. On May 9, Lucchini claimed his first Spitfire over Malta. Six days later, in another battle over Malta, he scored against a second Spitfire and damaged a third. The last 10 Gruppo mission over Malta, which came on May 19, was uneventful for Lucchini.

On May 26, 10 Gruppo was sent back to North Africa. Over the next five months, Lucchini flew 59 missions and scored six victories, two probables and shared eight kills. Most of these were Curtiss Tomahawks, but he did shoot down another Spitfire on the last day of August. On October 24, he claimed another Tomahawk and a Douglas Boston, but he was shot down himself and badly injured.

When Lucchini finally was released from the hospital to return to 10 Gruppo, the Axis had been defeated in North Africa and the focus was on defending Sicily from the impending Allied invasion. On July 5, having already flown seven sorties since his recuperation, Lucchini was on an air intercept mission against a strike force of American B-17 Flying Fortresses. He succeeded in shooting down one of the escorting Spitfires and started to attack the bombers when he was hit by fire from the bombers and went down in a plume of black smoke. His body was found at the crash site two days later.

Franco Lucchini had flown at least 262 missions and was awarded the Medaglia d'Argento al Valore Militare (silver medal) five times, four War Crosses and a German Iron Cross during his career. He was posthumously awarded with the Medaglia d'Oro al Valor Militare, Italy's highest decoration.

★
Franco Lucchini was Italy's second highest-scoring World War II ace, but with the addition of five victories scored in the Spanish Civil War, he matched Visconti's probable overall total of 26. Lucchini was killed in action on July 5, 1943. *Author's Collection*

# CHAPTER
## 08

# FRANCE

**B**EGINNING WITH ADOLPHE PÉGOUD AND ROLAND GARROS, French pilots were among the most colorful and storied aces of the First World War. The tales of their exploits are some of the greatest stories from the war that was then known simply as the "Great War." France produced 158 aces, men whose names were household words throughout the world in the early years of the twentieth century, and which are still well known icons of military aviation history. At the apogee of the list of French aces is the name of the great Ace of Aces, René Paul Fonck, who scored 75 victories, more than anyone in World War I except the "Red Baron," Manfred von Richthofen. Also on the list are Georges Guynemer with 54 victories and Charles Nungesser with 45.

For all the hardship that France suffered, it was a victor in World War I. Its capital was never occupied and it never tasted defeat. In World War II, however, France was defeated in a month and a half. Compared to the years of stalemate that had occurred in World War I, the German victories came with blinding speed.

By the time that France surrendered on June 22, 1940, French forces put up a resistance that was, at times, noble. Certainly the squadrons of the French Air Force, the Armée de l'Air, were among the most heroic of French combat units. Just as the French equipment was outclassed by that of the German armies on the ground, so too were French fighter aircraft. The Messerschmitt Bf 109 was easily superior to the Armée de l'Air's French-made Dewoitine D520s and American-made Curtiss Model 75 Hawks (equivalent to the P-36 in American service).

There were many Armée de l'Air aces during the brief Battle of France, but this is due in part to its method of counting victories. During World War I, the French were stricter about crediting scores for shared victories than they were in 1940. Full scores were given for assists and for probables to the point where all the pilots on the scene when an enemy was shot down received a full point for his overall tally. This created inflated scores, and more aces than there actually were, but it was certainly a propaganda measure which ensured that good news about the battles would be reported in the French media. However bracing this was for French morale at the time, it has left a great deal of uncertainty in looking back at French aces historically.

The top-scoring French ace of the short Battle of France was Edmond Marin la Meslée, who is credited with at least 16 victories while flying a Curtiss Hawk with the Escadrille (Squadron) 5 of the Armée de l'Air's Groupe de Chasse (Pursuit Group) I. Indeed, Groupe de Chasse I/5, which was based at Rheims in northeastern France, was the highest-scoring Armée de l'Air unit

★

Edmond Marin la Meslée was the highest-scoring ace of the Armée de l'Air Française during the 46 days of the Battle of France in May–June 1940. He shot down at least 16 enemy aircraft and probably more. He escaped to North Africa and was among those who joined the Free French forces in 1943. *Public Domain*

★
A restored Curtiss Model H75A Hawk in the markings of Groupe de Chasse II/5 of the Armée de l'Air Française as it would have appeared in June 1940 at the time of the Battle of France. On September 20, 1939, André-Armand Legrand had scored the first Allied victory on the Western Front in World War II while flying an H75A. Edmond Marin la Meslée scored 15 victories and five probables in such an aircraft. *Shutterstock*

# "L'ALLEMAGNE ATTEND LE BEAU TEMPS"

(GOEBBELS)

BILAN DES FORCES EN PRÉSENCE

MARIN LA MESLEE
L'AS DES AS FRANÇAIS

of the Battle of France, with 111 credited victories. Having scored a shared victory before the Battle of France, Marin la Meslée claimed a pair of Ju 87 Stukas on May 12. He would later join the Free French Air Force, with which he was flying P-47 Thunderbolts in the Alsace campaign when he was killed in action on February 4, 1945. He is credited with no victories while flying with the Free French.

When France surrendered, so too did the Armée de l'Air. Some of the pilots remained in France with the Armée de l'Air, which was taken over by the new Vichy government, which was set up as a puppet by the Germans. Others fled to Britain to carry on the war against the Germans alongside the British. These became the nucleus of the Free French forces under Charles DeGaulle. The Free French pilots would ultimately fly British and American aircraft and would operate under the Anglo-American command structure through the end of the war.

Other French pilots went east after the surrender to join the Soviet Voenno Vozdushnie Sily. They would ultimately be organized into the famed Normandie Niemen group under the VVS command structure. An important Normandie Niemen pilot was Marcel Albert, who is credited with 16 victories while flying with the Armée de l'Air, plus five with the Normandie Niemen group.

★ (Above)
The French illustrated weekly magazine 7 *Jours* (7 *Days*) carried a story about Edmond Marin la Meslée on the cover of its March 23, 1941 issue. *Photo by G. Garitan licensed under Creative Commons*

★ (Right)
Lieutenant Pierre Clostermann (left) congratulates Flight Lieutenant K.L. Charney in the cockpit of his Supermarine Spitfire Mk. IXB in the summer of 1944. They had just returned to Longues-sur-Mer (B11) in Normandy from an evening sortie in which they each shot down a Focke-Wulf Fw 190. On June 18, 1944, Clostermann had been one of the first Free French pilots to land on French soil when he arrived at Longues-sur-Mer. *UK Government*

# CLOSTERMANN: IN THE SHADOW OF RENÉ FONCK

**IN WORLD WAR II**, France's leading ace would not enjoy the glory and celebrity of the great René Fonck but he was, nevertheless, a colorful character who worked hard and made France proud. Generally regarded as France's leading ace in World War II, Pierre Clostermann scored all of his victories while flying with the British Royal Air Force, although the number is uncertain. Some sources list him with as few as 11, while in his autobiography Le Grande Cirque (The Big Show) he recounts a total of 33, plus 12 probable kills and 24 aircraft destroyed on the ground. He also participated in a successful attack on a German U-boat.

Clostermann fled to Great Britain in 1940 but did not became a pilot with the Royal Air Force until early 1943, when he was assigned to No. 341 "Alsace" Squadron, which was composed entirely of Free French airmen flying the Supermarine Spitfire Mk. IX. In August 1943, Clostermann shot down a pair of Focke-Wulf Fw 190s, his first two victories. He was subsequently transferred to the No. 602 "City of Glasgow" Squadron, composed of Belgian, Australian, Norwegian, Canadian and English—as well as French—pilots. On January 17, 1944, the squadron was transferred to the Orkney Islands where they would fly air defense for the naval base at Scapa Flow using Spitfire Mk. VIIIs.

As time for the June 6, 1944 invasion of northern France drew close, No. 602 Squadron was reassigned to attacking German antiaircraft positions in Normandy, a task which Clostermann despised. After the invasion, however, the squadron was able to go back to air-to-air work and he scored three victories in one day. For this he was awarded the Distinguished Flying Cross by the Royal Air Force. In the meantime, he and fellow pilot Jacques Remlinger were the first Free French airmen to land in France.

After he received his Distinguished Flying Cross, Clostermann was taken out of combat and given a desk job because he was diagnosed as suffering from battle fatigue. This lasted until December 1944, when he requested and received another combat assignment. This time he found himself back on the continent, specifically with No. 274 Squadron, which was flying Hawker Tempest Vs from a base at Volkel in the Netherlands. On May 3, 1945, after four months with No. 274 Squadron, Clostermann was given command of No. 122 Wing, but the war was over within a week. After the war he worked as an engineer, but reenlisted in the Armée de l'Air briefly in 1956–1957. He lived until 2006.

# POLAND

**W**ORLD WAR II BEGAN WITH GERMANY'S SUDDEN BLITZKRIEG invasion of Poland in the predawn hours of September 1, 1939. On the eve of the war, the Polish Air Force had seven fighter squadrons (Dywizjon Mysliwski) each equipped with about 20 aircraft, mainly PZL P-7s and P-11s produced by the Polish State Aircraft Factory (Panstwowe Zaklaty Lotnicze). These were assigned primarily to support the field armies. Only two reinforced squadrons, under the command of Colonel Stefan Pawlikowski, a World War I veteran pilot, were tasked with the air defense of Warsaw when the first attacks came.

At about 7:00 on the morning of September 1, airplane spotters alerted the Polish Air Force air defense units that a German bomber force was headed for Warsaw and interceptors were launched. The first Allied aerial victories of World War II occurred that morning. Stanislaw Skalski may have been the first, downing a Henschel Hs 126 on a reconnaissance mission at 5:32a.m. Within less than two hours, Wladyslaw Gnys shot down a pair of Dornier Do 17s, and a Heinkel He 111 was claimed by Lieutenant Alexander Gabszewicz.

Though the Luftwaffe fighters escorting the bombers took their toll on the Polish defenders, many of the bombers were forced to abort and the initial attack on Warsaw was less than a resounding success. In the coming weeks, however, the Polish Air Force was overwhelmed by the Germans, and Warsaw would suffer the terror of aerial bombing that was visited upon many major cities across the world over the coming six years.

The Polish Air Force was the first Allied air force in action during World War II, but for Poland the war would last just three weeks. After Poland was defeated, many of its best pilots escaped, some to the Soviet Union, but most to Britain. As for the Soviet Union, it should be recalled that on September 17, the Soviet Army also invaded Poland. Resistance had ceased by this time, and under the terms of the Hitler-Stalin pact of August 24, the Soviet invasion amounted to "dividing the spoils."

Many of the Polish pilots who escaped would fight again, flying as part of the Royal Air Force, the VVS, or the USAAF. There would ultimately be over 40 Polish aces in World War II. The top aces were Stanislaw Skalski, credited with 22 victories, Witold Urbanowicz with 18 and Eugeniusz Horbaczewski with 16.5. All flew with the Royal Air Force and Urbanowicz flew with the USAAF as well. Boleslaw "Mike" Gladych scored 14 kills with the USAAF and three with the RAF. Victor Kalinowski was the top-scoring Polish ace with the Voenno-Vozdushnie Sily, scoring nine victories.

★

Flying Officer Boleslaw Henryk Drobiński, an ace with the No. 303 Polish Fighter Squadron in the cockpit of his Spitfire on August 29, 1942. One of his seven aerial victories was against the great German ace Adolf Galland, though Galland walked away after his Messerschmitt went down. Drobiński survived the war and settled in England. *Wikimedia Commons*

★ (Right)
Pilot Officers Jan Zumbach (left) and Miroslaw Ferić, two aces of the No. 303 "City of Warsaw" Fighter Squadron, playing with the Squadron's mascot in October 1940. Beginning in September 1939, Ferić kept a personal diary, which became No. 303 Squadron's unit history. *UK Government*

★ (Below)
Comprised of Polish Air Force pilots who fled to Britain after Poland's defeat in 1939, No. 303 "City of Warsaw" Fighter Squadron of Britain's Royal Air Force was formed in the summer of 1940 and played an important role in the Battle of Britain. These are a few of the aces, gathered around the tail elevator of a Hawker Hurricane Mk. I at Northolt in Middlesex in October 1940. From left to right, they are Pilot Officer Miroslaw Ferić (8.66 aerial victories), Flying Officer Bogdan Grzeszczak, Pilot Officer Jan Zumbach (12.33), Flying Officer Zdzislaw Henneberg (8.5) and Canadian Flight-Lieutenant John Kent (12), who commanded "A" Flight of the Squadron at the time. *UK Government*

# SKALSKI: THE FIRST AND FINEST

**THE FIRST ALLIED ACE OF WORLD WAR II**, and the man who went on to be the highest-scoring Polish ace of the war, was Stanislaw Skalski. Having claimed his first victory on the first day of the war, he scored his second and third victories—two Do 17s—on September 2, and his fifth on September 4 to become Poland's first ace.

Born in October 1915 in Kodyma, Skalski earned his wings in 1938, and was assigned to the 142nd "Wild Ducks" Fighter Squadron in Torun. Flying P-11s with the Wild Ducks, he is credited with downing the two Do 17 bombers, two Hs 126s, a Ju 86 bomber and a Ju 87 Stuka. He also damaged three and had a shared victory. When he flew his last mission with the Polish Air Force on September 16, his total stood at 6.5.

With Poland's ultimate defeat now certain, a number of Polish Air Force pilots escaped from their country via Romania, hoping to regroup and fight the Germans from Britain and France. Skalski eventually made his way to Britain, where he joined the Royal Air Force in January 1940. He was assigned to No. 501 Squadron, which was equipped with Hawker Hurricanes. Skalski was in combat against the Germans in August 1940, during the Battle of Britain. In his first weeks back in action, he managed to down three enemy aircraft, bringing his total to 9.5. It must have seemed like déjà vu.

On September 5, Skalski's unit intercepted a strike force of He 111s, one of which was promptly claimed by his guns. He also managed to claim a pair of Messerschmitt Bf 109s, but his own Hurricane was shot down. He bailed out, but severe burns would keep him hospitalized for six weeks. The first Allied ace of World War II was also now probably the first man to achieve ace status with two separate air forces.

During 1941, the Royal Air Force had so many expatriate pilots within its ranks that it was possible to form entire squadrons of pilots who had formerly been with a specific air force. Skalski was assigned to No. 306 (Polish) Squadron as a flight commander in June 1941, and it was with this unit that he scored five victories during the summer. By now Skalski was the recipient of the Royal Air Force Distinguished Flying Cross, as well as the Silver Cross (Virtuti Militari)—Poland's highest decoration—and the Cross of Valor.

In April 1942, Skalski was placed in command of No. 317 (Polish) Squadron for five months before being reassigned to the North African Theater. In Tunisia, between March and May 1943, he commanded the Polish Fighting Team, flying Spitfire Mk. IXs as an autonomous component of No. 145 Squadron. The Fighting Team, which came to be known as "Skalski's Circus," claimed a large number of German aircraft, and Stanislaw Skalski added four to his own total. The first of these was a Ju 88 downed on March 28. Between April 2 and April 6, 1943, the Circus claimed eight Messerschmitt Bf 109s, two of which were shot down by Skalski. Skalski's fourth in North

★
In 1939, Stanislaw Skalski became the first Allied ace of World War II, and ultimately was the highest-scoring Polish ace. This photo from the summer of 1944 shows him with 21 aerial victories. By this time, he commanded No. 1 (Polish) Wing of the RAF. *Wikimedia Commons*

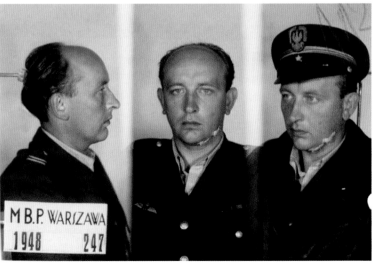

Africa came on May 6, 1943, on the last day of combat
for the Circus. A week later, the Germans surrendered in
North Africa and withdrew to Italy.

Skalski was promoted to command the Royal Air Force
No. 601 "County of London" Squadron, becoming the
first Pole to command a Royal Air Force fighter unit. With
No. 601 Squadron, he took part in Operation Husky, the
invasion of Sicily on July 9–10, 1943, and the subsequent
invasion of Italy at Salerno, which began on September 9.

Stanislaw Skalski returned to England in December
1943, where he was placed in command of No. 131 Wing,
which contained the Polish No. 302 Squadron, No. 308
Squadron and No. 317 Squadron. For exactly four months,
starting on April 3, 1944, he was in command of the No. 133
(Polish) Wing, which contained one British squadron, No.
129 Squadron, and two Polish units—No. 306 Squadron
and No. 315 Squadron. As commander of No. 133 Wing,
Skalski participated in the operations surrounding the
Operation Overlord invasion of France on June 6. On June
24, he scored two victories in an intense battle over Rouen
that netted the unit a total of six confirmed kills. From
August until the middle of October, Skalski commanded
No. 1 (Polish) Wing.

Stanislaw Skalski spent the final months of the war as
an instructor at the Royal Air Force Advanced Gunnery
School at Catfoss that was headed by the legendary Royal
Air Force ace Adolph Gysbert "Sailor" Malan. Skalski
ended the war as a national hero in Poland, also having
been awarded three Distinguished Flying Crosses and
a Distinguished Service Order by the British. His final
official score was 22 confirmed victories and one probable.

Returning to Poland after the war, Stanislaw Skalski
found that his British decorations and his stellar career
did not hold him in good stead with the Soviet-controlled
Communist government. In 1949, after the Communists
consolidated their power, they decided that Skalski was a
spy for the West and threw him into prison. When he was
finally released in 1956, the decorated hero of the skies
wound up as a taxi driver in Warsaw.

# HORBACZEWSKI:
## ON SKALSKI'S WING

Squadron Leader Eugeniusz Horbaczewski, commander of the No. 315 "City of Deblin" Polish Fighter Squadron, standing by his new North American Mustang Mk. III at Brenzett, Kent on August 2, 1944. He was shot down and killed on August 18, 1944, after destroying three Focke-Wulf Fw 190s. *UK Government*

**POLAND'S THIRD HIGHEST-SCORING ACE WAS AN INTERESTING CHARACTER.** He was a Ukraine-born Pole who chose to fight for Britain after the fall of his native country. In the course of his career with the Royal Air Force, he was among the cadre of pilots who were part of the group that flew with Stanislaw Skalski through much of the war. Eugeniusz Horbaczewski was actually the pilot who had the highest score while flying with the Polish Fighting Team—"Skalski's Circus"—in North Africa. If the four V-1 cruise missiles that he shot down were added to his ultimate score of 16.5 aircraft, he would have been second only to Skalski among Polish aces.

Horbaczewski was born in Kiev, the capital of Ukraine, in 1917. He grew up in Poland with an interest in flying and earned a Class C glider (highest) glider rating at age 18. The next step was powered flight, and he joined the Polish Air Force. He went on to become an aviation cadet at Deblin under Witold Urbanowicz, and he was part of the group who, along with Urbanowicz, was in the process of trying to get advanced fighters delivered to the Polish Air Force when the Germans attacked on September 1, 1939.

Along with Urbanowicz and Skalski, Horbaczewski escaped to Britain and joined the Royal Air Force. However, he was a relative latecomer. While Skalski, Urbanowicz and most other Polish pilots had been in combat during the Battle of Poland in 1939, and certainly during the Battle of Britain in 1940, Horbaczewski was not actually in combat until October 1941. He was assigned initially to No. 303 (Polish) "City of Warsaw" Squadron, a Spitfire unit which had earlier been involved in the heat of the Battle of Britain, and which was previously commanded by Urbanowicz.

Horbaczewski's first "probable" victory came on October 6, when the squadron was attacked by Messerschmitt Bf 109s while escorting bombers over France, but he would not get a confirmed kill until April 4, 1942 during another bomber escort mission over France. He attacked a Focke-Wulf Fw 190 that was on the tail of another Spitfire, opening fire at close range. The second victory came quickly. During another mission over France on April 16, he downed a Bf 109, again using close-in fire.

On August 19, Horbaczewski was in one of the Spitfires that was flying cover for the ill-fated Allied raid against Dieppe on the French coast. No. 303 Squadron intercepted a group of Fw 190s bent on attacking the landing craft and cut them apart. The unit ended the day with eight victories, one of them claimed by Horbaczewski.

In March 1943, Horbaczewski was sent to the North African Theater and assigned to the Polish Fighting Team, commanded by Stanislaw Skalski and known as "Skalski's Circus." Ultimately, Horbaczewski would claim five victories as part of the Circus, more than anyone else in the unit, including Skalski himself. The first of these, a Ju 88 bomber, came on March 28, the first day of combat for the Circus. On April 2, he would add a Bf 109 to his list of victories. Four days later, the tables were turned, and Horbaczewski found himself alone in a fight with five Messerschmitt Bf 109s. He was hit but managed a crash landing. Fortunately he was over allied territory at the time, and he was soon back in combat.

Horbaczewski's final action with the Circus came on April 22, when he downed a pair of Bf 109s in a massive dogfight over the Bay of Tunis. His combat record led to Horbaczewski being promoted to command No. 43 Squadron, making him the second Polish ace, after Skalski, to command a Royal Air Force fighter squadron. Like Skalski's No. 601 Squadron, Horbaczewski's No. 43 Squadron was involved in Operation Husky operations over Sicily, and in subsequent activities over Italy. At one point, he would shoot down two Bf 109s in less than a minute.

Having been sent back to Britain early in 1944, Horbaczewski was assigned to command No. 315 (Polish) Squadron, which was named "City of Deblin," after the city in Poland where many of the Polish aces in the Royal Air Force had originally earned their wings. Based at Coolham, it was also part of No. 133 (Polish) Wing, which was commanded by Stanislaw Skalski. In March 1944, the City of Deblin Squadron became operational with the Spitfire Mk. V, as well as the American-made North American Mustang III, the equivalent to the USAAF P-51C.

Horbaczewski and No. 315 Squadron took part in operations leading up to and following the June 6, 1944 Normandy Invasion. On June 22, Horbaczewski was involved in a rather dramatic display of heroism. When a squadron-mate was forced to make a crash landing in Normandy after a strafing operation, Horbaczewski landed his own aircraft and picked up the wounded pilot—who was unable to walk—and flew him back to Britain for medical attention.

Operationally, the squadron had a varied workload during the summer of 1944. In addition to their missions over Normandy, on June 30 they escorted a group of bombers against targets in Norway. Here they were jumped by a large number of Luftwaffe fighters. Although the Germans were much closer to their bases and the Polish pilots were at the limit of their range, the Poles managed to shoot down eight, and they suffered no losses. Horbaczewski himself shot down one Bf 109 before his guns jammed.

The summer of 1944 was also the time that the Germans began launching barrages of jet-propelled V-1 cruise missiles against Britain. While actual damage from the unguided "buzz bombs" was minimal, the morale implications in Britain were considerable, so all available resources were devoted to shooting them down. No. 315 Squadron was one of those resources. They managed to take out 53, including four downed by Horbaczewski himself.

Early on the morning of August 18, 12 City of Deblin Mustang IIIs were again on patrol over northern France when they surprised and engaged a larger group of Fw 190s belonging to JG 26. They shot down 16—possibly 17—of the Focke-Wulfs, three of them claimed by Horbaczewski. However, the defenders struck back, with three confirmed kills against the Poles. One of these was Eugeniusz Horbaczewski's Mustang.

The stone marker that still stands near the site of his death, outside the French village of Vellennes, records the fact that he was awarded Britain's Distinguished Service Order and Distinguished Flying Cross. It also notes that he was 26 at the time of his death.

★
Flight Lieutenant Eugeniusz Horbaczewski crash-landed this Supermarine Spitfire Mk. IX in Tunisia on April 6, 1943 after a dogfight in which he shot down a German Messerschmitt Bf 109. The aircraft is being salvaged by an RAF Advanced Servicing Unit. *UK Government*

★
Boleslaw Michal "Mike" Gladych joined the No. 303 Polish Fighter Squadron of the RAF in 1940 and flew two tours with them. In January 1944, he was invited by American ace Captain Francis "Gabby" Gabreski to fly P-47 Thunderbolts unofficially with USAAF 56th Fighter Group. He later few numerous missions with the 61st Fighter Squadron. *US Army Air Forces*

# GLADYCH: FIVE AIR FORCES AND THREE LIVES

**WHILE MOST OF THE POLISH PILOTS** who escaped after their country's capitulation wound up flying in "Polish" squadrons in Britain's Royal Air Force, Boleslaw Michel "Mike" Gladych began his expatriate career flying in a "Finnish" squadron in the French Armée de l'Air. His fourth and fifth air forces were the Royal Air Force and the USAAF.

Boleslaw Gladych was born in May 1918 in Warsaw and joined the Polish Air Force in 1938. He had learned to fly the PZL P VII and PZL P XI at Deblin when the war started, but he had not yet officially transitioned into a combat unit. He fled to Romania, where he was briefly interned at Turnu Severin, from which he escaped. When he arrived in France he joined the Groupe de Chasse I/145, a French squadron that was being sent to Finland to fight the Soviet forces. Designated as "Finnish," it also contained Polish volunteer pilots. While Finland was technically neutral in World War II, it had been attacked by the Soviet Union at the end of November 1939, two months after the Soviets had occupied the eastern half of Poland. For Poles in 1939 and 1940, the Soviet Union was almost as much of an enemy as Germany.

Groupe de Chasse I/145 would actually wind up fighting the Luftwaffe on the Western Front when the Germans launched their offensive against France in May 1940. Gladych first faced the enemy, flying an aging Caudron Cr 714 against Bf 109s, on June 10. As the story goes, the Messerschmitt pilot shot up Gladych's outclassed Caudron Cyclone, then dipped his wings and flew away, allowing the future ace to live to fight another day.

Gladych escaped to Britain when France fell. He eventually joined the Royal Air Force's No. 303 (Polish) "City of Warsaw" Squadron, which was commanded by Stanislaw Skalski and was the home, at one time or another over the coming years, to many major Polish aces. Gladych's first action with No. 303 Squadron came on April 26, 1941. This time, he was in the cockpit of a Supermarine Spitfire instead of a Caudron Cyclone, and his first victory was forthcoming. Statisticians recall his first kill as being the 250th by a Polish pilot flying with the Royal Air Force.

After having been injured in June, Gladych was back in action in October with another victory. Beginning in July 1942, he transferred to No. 302 "City of Poznan" Squadron, where he became a flight leader early in 1943. A few months later, a very strange thing happened. During a dogfight over northeastern France, Gladych was attacked by an Fw 190 pilot who shot up his Spitfire but dipped his wings and flew away. It was a replay of the incident that had occurred over France three years earlier. This time Gladych noticed a "13" on the side of the German aircraft and thought he recalled the same number from the previous incident.

In the autumn of 1943, Gladych was grounded by the Royal Air Force when he accidentally almost shot down the aircraft carrying British Prime Minister Winston Churchill. This led to his volunteering for his fifth air force. When he was with No. 303 Squadron, Gladych had met Francis "Gabby" Gabreski, a Polish-American pilot who had volunteered with the unit before the United States had entered the war. Now Gabreski was flying Republic P-47s with the USAAF 56th Fighter Group. With Gabreski's help, Gladych arranged a temporary duty transfer to the 56th Fighter Group and was soon flying combat missions with the group's 61st Fighter Squadron.

On March 8, 1944, the 61st Fighter Squadron was escorting bombers on a strike deep into Germany when Gladych had the strangest experience of his life—a third encounter with the mysterious German pilot with the mysterious number "13." Gladych had shot down one of the Fw 190s that attacked the bomber stream, but he was almost out of ammunition and separated from the rest of the squadron. Two Fw 190s cornered him and indicated that he should land at a nearby airfield. One of them was "13."

Gladych came in low, followed by the two Focke-Wulfs, and lowered his landing gear. When he was over the field, he opened fire, as though he was on a strafing run and gave his P-47 Thunderbolt full throttle. German anti-aircraft gunners returned fire, but they hit the Fw 190s instead of Gladych. On the way home, he ran out of fuel and had to bail out over southern Britain. His action earned him an American Silver Star.

Boleslaw Gladych's ninth, tenth—and last two—victories scored with the USAAF 56th Fighter Group were a pair of Fw 190s that he shot down on September 21, 1944. This would bring his final score with the USAAF to 14. His friend Gabby Gabreski, meanwhile, had the distinction of being the number two top-scoring USAAF ace in the European Theater, with 28.

When the war ended Gladych emigrated to the United States rather than returning to Poland, thus probably saving himself from some prison time as a guest of the Soviet-sponsored Polish government. His having volunteered to assist the Finns in fighting the Soviets would not have been well-received. In 1950, however, he did travel to Europe, where he happened to be in Frankfurt, Germany where a meeting of former German fighter pilots was taking place.

As would happen if the story were fiction—and truth can be as ironic as fiction—Mike Gladych found himself face-to-face with the man who had worn number 13 on all three previous encounters. Gladych finally shook the hand of Georg-Peter Eder, who had ended the war as an ace with 78 victories.

# THE OTHER ALLIED FORCES

# CZECHOSLOVAKIA

**CZECHOSLOVAKIA WAS CREATED IN 1918** as a union of Bohemia, Moravia and Slovakia that were part of the Austro Hungarian Empire, until its collapse in 1918. During the next two decades, Czechoslovakia evolved as the most democratic and economically developed nation in central or eastern Europe. However, Adolf Hitler used the presence of a sizable German-speaking population in the Sudetenland area of western Bohemia to demand that this area be absorbed into the German Reich. When France and Britain agreed at the famous Munich Conference in September 1938, Hitler was emboldened and Europe began slipping toward war. Then, in March 1939, Hitler sent troops to occupy Bohemia and Moravia in violation of the Munich Treaty.

The Czechoslovakia military ceased to exist and, as was the case with the Poles six months later, many Czech airmen escaped to fight the Germans in the uniforms of other nations. Some escaped to Poland, most eventually reached France, and then moved on to Britain when France surrendered. Their story is an amazing odyssey escaping the collapse of a series of independent nations, while serving in the air force of each as they went.

The highest-scoring Czech ace was Karel Miroslav Kuttelwascher. He scored at least three with the Armée de l'Air's Groupe de Chasse III/6 before being forced to evacuate to Britain. With the Royal Air Force, Kuttelwascher scored 18 victories while serving with both No. 1 Squadron and No. 23 Squadron.

★ [Above]
This Hawker Hurricane, number PZ865, is painted in the same colors and markings as the one flown by Karel Kuttelwascher during World War II. *Photo by Adrian Pingstone licensed under Wikimedia Commons*

★ [Opposite]
Karel "Kut" Kuttelwascher, seen here in April 1942 around the time of his eighth aerial victory while flying with the RAF, was the highest-scoring Czech pilot of World War II. He scored 18 with the RAF, and at least three while flying with the French early in 1940. *Wikimedia Commons*

★

Josef František was the second highest-scoring Czech ace of World War II, though his career was short. He was killed in a crash in October 1940 during the final week of the Battle of Britain. Having previously flown with the air forces of both Czechoslovakia and France, he flew with the No. 303 (Polish) Squadron of Britain's Royal Air Force. *Wikimedia Commons*

The second highest-scoring Czech ace with the Royal Air Force was Josef František, who scored 17 victories with No. 303 (Polish) Squadron before being killed in a flying accident on October 8, 1940. There are unconfirmed reports that he scored as many as 11 victories with the French Armée de l'Air before reaching Britain. If true, these would make him the highest-scoring Czech ace.

Born at Otaslavice near Prostejov in October 1913, František joined the Czech air force in 1934 and earned his wings at Prostejov in 1936. He was initially assigned to the 5th Observation Flight of the 2nd "Dr. Eduard Benes" Regiment at Olomouc. He was later picked for fighter pilot training because of his exceptional skill, and in June 1938 he was assigned to the 40th Fighter Flight. Based near Prague, the 40th Fighter Flight was equipped with Czech-manufactured Avia B 534 fighter aircraft, with which the Czech capital would have been defended if Czechoslovakia had not surrendered without a fight in March 1939.

František left Czechoslovakia for neighboring Poland, from which he had intended to move on to France, like many Czech pilots from his former unit. In July 1939, he had accepted an opportunity to join the Polish Air Force. When the Germans attacked in September, František was assigned to an observation unit and saw no combat. On September 22, 1939, he was one of three Czech pilots who participated in an operation aimed at evacuating Polish aircraft to Romania to avoid their being captured by the Germans.

František was interned briefly in Romania, but he escaped to Marseilles via Beirut, reaching France on October 20. In France, František became part a Polish unit within the Armée de l'Air. Some sources state that he scored as many as 11 kills during the Battle of France, but official documentation, if it ever existed, has been lost. One story suggests that he changed his name while he was in France to prevent German reprisals against his family in Czechoslovakia. If so, his Armée de l'Air victories may have been scored under this unknown assumed name.

When France fell in June 1940, František escaped again. This time to England. On August 2—still traveling with Polish pilots with whom he had been flying in two other air forces—he arrived at Northolt and reported for duty with the Royal Air Force's No. 303 (Polish) Squadron. Soon he was deep in the thick of the Battle of Britain.

František scored his first victory with the Royal Air Force on September 2 over Dover, downing a Bf 109 in a Hawker Hurricane Mk. I. He scored a second the following day, and five on September 6. His amazing success in so short a time suggests that he was not a beginner and that he must have had at least some previous combat successes, probably with the Armée de l'Air. On September 15, when No. 303 Squadron scored 16 victories, František was credited with a Bf 110.

František was one of the leading aces in all the Royal Air Force. He was a pilot with amazing skill and enormous potential, but he also had a tendency to break formation to hunt alone, which did not please his commanders.

On October 8 his flight was on patrol over Surrey when, as had become his habit, he peeled off to fly alone. Nobody saw what happened. His Hurricane crashed near the village of Ewell, but there was no evidence that he had been shot down. His body was found near the crashed aircraft with no visible injuries except the broken neck which was the cause of his death.

# NORWAY

**NORWAY,** like Denmark and Sweden, had remained neutral in World War I and hoped to do so in World War II. However, like Denmark, Norway was invaded on April 9, 1940. Sweden, unlike the others, had prepared for war and was not attacked. Both Denmark and Norway were overwhelmed, and the capitals of both countries were captured in a matter of days. British troops landed in the north of Norway and held on until June, when they were forced to withdraw. Norway's King Haakon VII, who had fled to Britain, formally surrendered his country on June 9.

Many Norwegian pilots escaped to join the Royal Air Force, and among them was Svein Heglund, who flew with No. 331 Squadron and No. 85 Squadron. He became Norway's only World War II ace, with at least 14 victories.

★
Kaptein Svein Heglund, seen here in August 1943, was Norway's highest-scoring ace of World War II. He flew with No. 85 and No. 331 Squadrons of Britain's Royal Air Force. *Wikimedia Commons*

★
The insignias of several of the countries whose pilots became aces while flying for the Allied cause. From left, they are Czechoslovakia, Norway, the Netherlands and Belgium. *Author's Collection*

# NETHERLANDS

**WORLD WAR II BEGAN WITH GERMANY'S THRUST TO THE EAST AGAINST POLAND,** and it was assumed to be only a matter of time before Hitler turned west to attack France, which German armies had invaded twice since 1870. However, between the two lay the "low countries" of Luxembourg, the Netherlands and Belgium. Luxembourg and Belgium were badly mauled in World War I, but the Netherlands had remained neutral and, like the Scandinavian countries, hoped to do so again. However, the Netherlands' very name, which means "low country," explains why it is virtually indefensible. It is flat, with no natural barriers to invasion. The terrain is naturally suited to the kind of blitzkrieg tactics that the Germans had developed and used so effectively in Poland.

When the German invasion of Western Europe began on May 10, 1940, Belgium and the Netherlands came first. The Dutch city of Rotterdam was flattened by the Luftwaffe and the Netherlands army surrendered after just four days. Following the defeat, many of the former Royal Netherlands Air Force pilots went to Britain to fly with the British Royal Air Force. One, Gerald Kesseler, became an ace with 16 victories. In 1944, when Germany launched its air offensive against Britain with the V-1 cruise missiles, a number of Dutch pilots were involved in the interception effort. The highest-scoring Dutch pilot during this phase of operations was probably Rudolph Frans "Rudy" Burgwal, who claimed 21. He was killed on August 12, 1944 while flying a bomber escort mission.

# BELGIUM

**IN BOTH WORLD WARS**, Belgium was seen by Germany as merely a steppingstone to France, and in both wars, Belgian resistance to the invasion lasted but a few weeks. In World War II, Belgium was invaded on May 10 and it surrendered on May 28. Through most of both world wars, Belgian pilots found themselves fighting the invader of their country from the outside, after Belgium was occupied by German armies. In World War I, the Belgian air force retired to France to fight for four long years. There were several important Belgian aces during the first war, with the highest scoring, by far, being Willy Omer Francois Jean Coppens, who scored 37 victories.

The Belgian ace to achieve the highest score during World War II was a nobleman named Yvan Georges Arsene Felician du Monceau de Bergandael. He fought briefly against the German offensive during the spring of 1940, and later escaped to Britain by way of Gibraltar. He joined the Royal Air Force and was assigned initially to No. 253 Squadron but was soon instrumental in helping to organize the Belgian contingent within No. 609 Squadron. He later served with both No. 349 and No. 350 Squadrons. Referred to by his squadron mates as "Duke," because of his family's nobility, Monceau de Bergandael scored a total of eight victories.

★
Yvan Du Monceau de Bergendal was a Belgian nobleman who was his country's highest-scoring ace. He flew in the defense of his country during the 18 days between the German invasion and the final collapse. He then escaped to Britain, where he flew with Belgian expatriates in several RAF squadrons. *Author's Collection*

# THE OTHER AXIS FORCES

# SLOVAKIA

**IN MARCH 1939**, when Bohemia and Moravia were incorporated into the German Reich and Czechoslovakia disappeared, Slovakia declared itself an independent ally of Nazi Germany. When World War II began six months later, the pilots of the former air force of Czechoslovakia went two ways. As noted in the previous chapter, the now-stateless Czech pilots went—by way of Poland and/or France—to Britain to fight against Germany with the Royal Air Force. The Slovaks formed their own air force, the Slovenské Vzdušné Zbrane (SVZ). It was equipped by Germany and placed under the operational control of the Luftwaffe.

By 1944, however, it was clear that Germany was going to lose the war, and a movement got underway to change sides. This was pragmatic as well as idealistic. Slovakia could see that it was going to be occupied by Soviet troops and it was obviously better to be an anti-German country "liberated" by the Soviets rather than a pro-German country "defeated" by the Soviets. In August, a Slovak National Council was formed, and an uprising against the Tiso government began. The Slovak National Uprising was declared on August 29 and it allied itself with the Czechoslovakian government in exile in Britain. Many of the pilots of the SVZ, who had fought with the Luftwaffe, switched sides and began fighting against the Luftwaffe. German forces, however, were superior to those of the Slovak National Council, and the uprising was contained. Slovakia was occupied by Soviet forces in 1945, and not reunited with Czechoslovakia until 1993.

Though records are incomplete, it is known that there were at least 14 aces in the SVZ. All of them flew under Luftwaffe Jagdgeschwader control, and almost all of their victories were scored against the Soviet Voenno-Vozdushnie Sily. The highest-scoring aces were all under the control of JG 52. Ján Reznák was the top Slovak ace. He is credited, according to various sources, with 32 or 33 victories while flying with JG 52. In second place was Izidor Kovárik, who scored 28 or 29 kills with JG 52 before being shot down and killed on July 11, 1944, a month before the Slovak National Uprising.

★
Leading Slovak ace Ján Reznák in the cockpit of his Bk-534 (B-534) fighter in June 1941. The aircraft was manufactured by Avia, the largest planemaker in Czechoslovakia before the war, and a manufacturer of German-designed aircraft during and after the war. *Author's Collection*

★
Izidor Kovárik and Ján Reznák, the two highest-scoring Slovak aces scored their aerial victories while flying with the German Luftwaffe. This photo was taken on April 25, 1944, three months before Kovárik was killed in action. *Author's Collection*

A model of a
Messerschmitt Bf 109
in wartime Hungarian
markings is the
centerpiece of the tomb
of Dezso Szentgyörgyi,
located in Budapest's
Farkasréti Cemetery.
He was Hungary's
leading ace. *Photo
by Szenti Tamás,
licensed under Creative
Commons*

# HUNGARY

**IN THE EARLY YEARS OF WORLD WAR II**, Hungary was probably the most staunchly loyal of the second tier Axis powers. The strongly nationalistic dictator of Hungary, Admiral Miklós Horthy de Nagybánya, enthusiastically emulated Hitler and Mussolini. He saw an alliance with them as a good route to restoring the national pride lost when 1920's Treaty of Trianon had taken away nearly three quarters of the territory that it had as a kingdom within the old Austro-Hungarian Empire. Horthy had been the last commander in chief of the Austro Hungarian Navy and he became regent of Hungary in 1920, ruling with the proverbial iron fist until 1944. In that year, sensing that Germany would lose to the Allies, he attempted through secret negotiations to switch sides. However, the Germans got wind of his plans and jailed him. After the war he retired to Portugal, where he would live until his death in 1957.

Hungary was the last Axis power in Europe to stand by Hitler, fighting on until May 1945.

During World War II, Horthy's air force fought alongside the Germans, first against the Soviet VVS, and later against the USAAF. Hungary's first ace was Imre Panezel, who scored his five during 1942 and who was declared missing in action during a mission on January 11, 1943. The leading Hungarian ace was Dezso Szentgyörgyi, who scored at least 32 (some sources say 34) victories. He first saw action on the Eastern Front in 1942 and scored his first victory on June 5, 1943.

During 1944, Hungary itself started to come under air attack by long-range heavy bombers of the USAAF Fifteenth Air Force, based in Italy. With this, the Royal Hungarian Home Defense Air Force had to reorient its priorities to air defense of the homeland rather than offensive operations against the Soviet Union. During this period, Szentgyörgyi flew with 2 VSzd of 101 Regiment and claimed five USAAF aircraft, four of them B-24 Liberators.

The air defense mission soon also included the Soviet VVS, as Soviet aircraft began flying over Hungary by winter. Szentgyörgyi continued to fly against the Soviets until Hungary capitulated early in 1945, scoring 20 victories against Soviet aircraft. For this, he was imprisoned by the Soviet Union for many years, but he was eventually "rehabilitated." He went on to fly as an airline pilot until his death in an air crash in 1971.

He is honored today by the modern, post-Communist Hungarian air force, who named a regiment after him. The 59th "Dezso Szentgyörgyi" Tactical Fighter Regiment based at Kecskemet is considered to be the most important unit in the air force.

# CROATIA

**CROATIA TOOK ADVANTAGE OF GERMANY'S INVASION OF YUGOSLAVIA IN 1941** to declare its independence, and remained so until 1944. It would then go back into the Yugoslav federation after World War II, but again declare its independence in 1991. Between 1941 and 1944, Croatia was ruled by the cruel nationalist Ante Pavelic, who allied himself closely with Fascist Italy and gladly associated himself with Nazi Germany. During those years, Croatian pilots fought against Serbs, Greeks and Soviet forces. They were organized into special Croatian squadrons within the Luftwaffe, especially Kroaten Staffeln 15 of the Luftwaffe's JG 52, and were equipped with Messerschmitt Bf 109s. The leading Croatian ace was probably Cvitan Galic, who flew with Kroaten Staffeln 15 until he was killed in action on April 6, 1944. He is credited with at least 36 victories, although some sources list him with 38.

★
Izidor Kovárik in his Messerschmitt Bf 109G-4 in the spring of 1943, when he was flying with the Luftwaffe on the Eastern Front. *Author's Collection*

★
Captain Constantin
Cantacuzino (left)
was a nobleman and
prewar aerobat who
became Romania's top-
scoring ace of World
War II. He is seen here
in Lucenec, Slovakia
on April 10, 1945 as
the war neared its end.
He is with Captain
Mircea Badulescu
and General Traian
Burduloiu, who had
assumed command
of the Romanian
Air Force a month
earlier. *Photo from
Mircea T. Badulescu,
licensed under Creative
Commons*

# ROMANIA

**LIKE HUNGARY,** Romania entered World War II ruled by a powerful nationalist faction that was in sympathy with the goals and philosophy of Nazi Germany and Fascist Italy. Beginning in 1938, King Karol II attempted to rule as an absolute monarch, but in 1940 the government was taken over by the fascist Iron Guard under General Ion Antonescu, who kept Karol as a mere figurehead. Antonescu joined the Axis when Romania was forced to cede Bessarabia and Bucovina to the Soviet Union and northern Transylvania to Hungary. When Germany invaded the Soviet Union in June 1941, Antonescu supplied troops that took a full and active part in offensive operations.

Romanian forces fought shoulder to shoulder with the Germans until 1944, when the Soviet counteroffensive finally pushed them out of Soviet territory and into Romania itself. Facing the most unpleasant prospects of being occupied by the Soviet army as a conqueror, King Michael (Karol's son) formed a coalition with the Romanian Communist party and other factions to successfully overthrow Antonescu. In August 1944, Romania joined the Allies, but in March 1945, King Michael was forced to accept a Communist dominated Soviet puppet government, and eventually to abdicate when the monarchy was abolished in 1947.

Between 1941 and 1944, the Royal Romanian Air Force produced as many as 20 aces on the Eastern Front, and in the air defense of Romania against USAAF Fifteenth Air Force long-range bombers. The actual number is unclear for a number of reasons, loss of accurate records being one. Another is the strange and complicated Royal Romanian Air Force practice of awarding multiple points depending on the type of aircraft shot down. This practice, which was probably not instituted in its final form until 1944, called for awarding three "victories" to a pilot that claimed a four-engine bomber, and two victories for downing a twin-engine aircraft. Shooting down a fighter in a dogfight, however, merely counted as one. The purpose of this practice was obviously for domestic consumption, to keep morale up when the big bombers started showing up over Romania's major cities.

The highest-scoring Romanian ace also has the distinction of being the highest-scoring ace of noble birth. The colorful Count Constantin Cantacuzine (or Cantacuzino) was an extraordinary pilot who had flown in aerobatic meets before the war and who would do so again after the war, well into the 1950s. The count's actual count, however, is uncertain because of the usual discrepancies in record-keeping and the complex method of counting multiple-engine victories. He is often listed with as many as 56 to 60 victories, but his actual number of aircraft shot down is probably closer to the 43 that is often suggested.

★
Romanian aces Alexandru Serbanescu and Ioan Dicezare in a wartime press photo. Serbanescu was Romania's second highest-scoring ace, with at least 47 victories, while Dicezare achieved 16. Both men were killed in action in August 1944, shortly before Romania capitulated to the Allies. *Wikimedia Commons*

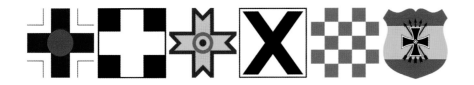

★
The insignias of several of the countries whose pilots became aces while flying in support of the German war effort. From left, they are those of Slovakia, Hungary, Romania, Bulgaria, Croatia, and of the Spanish Blue Division. *Author's Collection*

# BULGARIA

**THOUGH IT WAS A MEMBER OF THE AXIS**, Bulgaria was less aggressive than either Hungary or Romania in contributing to the Axis war effort. King Boris III ruled with a strong hand internally, but after he died in 1943 there was a power vacuum. The Soviet Union invaded in September 1944 and occupied the country in a matter of months.

As with the Royal Romanian Air Force, the Bulgarians adopted the practice of awarding multiple points depending on the number of an enemy aircraft's engines. However, not only did the Bulgarians award three "victories" to a pilot that claimed a four-engine bomber, they would give him two victories for just damaging it. The leading Bulgarian ace was Stoyan Iliev Stoyanov, who flew with the 682 Jato (Squadron). He is credited with 14 victories under the Bulgarian system, but is believed to have actually shot down four, shared in a fifth, and damaged four.

# SPAIN

★
Angel Salas-Larrazábal [far right] in seen here with a group of Spanish pilots who flew in support of the Luftwaffe on the Eastern Front in World War II. He was a leading ace flying with the Nationalists in the Spanish Civil War, and added to his score while flying with the Escuadrilla Azul (the Spanish Blue Squadron) on the Eastern Front in World War II. The Escuadrilla Azul included pilots from five Spanish squadrons who rotated through the Eastern Front between September 1941 and May 1943. They were attached to the Luftwaffe's Jagdgeschwader 27 and 51. The man in black is the Spanish ambassador to Berlin, José Finat.
*Wikimedia Commons*

**BETWEEN 1936 AND 1939**, the Spanish Civil War tore the country apart, with bloodshed on a scale that exceeded any European conflict of the twentieth century except during the two world wars. The two sides became so polarized that they invited the killing machines of Germany, Italy and the Soviet Union to come to Spain and kill other Spaniards. Nationalist leader General Francisco Franco won the war with the help of Germany and Italy, but Franco never officially intervened in World War II to return the favor.

In June 1941, when Germany invaded the Soviet Union, however, Franco was anxious to get back at his old enemy, and he supplied ground troops in the form of the famous Spanish Blue Division. A number of Spanish pilots also served in the Luftwaffe, especially with the Spanish Escuadrilla Azul (Blue Squadron) during World War II. One Spanish Civil War Nationalist ace who also scored victories in World War II was Angel Salas-Larrazábal, who had 16.33 victories in Spain and would add seven to his score in World War II. He remained with the Ejército del Aire (Spanish Air Force) after the war, retiring in 1972. In 1991, he was made an honorary Captain General of the Ejército del Aire. He died in 1994.

# CHAPTER

## 12

# FINLAND

**D**URING WORLD WAR II, Finland had the distinction of being the only small country in Europe that successfully resisted both the Soviet Union and Germany. As Josef Stalin, whose armies defeated Germany but not Finland, said in 1948 with a great deal of irony, "Nobody respects a country with a poor army, but everybody respects a country with a good army. I raise my toast to the Finnish Army."

The Finnish Air Force, known as the Ilmavoimat, also had the ace who out-scored the top aces of every country in the world except Germany. With a score of 94.17, Eino Ilmari Juutilainen had more confirmed kills than any non-Luftwaffe ace, although Japan's Hiroyoshi Nishizawa and Tetsuzo Iwamoto had unconfirmed claims that may have put them over the 100 mark. Juutilainen was also the only non-Axis ace to exceed the World War I score of 80, achieved by the "Red Baron," Manfred von Richthofen.

Finland had nearly 100 aces, more than any country other than the biggest three Allied and biggest three Axis nations. Behind Juutilainen, the leading Finnish aces were Hans Henrik Wind, with 75 victories; Eino Antero "Ekka" Luukkanen (a boyhood friend of Juutilainen) with 56; Urho Sakari Lehtovaara with 44.5; Oiva Emil Kalervo Tuominen with 44; Risto Olli Petter Puhakka with 42; Olavi Kauko Puro with 36, and Nils Edvard Katajainen with 35.5. As an added footnote, both Juutilainen and Jorma Sarvanto (16.83 total victories) would each score six in one day.

The famous "secret protocol" to the Hitler-Stalin non-aggression pact of August 24, 1939 stated that Finland, Estonia, Latvia and Lithuania belonged to the Soviet sphere of interest. In October, the latter three decided to become part of the Soviet Union rather than risk war, and so they would remain for 51 years. Finland rejected Stalin's demands and on November 30, the Soviet army attacked. During the ensuing "Winter War," the Soviet forces captured the Karelia and Salla areas, but the Finns fought them to a standstill. A ceasefire signed on March 13, 1940.

On June 25, 1941, three days after the German invasion of the Soviet Union, Finland was again attacked. With the help of Germany, Finland would manage to continue to resist the Soviet armies for more than three years. For Germany and Finland, it was a marriage of convenience rather than an alliance. The Soviet Union was a common enemy. Finland never joined the Axis, and was never at war with any Allied power other than the Soviet Union.

During the "Continuation War" (as the conflict after 1941 was called), Germany supplied Finland with materiel—including Messerschmitt Bf 109s for the Ilmavoimat, and Finland allowed Germany access to facilities in Lapland—the far north of Finland—which was adjacent to German bases in occupied Norway. For Germany, the value of having Finland on its side was that the Finns were tenacious and effective fighters, and they kept sizable numbers of Soviet troops and aircraft tied down and unavailable for combat against the Germans. The Soviet Union was never able to defeat the Finns.

★
Finnish fighter ace Sergeant Oiva Tuominen, photographed on October 10, 1941. He was one of several aces to be a recipient of the Mannerheim Cross. *Sotamuseo photo licensed under Creative Commons*

★
Hasse Wind steps out of his Brewster B239 fighter at Suulajärvi Airfield on August 26, 1943. He scored more than half of his aerial victories in the American-made fighter that was considered obsolete by many air forces. *Wikimedia Commons*

★ (Right)
Finnish fighter
ace Sergeant Nils
Katajainen of Fighter
Squadron 24 prepares
to take off from the
airfield at Lappeenrant
for a mission in his
Messerschmitt Bf
109G-8. *Wikimedia
Commons*

★ (Below, left)
Lieutenant Jorma
Kalevi Sarvanto of
Squadron 24 returns
to Selkäpää Airfield
after scoring a victory
on June 24, 1941.
*Wikimedia Commons*

★ (Below, right)
Lieutenant Olli
Puhakka returning
from a winter 1942
patrol flight between
the airfields at
Äänisjärvi and Viitana.
After the war, he had
a long career as an
airline pilot. *Sotamuseo
photo licensed under
Creative Commons*

# JUUTILAINEN:
## FINLAND'S ACE OF ACES

**THE ACE WITH THE GREATEST SCORE OF ANYONE OUTSIDE GERMANY** was born on February 21, 1914 in Lieksa and grew up in Sortavala, where there was an Ilmavoimat base. Eino Ilmari Juutilainen's interest in military aviation came from watching aircraft at this base as a youngster. When it came time for his required military service at age 18, he was assigned as a mechanic with the 1st Separate Maritime Squadron, but he learned to fly on his own and joined the Ilmavoimat in 1933. After initial military flight training, he went through an intensive fighter pilot school at Utti, which—if the performance of the Ilmavoimat in World War II is any indication—was one of the best in the world.

In March 1939, Juutilainen was assigned to Lentolaivue 24 (Squadron 24), also at the base at Utti, the squadron with which he would remain until 1943. On the eve of the war Lentolaivue 24 was equipped with Fokker D-21s, which were built in the Netherlands and did not represent the leading edge in fighter aircraft technology.

By October 1939, as the Soviet Union began to demand territorial concessions from Finland, war was seen as inevitable. Finnish military units were put on alert and prepared for combat. Lentolaivue 24 was deployed to Immola, so as to be close to the border with the Soviet Union, and camouflaged shelters were prepared. When the Winter War began at the end of November, the Ilmavoimat was as ready as it could be to meet the Soviet offensive. The Fokker D-21s were inferior to the Soviet Polikarpov I-15s and I-16s, but Finnish pilot training was superior.

Most aerial combat in the Winter War was governed not by hardware but by the weather. For much of the first two weeks of the war, aircraft on both sides were grounded.

Juutilainen's combat action did not take place until December 19, when an element of Lentolaivue 24 intercepted a strike force of Ilyushin DB 3 bombers. When attacked, the bombers turned to run and Juutilainen quickly shot one down. The others were damaged, but the Fokkers turned back when their ammunition was exhausted and did not observe the Soviets crash. Four days later, Juutilainen participated in another intercept, and on New Year's Eve he found himself in his first dogfight. The Soviet I 16 had the technical advantage but Juutilainen outflew him and, through superior marksmanship, outgunned him as well.

When the Winter War ended in March 1940, the Ilmavoimat had been molded into a very effective force. It was certainly respected by the Soviet VVS. Finland attempted to acquire better aircraft from Britain and France, but they were gearing up for their coming fight with Germany, so the best that Finland was able to do was a small number of Gloster Gladiators. They turned to the United States, where they were able to acquire 44 Brewster Model B239 Buffalos, a type which had entered United States Navy service under the designation F2A-1. The Finns would retrofit their Buffalos with extra armor aft of the cockpit that was not present in the stock F2A-1.

★
Ilmari Juutilainen, seen here on June 26, 1942 after his 20th aerial victory, was Finland's top-scoring ace and probably the highest-scoring non-German ace in history. *Blomberg photo licensed under Creative Commons*

Today, the Buffalo is recalled as having been a cumbersome and inferior aircraft, but in 1940 it was a major improvement to the Ilmavoimat fighter force.

On June 25, 1941, three days after Germany launched its massive invasion against the Soviet Union, Soviet bombers appeared over Finland. The so-called "Continuation War" had begun. Now based at Rantasalmi Air Base, Lentolaivue 24 first saw action on July 9, when it was tasked with intercepting a VVS bomber force. It was on this morning that Juutilainen flew in his first combat action of the war, and his first with a Buffalo. He attacked an element of Polikarpov I 153s that were escorting the bombers and shot one down only to be attacked by another. He evaded the second I-153, which turned off, formed up with a second Soviet fighter, and started running for the border. Juutilainen chased the two enemy fighters and brought down one as the other escaped. In its first day of combat in the resumed war, Lentolaivue 24 had downed nine enemy aircraft, among them two for Juutilainen.

His next victories came on August 18, when Lentolaivue 24 was involved in a huge aerial battle over the Gulf of Finland. In the early stages of the fight, Juutilainen shot down an I 16, which was his fifth victory, the one that made him an ace. However, the fight was not yet over. He was attacked again and again by aggressive I-16 pilots, both of whom fell to the Buffalo's guns. If the Polikarpovs were superior to the D-21, they were clearly outclassed by the Buffalos. Lentolaivue 24 would claim 16 aircraft for the day, and new ace Ilmari Juutilainen had three of them.

On September 20, Juutilainen would shoot down a fighter that was absolutely superior to the Buffalo. By this time, the British had delivered Hawker Hurricanes and a small number of Supermarine Spitfires to the VVS, and the aircraft that Juutilainen shot down on this date is believed to have been one of these Spitfires.

Juutilainen had experienced engine trouble during a fight and was making his way back to base when the aircraft thought to be a Spitfire attacked from behind. Juutilainen waited until the last possible moment, when he expected the Soviet pilot to open fire, and then he threw the Buffalo into a quick roll. This unexpected maneuver threw the enemy off guard and he overshot Juutilainen, who then came in behind and opened fire, sending the Spitfire down in flames. Another Spitfire attacked, but Juutilainen out-maneuvered him and he broke off the attack.

As Juutilainen continued to nurse the crippled Buffalo toward his base, he was bounced by a MiG-1. After a tight, turning fight, which was at slow speed because that was all the Buffalo could muster, Juutilainen saw an opportunity for a shot and took it. He had now scored twice in a malfunctioning aircraft.

Juutilainen's skills—and his growing number of victories—attracted a great deal of attention, both from the Ilmavoimat community and from a grateful nation. On April 26, 1942, he was awarded the Mannerheim Cross, Finland's highest decoration for bravery. He was also coming to be well known in the Soviet Union. After the war he learned that VVS pilots considered him a pilot to avoid.

The Buffalo was good to Juutilainen, and to the Ilmavoimat, but as the months wore on it was clearly becoming obsolete in the same skies as the generation of fighters that was coming on line in 1943. The Ilmavoimat high command knew this and negotiated with the Germans to acquire the aircraft with which the Luftwaffe was tearing the VVS to shreds, the Messerschmitt Bf 109.

In February 1943, the Ilmavoimat organized a new squadron, Lentolaivue 34, to operate the new fighters and, naturally, Juutilainen was assigned as one of the pilots. He was also among those that were sent to Germany to familiarize themselves with the aircraft, specifically the Bf

109G 2 model, and to begin flying them back to Finland. The Messerschmitt was vastly superior to the Buffalo, and in the hands of the well-trained and battle-hardened Finnish pilots, it was an extraordinary weapon. The Bf 109G-2 made it possible for Juutilainen to build his score into the 80s and 90s, and for the Ilmavoimat to keep the much larger VVS at bay.

It was not until the VVS started deploying the Lavochkin La 5 and the Yakovlev Yak 9 that there were Soviet-built warplanes in the skies over Finland capable of challenging the Messerschmitts. It was on August 31, 1943 that Juutilainen first encountered the Lavochkin fighter. For him, being attacked by an La-5 was just like fighting an I-15 in a Buffalo. It was a turning battle in which he kept the VVS pilot from getting a clear shot until he managed to get behind the Soviet aircraft and line him up in the gunsight.

Juutilainen's best day of the war came on June 30, 1944, when he succeeded in shooting down six enemy aircraft in a single day. First came a battle in which he claimed a pair of P 39 Airacobras, and next a pair of Yak 9s. The Lentolaivue 34 formation was just running low on fuel when they encountered a bomber strike force, escorted by La-5s, headed for Viipuri. The Finnish Bf 109s made the intercept and Juutilainen downed a Sturmovik attack bomber and one of the Lavochkins.

By the autumn of 1944, the Soviet Union was locked in its massive life and death Great Patriotic War with Nazi Germany. The sideshow war with Finland—which was neither "great" nor "patriotic"—was a stalemate that offered little more than a drain on resources, so Stalin made the decision to call it off.

The war would officially end on September 4, and Juutilainen's last combat mission—and 94th victory—came the day before. His patrol was bounced by a VVS fighter over Carelia, possibly hoping to get a kill before the war ended, but the fighter broke off after one pass, and in the course of looking for him, Juutilainen encountered and shot down a Lisunov Li 2 transport. It was a rather anticlimactic close to a stellar career.

In 437 missions, Juutilainen had scored 54 victories in the Messerschmitt Bf 109G-2, 36 in the Brewster Buffalo and his first four—plus a shared victory—in the old Fokker D-21. He was awarded his second Mannerheim Cross on June 28, 1944, making him one of only four people to be awarded two. One of the others was Hans Wind, Finland's second highest-scoring ace.

Juutilainen retired from the Ilmavoimat in May 1947 and would pursue a career in commercial aviation, while flying his own private plane on the side. He would live to see the collapse of his old nemesis, the Soviet Union. He died on February 21, 1999 in Tuusula.

★
Ilmari Juutilainen taxiing his Brewster B239 fighter at Tiiksjärvi Airfield, Eastern Karelia during the winter of 1942-1943. *Finnish Heritage Agency photo licensed under Creative Commons*

# WIND: FINLAND'S SECOND HIGHEST-SCORING ACE

**HANS HENRIK "HASSE" WIND** was born on July 30, 1919 in Tammisaari and joined the Ilmavoimat as a reserve pilot in 1938. A shortage of aircraft kept him out of action during the Winter War, but he joined the active Ilmavoimat in 1941, so he was on hand when the war resumed in June 1941. This was less than a week after Wind was commissioned as a lieutenant.

In August 1941 he was transferred to Lentolaivue 24, where he would fly Buffalos alongside Juutilainen. His first victory, against a Polikarpov I-15, came in September, but he progressed rather slowly, adding only two kills through July 1942, when Lentolaivue 24 was transferred to Rompotti on the Gulf of Finland. At this point, things began to pick up for Hasse Wind. He achieved ace status on August 14, shooting down a pair of Hawker Hurricanes. Four days later, Lentolaivue 24 tangled with a large force of VVS aircraft and Wind claimed another Hurricane and two I 16s.

Wind's ninth came on October 10, when his three-Buffalo patrol was attacked by a dozen MiG-3s. One of them got on his tail and he was unable to out-turn him to get into firing position, so he maneuvered the turning battle lower and lower until the Soviet fighter crashed into the ground. By the end of 1942, his score stood at 14.5.

The Messerschmitt Bf 109s entered service with the Ilmavoimat in February 1943, but Wind remained with Lentolaivue 24 and continued to fly the Buffalo. He had become certainly the best Buffalo pilot in the world. American and British Commonwealth pilots who were using them against the Japanese in the Far East at exactly this same time frame were completely overwhelmed by the Mitsubishi A6M Zero, but Wind became a Buffalo expert.

On April 5, 1943, Wind shot down three Il 2 Sturmovik attack bombers, which were considered to be very difficult because they were so heavily armored and had a rear-firing gunner who made attacks from behind difficult. Nine days later, he managed to shoot down a pair of Supermarine Spitfires, an aircraft that was far superior to the Buffalo—but, of course, only in the hands of a superior pilot.

On his 24th birthday in July 1943, Hasse Wind was awarded his first Mannerheim Cross. His score now stood at 33.5, and in October, Wind was promoted to Captain. Over the winter he would add another sort of achievement to his resume. In the course of training new pilots, Wind wrote a manual that would remain in use at the Ilmavoimat for the next three decades.

Lentolaivue 24 had begun to convert to Bf 109G-2s in the summer of 1943, but Wind continued to fly his

★
Finnish ace and Knight of the Mannerheim Cross, Lieutenant Hans Henrik "Hasse" Wind (center) with his ground crew on September 12, 1943. *Wikimedia Commons*

Buffalo until May 1944. His first victory in the Messerschmitt came on May 27, when he claimed a pair of La 5s. When the Soviet offensive in the Isthmus of Carelia began on June 9, a badly outnumbered Lentolaivue 24 and Lentolaivue 34 were tasked with intercepting the VVS bombers that accompanied the ground attack.

Flying as many as seven missions a day, the Ilmavoimat pilots were nearly overwhelmed by this effort to inflict a final defeat on Finland. But the Ilmavoimat took its toll. June 13 was not a lucky day for the VVS in the sector patrolled by Hasse Wind's flight of six Messerschmitts. During the morning they sighted a force of Petlyakov Pe 2 bombers and quickly shot down eight—three of them claimed by Wind himself, one after the other in quick succession.

The day was not over. During the afternoon, Wind's patrol shot down four more Pe-2s out of a flight of six—with Wind claiming two for himself—and escaped before the escort fighters could even engage them. It was days like June 13 that made Stalin decide to give up on Finland.

Hasse Wind was on a streak. Over the next 11 days he subtracted more of Stalin's assets, while adding 25 kill marks to the tail of his Bf 109G-6—three more Pe-2s, a Sturmovik, two DB-3s, two Spitfires, three Airacobras, two Yak-7s, five Yak-9s and seven La-5s. In a span of less than two weeks, Wind had shot down 30 VVS aircraft, and had three days on which he shot down five.

Streaks like this never last, and time was running out for Hasse Wind. He claimed another three Yak-9s on June 26, but two days later it all came to an end. He and his wingman, Nils "Nipa" Katajainen (an ace with 30 victories to Wind's 72), were ordered to undertake an armed reconnaissance deep into enemy territory south of Vyborg. Nearing the target, Wind led an attack on seven Yak 9, only to be bounced by another 20 VVS fighters.

Wind managed to shoot down three of the Yaks, but he was, in turn, fired on by an Airacobra. A 37mm shell exploded in the cockpit, badly wounding him. The Messerschmitt was on fire and spiraling down. To the Soviets, it probably looked like a kill for their side. However, Wind managed to pull out and struggle back to his base at Lappeenranta. He assumed that Katajainen had been shot down.

When he landed, Wind was so weak from loss of blood that he had to be lifted from the cockpit of his Messerschmitt. He would not know, until he woke up in the hospital a week later, that Katajainen had also survived the melee. On June 26, Katajainen also assumed that Wind was dead. After he saw Wind's Bf 109 go down, Katajainen claimed one of the Airacobras, and on his way home surprised a flight of Sturmoviks and shot down two. Five days later he too was badly wounded, and soon found himself in a hospital bed next to Wind.

His last battle earned Wind his second Mannerheim Cross. His final score was 75 victories in 302 missions. Second only to Eino Juutilainen among Finnish aces, Wind still had a higher score than any ace in the opposing Soviet VVS. He was also the highest-scoring Buffalo ace in any air force, with 39 of his kills flying the Brewster B239.

He recovered from most of his wounds, but the small splinters from the shattered cockpit glass would remain a painful legacy for the rest of his life. He was married on August 26, 1944 and resigned from the Ilmavoimat in May 1945. He went on to attend the Helsinki School of Business. For most of his life he did not discuss his wartime exploits, but he finally did consent to a biography by Borje Sjogren that was published in 1990. He died in Tampere on July 24, 1995.

# INDEX

## N

Netherlands, *218*
Neumann, Eduard "Edu," *119, 121*
Niclot, Furio, *150*
Night Witches, *189*
Nishizawa, Hiroyoshi, *11, 166, 170–172, 174*
Nooy, Cornelius, *60*
Norway, *217*
Nowotny, Walter, *99, 104–107*
Nungesser, Charles, *201*

## O

O'Hare, Edward H. "Butch," *65–68*
Okumura, Takeo, *166*
Operation Barbarossa, *93–94, 101, 102, 104, 180, 184*
Operation Bodenplatte, *48, 51, 111*
Operation Compass, *153*
Operation Crusader, *157*
Operation Dynamo, *138, 140, 141, 146*
Operation Husky, *160, 208, 210*
Operation Torch, *69*
Osipienko, Polina, *189*
Osterkamp, Theo, *97*

## P

Pattle, Marmaduke Thomas St. John "Pat," *11, 102, 129, 132–133, 153, 154, 161*
Pavelic, Ante, *223*
Pawlikowski, Stefan, *205*
Pearl Harbor, *22, 165, 168, 170, 173*
Pégoud, Adolphe, *8, 201*
Peron, Juan, *100*
Philipp, Hans, *42*
Pokryshkin, Aleksandr Ivanovich "Sasha," *184–187*

Poland
    Boleslaw Michel "Mike" Gladych, *38, 205, 212–213*
    Eugeniusz Horbaczewski, *205, 209–211*
    Stanislaw Skalski, *205, 207–208, 209, 210, 212*
Power, Tyrone, *161*
Preddy, George, *17, 50–51*
Prentice, George, *45*
Puhakka, Risto Olli Petter, *229*
Puro, Olavi Kauko, *229*

## R

Rall, Günther, *56, 89, 92, 102–103, 114*
Randolph Field, *30*
Raskova, Marina, *188–189, 192*
Rechkalov, Grigori Andreevich, *184, 186–187*
Reiner, Giulio, *196*
Remlinger, Jacques, *203*
Republic Field, *47, 50*
Reznák, Ján, *221*
Richthofen, Manfred von, *89, 95*
Rickenbacker, Edward V. "Eddie," *16, 27, 29, 31, 38, 74, 78*
Rittmayer, Jack, *32, 33*
Robbins, Jay T., *18*
Romania, *224–225*
Rommel, Erwin, *118, 119, 121, 123, 149, 154*
Roosevelt, Franklin D., *64, 74, 165*
Rudorffer, Erich, *100, 108–109*
Republic Field, *47, 50*
Rushing, Roy, *63*
Russo-Japanese War, *164, 165*
Ryan, John Dale, *49*
Rychagov, Pavel "Pablo Palencar," *178*
Rykov, A. I., *188*

## S

Safonov, Boris, *181*
Saito, Fred, *175*
Sakai, Saburo, *166, 170, 171, 172, 173–175, 174*
Salas-Larrazábal, Angel, *226*
Salomatin, Alexei, *192, 193*
Sarvanto, Jorma, *229*
Sasai, Junichi, *166*
Sasaki, Isamu, *166*
Sasebo Naval Base, *173*
Schilling, David C., *16*
Schroer, Werner, *156*
Scott, Robert, *21*
Selfridge Field, *39*
Serov, Anatoli "Carlos Castejon," *178*
Shinohara, Hinomichi, *166*
Sino-Japanese War, *11, 20–21, 77, 164–165, 168, 173*
Sjogren, Borje, *233*
Skalski's Circus, *207, 209, 210*
Skalski, Stanislaw, *205, 207–208, 209, 210, 212*
Slovakia, *221*
Slovenské Vzdušné Zbrane (SVZ), *221*
Smith, John, *61*
Soviet Union
    Aleksandr Ivanovich "Sasha" Pokryshkin, *184–186*
    Grigori Andreevich Rechkalov, *184, 186–187*
    Ekaterina (Katarina) Vasilyevna "Katya" Budanova, *190, 191, 193*
    Ivan Nikitich Kozhedub, *11, 181, 182–183, 186*
    Lidiya Vladimirovna "Lilya" Litvyak, *190–193*
Spaatz, Carl "Tooey," *55*
Spain, *226*
Spanish Civil War, *19, 84, 93, 96, 178, 195, 196, 198, 226*
Spears, Harold, *80*
Spring Offensive (1942), *180*
Stalin, Josef, *91, 92, 178, 180, 188, 189, 191, 229, 233, 235*

Steinhoff, Johannes "Macky," *99, 100, 101, 113–115, 118, 190*
Stevens, R.W., *107*
Stoyanov, Stoyan Iliev, *226*
Sugimoto, Akira, *33*
Sugita, Shoichi, *166*
Szentgyörgyi, Dezso, *222*

## T

T-4 project, *95*
Takali Field, *149*
Tanaka, Kuniyoshi, *165*
Thach, John, *65, 67*
Thomas, Wilbur J., *61*
Thropp, Douglass, *32, 33*
Tinker, Frank Glasgow, *19*
Trammell, Park, *62*
Trumball Field, *47*
Tuck, Robert Roland Stanford "Bob," *8, 128, 130, 139, 140–144*
Tuominen, Oiva Emil Kalervo, *229*

## U

Udet, Ernst, *94, 95, 98*
Urbanowicz, Witold, *205, 209, 210*
US Army Air Forces (USAAF)
    Albert J. "Ajax" Baumler, *19*
    Boyd D. "Buzz" Wagner, *22–23*
    Charles H. "Mac" MacDonald, *18, 44–46*
    David Lee "Tex" Hill, *21*
    Dominic Salvatore "Don" Gentile, *17, 18, 53–54*
    Frank Glasgow Tinker, *19*
    George Preddy, *17, 50–51*
    Hubert "Hub" Zemke, *37, 39, 55–57*
    introduction, *16–18*
    John C. Meyer, *17, 47–49*
    Neel Kearby, *31, 34–35*

# V

# W

# Y

# Z

# BILL YENNE

**BILL YENNE IS THE SAN FRANCISCO-BASED AUTHOR** of more than two dozen books on military and historical topics. He is also a member of the American Aviation Historical Society and has contributed to encyclopedias of both World Wars.

Walter J. Boyne, the former head of the Smithsonian National Air and Space Museum, has recommended Mr. Yenne's work, writing "I can guarantee that you will be engaged by his master storytelling from his opening words to the very last page."

His work has been selected for the official Chief of Staff of the Air Force Reading List, and he is the recipient of the Air Force Association's Gill Robb Wilson Award for his "most outstanding contribution in the field of arts and letters [and for his] work of over two dozen airpower-themed books and for years of effort shaping how many people understand and appreciate airpower."

Among his books about airpower are *Big Week: Six Days That Changed the Course of World War II*, and detailed histories of such aircraft as the B-17, B-29, and the B-52. He had also written corporate histories of planemakers Boeing, Convair, Lockheed, McDonnell Douglas, North American Aviation, and Rockwell International.

Aviation biographies penned by Mr. Yenne have included *Hap Arnold: The General Who Invented the US Air Force*, which General Craig McKinley, president of the Air Force Association described as "a superior job helping the reader better understand General Arnold."

His biographies of aces have included a dual biography of Dick Bong and Tommy McGuire, *Aces High: The Heroic Story of the Two Top-Scoring American Aces of World War II*, which was described by pilot and best-selling author Dan Roam as "The greatest flying story of all time," as well as *The White Rose of Stalingrad: The Real-Life Adventure of Lidiya Vladimirovna Litvyak, the Highest Scoring Female Air Ace of All Time*, which has been published in four languages.

Mr. Yenne has appeared in documentaries airing on the History Channel, the National Geographic Channel, the Smithsonian Channel, ARD German Television, and NHK Japanese Television. Visit him on the web at www.BillYenne.com.